2995

D1345870

TWENTIETH-CENTURY
Piano Music

TWENTIETH-CENTURY
Piano · Music

David Burge

Eastman School of Music

SCHIRMER BOOKS

A DIVISION OF MACMILLAN, INC.
New York

COLLIER MACMILLAN CANADA
Toronto

MAXWELL MACMILLAN INTERNATIONAL
New York Oxford Singapore Sydney

Schirmer Books
A Division of Macmillan, Inc.
866 Third Avenue, New York, N.Y. 10022

Collier Macmillan Canada, Inc.
1200 Eglinton Avenue East, Suite 200
Don Mills, Ontario M3C 3N1

Library of Congress Catalog Card Number: 90-8663

Printed in the United States of America

printing number
1   2   3   4   5   6   7   8   9   10

Library of Congress Cataloging-in-Publication Data

Burge, David.
    Twentieth-century piano music / David Burge.
        p.   cm.—(Studies in musical genres and repertories)
    Discography: p.
Includes bibliographical references (p.   ) and index.
ISBN 0-02-870321-9
    1. Piano music—20th century—History and criticism.   I. Title.
II. Series.
ML707.B87   1990
786.2'09'04—dc20   90-8663
                                                      CIP
                                                      MN

Dedicated
with affection
to my students

Contents

Preface

It has been my good fortune during the past four decades to be associated with hundreds of composers from all over the world. I have performed, recorded, listened to, taught, and written about their piano music, rejoicing in the beauty and expressiveness of the best of it, happy that the twentieth century has provided such rich fare for my instrument.

This brief book is a personal study of some of these riches. I am aware that many pianists today have not had the opportunity to become acquainted with more than a small fraction of this repertoire. This is due, to a considerable extent, to the unfortunate limitations of our present educational perspectives, which tend to enshrine that which is already established and to regard all else as peripheral. My aim is that what follows—a tour of what I consider the better repertoire for solo piano from the first nine decades of this century—will help to change these attitudes by awakening interest in this wonderful music. I also hope that pianists will come to see that if piano playing is to remain a living, relevant art, the performance of this music is essential.

I am aware, of course, that the views I express concerning some of the compositional developments since 1900 will not be acceptable to all. Some readers will find certain omissions inexcusable and selected points of view infuriating. In any case, I *hope* this is true, for I would not ever wish to think that we all agree.

In any case, there has been no attempt to make this book "complete." Those searching for the closest thing to a list of everything written for the piano during the twentieth century will do well to examine Maurice Hinson's amazing and invaluable *Guide to the Pianist's Repertoire*, to which I have continually referred in my labors. Nor have I, even in chapters devoted to a single composer, discussed every piece written for the keyboard by that person. Rather, I have tried to explain why I, as a performing pianist and experienced teacher, find specific works particularly impressive, moving, and beautiful. In so doing I have been honest and true to my own feelings and experience, and I trust no one will deny me that privilege.

I would like to thank the dozens—or hundreds, I should say—of composers, performers, colleagues, students, and friends who have been so continuously encouraging to me in so many vital ways for so long. A great debt of gratitude is owed to the late William H. Bailey, my colleague at Whitman College in the 1950s, for his often gentle and sometimes severe persuasions concerning musical values; I shall never forget what he taught me. The men and women who took on thankless administrative tasks while I was chairman of the American Society of University Composers in the early 1970s, especially Gerald Warfield, were all, in their individual ways, instrumental in plugging me in to the realities of the life of today's composer.

Tom Darter and Jim Aikin at *Keyboard Magazine* must be thanked many times over for alternatingly threatening and cajoling me into writing the nearly one hundred and fifty articles on contemporary piano music I have scribbled out for that magazine; I particularly thank them and others at *Keyboard* for allowing me to draw heavily on my own previous work in certain portions of what follows. I also wish to acknowledge the assistance of the vast resources of the Sibley Music Library of the Eastman School of Music which, on the rare occasions when they do not include everything one might wish to see, can inform one as to how to find it elsewhere.

Pianist Bradford Gowen was kind enough to read the manuscript in an early draft. His meticulous comments, suggestions, and corrections are greatly appreciated, as are those of R. Larry Todd, the series editor. My thanks to Maribeth Anderson Payne, editor-in-chief of Schirmer Books, for encouraging me to undertake this project, and to her associate editor, Robert Axelrod, for his professional assistance in the details of preparing the manuscript and, even more, for his keen insights concerning the shape and focus of the book.

Finally, I must commend Becky Chapman-Winter and her associates at A-R Editions, Inc. in Madison, Wisconsin for the meticulous manner in which they have produced this volume. In particular, their care in the reproduction and arrangement of the numerous and often tricky musical examples deserves the highest accolades. Their exemplary efforts have my sincerest gratitude.

D. B.
Summer 1990

TWENTIETH-CENTURY
Piano Music

PART 1

From 1900 to the End of World War I

CHAPTER ONE

Claude Debussy

Between the spectacularly mourned death of Victor Hugo in 1885 and the commencement of World War I nearly thirty years later, no European city provided a better stage for artistic revolution than Paris. The word *stage* is particularly apt: There was not only great public interest in the arts—painting, literature, theater, dance, and music—but also a decidedly theatrical sense of participation. People dressed to be seen; they walked and gestured to be observed; and conversation was an art to be cultivated and admired. In the exclusive salons the arts vied with politics and morality for a place in sophisticated, if not always profound, discourse. For the less well heeled, the cafés of the grand boulevards and the Latin Quarter became centers of heated debate on every possible artistic subject. An unprecedented cross-pollination between painters, poets, writers, and composers took place in this fertile milieu.

In a relatively short time new kinds of artistic thought and stimuli, far removed from the Germanic traditions of the academy, came together in this remarkable city. Interest in things non-European led Paris museums to fill up with marvels of African and Egyptian art as well as every sort of decorative splendor from China and Japan. The International Exposition of 1889 included not only the Hall of Industry with its remarkable scientific exhibits, but also performances by dancers from the island of Java, until then perceived only as a hazy place somewhere on the other side of the world. These dancers were accompanied by *gamelan* players, whose metallophones and gongs produced exotic sounds that excited the imagination and uncovered new possibilities for western musical composition.

The need for new ways of seeing, thinking, feeling, and doing was in the air. Sarah Bernhardt declared and then proved that a woman could play Hamlet; Gauguin went to Tahiti to find a "new vision"; the Schola Cantorum peered back into history and revived the church modes; and—more important than any of these—artists looked within themselves, examining their dreams and subconscious selves and forging a new esthetic that allowed them to break from the conventions that had governed them.

Striking out against the academy, members of the Société des Artistes Indépendants made a virtue of unfettered artistic individualism; these artists let it be known that no sin was unforgivable except that of not feeling. And, striking out against the conformity of a hierarchical society, anarchists of the mid-1880s, not unlike their counterparts a century later, tossed bombs and vented their hatred of political and intellectual coercion. In so doing they challenged the esthetics of the time as well, a challenge that was not lost on the creative men and women who argued their nights away in the cafés of the Left Bank.

By no means did all of Parisian society sympathize with such advanced tendencies. It was a time of relative political stability. Social conformity was the norm in the upper classes, and the nonconformity of the Société and the spiritual defiance of the Symbolists posed almost as much a threat to bourgeois complacency as the bombs of the anarchists. This complacency served only to heat up the artistic community, driving them closer together into what was soon to be called the *avant-garde*.

Born on the outskirts of Paris to poverty-stricken parents, Claude Achille Debussy (1862–1918) showed an extraordinary affinity for music at a very early age. Due not only to his talent but also to fortuitous circumstances, he was able to enter the Paris Conservatoire at the age of ten. There, in spite of his truculent behavior and well-documented dislike for the accepted rules of harmony and musical composition, he emerged more than a decade later as the winner of the Prix de Rome.

At the age of 25 he returned to France after two unhappy years in Italy and soon became a member of the Parisian avant-garde. Finding few musicians in whom he could confide, he regularly attended meetings of the Symbolist poets, especially the "Tuesdays" held at the home of Stéphane Mallarmé. There he met writers such as Paul Verlaine, painters such as James McNeill Whistler and Odilon Redon, and others. He immediately felt an affinity for the Symbolists' attempts to explore the writer's psychological state rather than for the emphasis on objective description and technical perfection, the aim of the earlier Parnassians. And he instantly understood the new painters' desires to translate their immediate, subjective impressions of a scene onto canvas rather than to continue formal transcription of exact likenesses, the object of older artists.

Thinking of applying these ideas to music, Debussy journeyed to Bayreuth in the summers of 1888 and 1889 and, for at least a brief period, felt an overwhelming stimulus from the colorful, heavily chromatic music of Wagner's music dramas, especially *Parsifal* and *Tristan*. Although Debussy soon recognized that the Wagnerian *Gesamtkunstwerk* (universal art work) did not have the same aims that had attracted him to the Symbolists, the music itself left its mark on his own developing style.

Also in 1889 he heard for the first time the Javanese gamelan at the International Exposition in Paris. These sounds and the free-flowing musical forms had a profound effect, and Debussy was soon to become the first of many western composers whose work showed the influence of the East.

Although perceptible changes in Debussy's style occurred throughout his career, certain unmistakable characteristics are found in all of his music. Especially in matters of harmonic treatment and timbre he was to leave an indelible impression on the history of music. As is the case with every great composer, not everything he did was understood at first, not even by his most ardent admirers, who perceived that his music was sensitive and well wrought, but often rather vague. Perhaps inevitably, a newspaper critic linked his music with the work of that group of late nineteenth-century French painters who also had achieved a certain vagueness, "what those imbeciles call Impressionism,"[1] as Debussy commented wryly.

Indeed, *impressionism*, a term more applicable to painting than to music, was a word he never found appropriate. Rather, following the lead of the Symbolists, he wished to go beyond the "impression" in order to express his inner feelings *about* the impression. To do this he created what was virtually a new musical language, free of superimposed formal constraints and deterministic tonal harmony; a language, in short, that reached into the subconscious and was uninformed by overemphasis or rhetoric. In a statement that would have appealed to Freud and Jung, Debussy declared he wanted music "to appear as though it came from a shadow."[2]

In the mid-1890s, by then the composer of *Prélude à "L'après-midi d'un faune"* and a brilliant string quartet, Debussy was established. By the time of his opera, *Pelléas et Mélisande*, completed in 1902, he was France's most famous composer.

Debussy wrote piano music throughout his lifetime. The early *Suite bergamasque* (completed, 1890), though not demonstrating the forward-looking tendencies of works written a decade or so later, displays Debussy's control over the diatonic harmonic style then still in vogue in Paris. The beautiful third movement, "Clair de lune," certainly deserves its fame, if not the maudlin treatment it still receives in countless arhythmic performances. Has any composer appropriated to himself a single sound more firmly than the young Debussy with the perfectly spaced pianissimo chord that begins measure 15 (example 1.1)?

Although the opening tune of the fourth and last movement, "Passepied," seems quite ordinary, Debussy imbues it with a distinctive flavor through subtle use of staccato and legato in the first few measures and through wisps of counterpoint further on (example 1.2).

A considerable change in style is evident in *Suite: Pour le piano*

EXAMPLE 1.1. Debussy, *Suite bergamasque*, "Clair de lune," mm. 15–16.

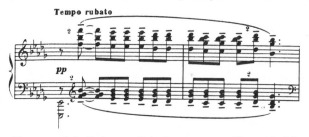

EXAMPLE 1.2. Debussy, *Suite bergamasque*, "Passepied," mm. 1–11.

(1901), the single-movement *L'isle joyeuse* (1904), and particularly in the three-movement *Estampes* (1903). In these works Debussy becomes more adventurous in his choice of subject material, mirroring his continuing exploration of new sounds and sound combinations. In the first movement of *Estampes*, "Pagodes," for example, we hear the composer's reflections on the harmonic style of the Javanese gamelan; in the second movement, "La soirée dans Grenade," we hear his reflections on the singular rhythms of the folk music of Spain. The third movement, "Jardins sous la pluie," is a particularly interesting display of the manner in which Debussy found it possible to suspend tonality for lengthy passages within an otherwise tonal work. Debussy may have heard passages of a similar nature in Wagner's late operas, passages that usually serve to link a dominant sonority to its distant resolution and for which conventional tonal analysis is difficult. Debussy's lithe treatment of nontraditional harmonies, however, is much different from what he heard at Bayreuth—it depends far less on the eventual gravitational effects of a long-delayed return to a tonic.

Although Debussy had decided opinions on all musical matters,[3] as a composer he was not trying to form a new system or champion one particular style over others. Rather, his harmonic genius allowed him to see that it was possible to move from one tonality to another without employing the conventional modulations taught at the Conservatoire. Sometimes, in fact, he was able to set up a long, schematic pattern in lieu of a traditional modulation, and this pattern could be repeated in sequence at length with great dramatic effect. Example 1.3, from "Jardins sous la pluie," is relatively short; the full score reveals a much longer non-tonal sequence beginning after measure 56.

EXAMPLE 1.3. Debussy, *Estampes*, "Jardins sous la pluie," mm. 49–56.

Notice the disarmingly simple succession of unrelated major triads in measures 52 and 53 of example 1.3. Measures 54 and 55 repeat the chords exactly, only a half step higher. It all flows so easily that one is unaware of the daring nature of the progression. As Peter Yates comments, "his music seems in our ears less courageous than it is."[4]

Debussy's keen ear for pianistic sonority had already brought forth a simple, lucid beauty in such passages as the opening moments of the early "Clair de lune." In his later works this sense was developed to such an extent that Debussy was able to create a magical atmosphere and capture a psychological setting in a manner that was not only ravishing to the ear but evocative of place and reminiscent of dreams. The beginning of "La soirée dans Grenade," a habanera that, in Debussy's words, begin "slowly with a nonchalantly graceful rhythm," soon covers the entire keyboard and quickly conjures up the heartbeat of Spanish dance. Growing in intensity, the work quickly arrives at a climax and then, more quietly, ruminates on the subtler innuendos of this prototypical medium of Spanish cultural expression. But what is one to think of the mysterious interruptions, "light and distant" and in another rhythm, that one hears just as the habanera ostinato is about to disappear into the "shadow" near the end? (example 1.4). A dreaming guitar player? A horse barely heard, galloping across the horizon? The fleeting reminiscences of a dancer no longer able to dance? Debussy, of course, does not say, and the closing sonorities are more mysterious than when they first appeared. Referring to Debussy's sense of sonority and power of evocation, Manuel de Falla was to exclaim that the greatest composer of Spanish music was a Frenchman who had never visited Spain!

EXAMPLE 1.4. Debussy, *Estampes*, "La soirée dans Grenade," mm. 106–112.

In his ensuing compositions Debussy continued to juxtapose passages of diatonic, chromatic, and occasionally non-tonal harmony. The results are so natural and unforced that one forgets to notice the composer's presumption in combining what otherwise might be considered irreconcilable styles. One would hardly expect to find the pandiatonic measures shown in example 1.5 followed first by a progression of parallel chromatic sevenths and tritones (example 1.6), then by a nearly atonal measure (example 1.7), and finally by the *completely* atonal scheme in which inverted parallel ninth chords move up by leaps of minor thirds (example 1.8). This, however, is exactly what happens in the first few moments of "Reflets dans l'eau," the first of three movements in the first book of *Images* (1905). This glistening work not only demonstrates Debussy's ability to balance tonal and non-tonal writing, but admirably shows the kind of harmonic daring that caused him to be one of the principal influences on composers half a century later.

EXAMPLE 1.5. Debussy, *Images I*, "Reflets dans l'eau," mm. 1–2.

EXAMPLE 1.6. Debussy, *Images I*, "Reflets dans l'eau," mm. 9–10.

EXAMPLE 1.7. Debussy, *Images I*, "Reflets dans l'eau," m. 14.

EXAMPLE 1.8. Debussy, *Images I*, "Reflets dans l'eau," mm. 20–21.

A brief examination of some of Debussy's harmonic practices is appropriate here. Every description of his music inevitably mentions his use of the whole-tone scale, certainly he often made effective use in many ways of the entire six-note scale or of chords and intervals derived from it. Parallel major thirds a whole step apart and augmented triads, both trademarks of the whole-tone scale, are frequently employed, as is the interval of the tritone. Of particular interest, but perhaps too seldom discussed, is the composer's unprecedented use of whole-tone chords within progressions involving more traditional chords. Most important is his daring in moving freely from one chord to another, traditional or not. This latter characteristic in Debussy's writing led composers two generations after him to declare that he had accomplished, above all, "the emancipation of sound," freeing individual chords from their traditional functions.

In example 1.9, from near the end of "Reflets dans l'eau," Debussy establishes E-flat major rather forcefully. Measure 59 contains an E-flat ninth in root position. But in measure 60 there is a sudden shift: all the notes in the measure derive from a whole-tone scale. It is difficult to confirm any root pitch because there are no perfect intervals with strong root-defining tendencies and no leading tones with inherent resolving characteristics. Debussy makes use of this ambivalence, somewhat in the way earlier composers—Mozart, Beethoven, Schubert, Weber, and Liszt, to name just a few—had exploited the undetermined harmonic fate of the diminished-seventh chord, made up, like the whole-tone scale, of equal intervals.

Measure 61 reintroduces the E-flat ninth, which moves in the next measure to a D-flat ninth. This, in turn, is altered in measure 63, changing it into a whole-tone chord again, now more clearly rooted on D-flat. Prolonged through measure 64 and serving enharmonically as an altered dominant on C-sharp, the whole-tone chord resolves traditionally to F-sharp minor on the first beat of measure 65. Slipping chromatically to an unrelated D-minor chord on the next beat, there is a plagal cadence to A major in measure 66, but this is followed abruptly in measure 67 by a C-minor arpeggio, the surprise of which is enhanced by its being triple piano. Returning in measure 68 to the same A-major chord with the same figurations as two bars earlier, Debussy, having made the radical color change from A major to C minor in measures 66–67, now smoothly glides down a half step to an A-flat ninth in measure 69. This prepares for the return of the work's opening idea in D-flat major; in other words, the A-flat ninth serves as a dominant preparation just as in a traditional classical retransition, though it is approached in a decidedly nonclassical manner.

A full appreciation of Debussy's skill and boldness in creating new language from old materials requires more than a brief glance at a succession of harmonies. One could also refer to Debussy's handling of

EXAMPLE 1.9. Debussy, *Images I*, "Reflets dans l'eau," mm. 57–72.

motive, line, common tones and cross relations, dynamics, and tempo adjustments. In any case, clearly by the time of "Reflets dans l'eau," Debussy was completely at ease in this new language.

In the second book of *Images* (1907), Debussy's titles became more imaginative, and his written indications to the performer, always discreet, become increasingly specific with regard to the manner of playing, thereby telling the performer more than ever about the interpretation he favored. Thus, in "Cloches à travers les feuilles" ("Bells Heard through the Leaves"), a bass figure is marked *presque rien* (almost nothing); a melody is *expressif et doucement appuyé* (expressive and sweetly pressed—that is, keys are to be pressed gently rather than struck, probably the most outstanding feature of Debussy's own playing); and an underlying figuration is designated *très égal—comme une buée irisée* (very equal—like an iridescent mist). In a pianissimo passage in the next piece, "Et la lune descend sur le temple qui fut" ("The Moon Goes down on the Ruined Temple"), the performer is instructed, *frappez les accords sans lourdeur* (play the chords without heaviness—again a characteristic of Debussy's own performances). And always there are the carefully placed markings by which Debussy sets off a phrase or a special harmonic event: *cédez* (literally, "give in," i. e., hold back), *un peu retenu* (held back a little), and—quite rarely—*rubato*. In short, Debussy's is a highly refined style involving delicately balanced forces, understated enough so that the occasional emotional outburst has telling effect, structurally clear enough even as the music's inner message appears "as though it came from a shadow."

In his next work for piano, *Children's Corner* (1908), Debussy deliciously captures the intimacy, candor, and innocence of childhood in a manner equalled only in Robert Schumann's wonderful *Kinderszenen*. If Debussy was aware of the beginnings of the illness that was to result in his death only ten years later, or if he listened to the political and economic rumblings to the east that were to erupt into a cataclysmic war, he does not reveal his apprehension in a single measure of this charming set of pieces. The touching simplicity of "The Snow Is Dancing" and "The Little Shepherd" reflects his extraordinary sensitivity to harmonic and melodic nuance. His somewhat less subtle sense of humor, which was to surface more boldly in the second book of *Preludes* a few years later, is apparent in "Jimbo's Lullaby" (subtitled "Berceuse des éléphants"), in which the low opening melody, played by the left hand, is marked *doux et un peu gauche*, a pun that is something less than sly, *gauche* meaning both "left" and "clumsy" in French (example 1.10).

In the first book of *Preludes* (1910) Debussy, his pianistic imagination soaring, continued to produce lucidly wrought, beautifully shaped character pieces. In most cases the basic material for each prelude is relatively simple, and its working out seems natural, colorful, and unforced. One remains unaware of the manipulations of a strong-willed

EXAMPLE 1.10. Debussy, *Children's Corner*, "Jimbo's Lullaby," mm. 1–8.

composer whose intuition leads him to expand or contract phrases, to elide, transform, or introduce features that in lesser hands would seem out of place, not all the time, just often with an insistence all the more convincing for being pianissimo.

Most of these first twelve preludes are well known, the most famous being "La cathédrale engloutie" ("The Sunken Cathedral"), "Minstrels," and "La fille aux cheveux de lin" ("The Maid with the Flaxen Hair"). In the last-mentioned piece, the unpretentious opening melody seems to have emerged as much from the tactile experience of playing on the black keys as from anything else (example 1.11).

EXAMPLE 1.11. Debussy, *Preludes I*, "La fille aux cheveux de lin," mm. 1–4.

This is, admittedly, a subjective reaction, yet if one transposes these three bars up a half step to G major, one may find that some of the phrase's magic has been drained away by the removal of that special aura that the *feeling* of the black keys imparts to a sound. Similarly, in the prelude called "Voiles" ("Sails"), most of which remains exclusively in a whole-tone scale, Debussy moves for a few climactic measures from whole-tone to black-key pentatonic, which again exploits a specific pianistic sound and a particular sentient experience, both of which would be lost if transposed (example 1.12).

EXAMPLE 1.12. Debussy, *Preludes I*, "Voiles," mm. 41–44.

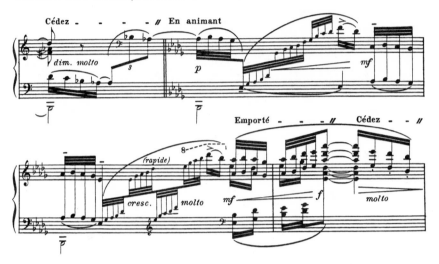

These are obvious instances of the composer's willingness to be guided by the idiosyncrasies and feel of the keyboard; more subtle examples abound. Not surprisingly, Debussy—friend of the Symbolist poets, for whom a single word could have myriad evocations, and with firsthand knowledge of the Impressionist painters, whose aim was not so much to capture the object as the atmosphere surrounding it—involved the sensuousness of the piano keyboard itself in the aggregate effect of his music.

It is the usual practice of performers to make selections, playing a group of two, three, or more preludes in a "Debussy group," a procedure with which the composer would probably have found no fault. Nevertheless, a performance of an entire set—all of the first book or all of the second—played in the order in which they were arranged by the composer, is an experience of a magnitude that cannot be explained only by sheer length. That "the whole is more than the sum of its parts" seems in this case to be true. Individual preludes tend to emphasize a few basic colors and some related tints and shades. An entire set of twelve, however, lasting close to forty-five minutes, eventually provides not only all of Debussy's impressive spectrum of sonorities but also, more importantly, a cumulative sense of emotional completeness.

Some of this expressive richness is reflected in the titles, but these, placed at the end of each prelude rather than at the beginning, can hardly be taken as more than suggestions about the interpretive approach that might best suit individual pieces. "Des pas sur la neige" ("Footsteps in the Snow") is a title that has numerous connotations—perhaps mysterious winter apparitions, Christmas visitations, a desolate Arctic path, cheerful and crisp open spaces—each with different emotional resonances. Debussy's reference to "a sad and frozen landscape" at the opening is more specific, but the music itself, with its repeating ostinato and plaintive tune, varied over and over, conjures up the sense of desolation and regret that informs the piece. This sense would be there without the title or the directions (example 1.13).

EXAMPLE 1.13. Debussy, *Preludes I*, "Des pas sur la neige," mm. 1–3.

Still, the composer's written directions go far beyond convention in relaying the emotional landscape of his music. "The Sunken Cathedral" is indeed, as he says, *profondément calme* at the outset, and "Minstrels" does not come off if it is not played *nerveux et avec humour*, as requested.

The cabaret-type melodies that occasionally surface in the first book of *Preludes*, as in the middle of "Les collines d'Anacapri" ("The Hills of Anacapri") and near the end of "Minstrels," also brighten "Général Lavine—eccentric" in the second book of *Preludes* (1913). Less subtle is Debussy's elephantine version of "God Save the King" in "Hommage à S. Pickwick, Esq., P.P.M.P.C." Erik Satie once said to Debussy, lightly dismissing Wagner's leitmotif technique, "there is no need for the orchestra to grimace when a character comes onstage." Notwithstanding that bit of advice, Debussy found it possible to "set a scene" with bits of popular melodies when it served his purpose. In like manner, he employs the harmonies and rhythms of the habanera to call forth the flavor of Spain in the tumultuous prelude "La puerta del vino" from the second book.

The second book demonstrates a further refinement and enrichment of Debussy's art, pointing toward *Douze études* (1915) and the sonatas for two or more instruments that he was to produce in the tragic final years of his life. Each book of preludes includes twelve pieces, and the playing time for each is approximately equal; nevertheless, in the original Durand edition the second book takes up half again as many pages as the first, giving a rough indication of the additional wealth of figurative detail therein. The composer's candid simplicity can still be found: "Feuilles mortes" ("Dead Leaves") in the second book compares, emotionally and musically, with " 'Les sons et les parfums tournent dans l'air du soir' " (" 'Sounds and Perfumes Mingle in the Evening Air' ") from the first; "Bruyères" ("Heather") has echoes of "La fille aux cheveaux de lin." But all in all the second volume explores the resources of the piano more than the first and is therefore more challenging to the performer, requiring more control and more dexterity.

At the outset of the first prelude from book two, "Brouillards" ("Mists"), the composer's repertoire of seamless, atmospheric pianistic inventions is enriched by a new white-against-black figuration (example 1.14). It is in fact only a few steps away from the famous whirling figure that opens the final prelude, "Feux d'artifice" ("Fireworks") (example 1.15).

EXAMPLE 1.14. Debussy, *Preludes II*, "Brouillards," m. 1.

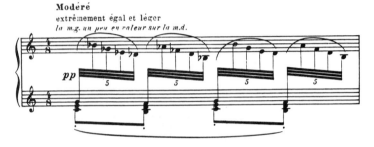

EXAMPLE 1.15. Debussy, *Preludes II*, "Feux d'artifice," mm. 1–4.

One of the most spellbinding figural passages in all of Debussy's piano music occurs in the middle of "Ondine," in which a beautifully spaced sonority builds from the center out, hands interlocked in a "murmuring" rhythm (example 1.16).

Harmonically, too, Debussy continues to refine and explore. Parallel unrelated triads consistently provide the ear with the maximum

EXAMPLE 1.16. Debussy, *Preludes II*, "Ondine," mm. 41–47.

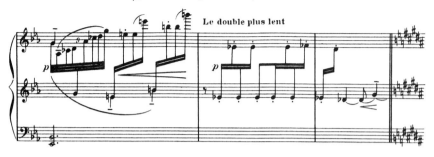

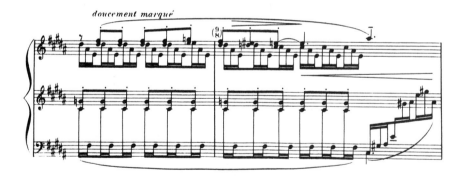

number of cross-relations in the opening motive of "Général Lavine—eccentric" (example 1.17), though by this time the concept of *unrelated triads* no longer applies—Debussy seems able to relate almost any succession of triads or seventh chords. In like manner, the term *false relation* has become meaningless, melodic and chord-quality concerns having long since taken precedence over adherence to a particular mode or scale. For example, in "La terrasse des audiences du clair de lune" ("The Moon's Court") (example 1.18), the melody, clearly in F-sharp major, would probably look like example 1.19 if written alone. Debussy, however, scores it as is most convenient to the eye—a B-flat seventh chord is easier to read than an A-sharp seventh—and lets the accidentals cross-relate where they may.

EXAMPLE 1.17. Debussy, *Preludes II*, "Général Lavine—eccentric," mm. 1–4.

EXAMPLE 1.18. Debussy, *Preludes II*, "La terrasse des audiences du clair de lune," mm. 3–4.

EXAMPLE 1.19. Conventional spelling of melody in example 1.18.

"La terrasse" is, indeed, one of Debussy's most stunning works for the piano. From the opening diminished-seventh chord (immediately filled chromatically, first the top third, then the bottom third, by an eight-tone scale high in the treble, an extraordinarily clever and apposite linkage), through tentative, ghostly dance figures and a brief but sonorous climax, to its mystical conclusion in a unique dotted-sixteenth note sequence, this ravishing piece creates a musical *chiaroscuro*, moving from pastel to pastel, changing colors deftly and imperceptibly, as clouds change their shapes in the night sky (examples 1.20 and 1.21). Preceded by General Lavine's ribald cakewalk and followed by the sprightly, mercurial forms of "Ondine," the work beautifully displays Debussy's ability to focus on the most evanescent scenes and feelings, conclude, and move on.

Included in most of Debussy's major works mentioned thus far are movements of particular technical difficulty: one thinks of the "Toccata"

EXAMPLE 1.20. Debussy, *Preludes II*, "La terrasse des audiences du clair de lune," mm. 1–2.

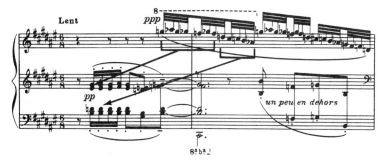

EXAMPLE 1.21. Debussy, *Preludes II*, "La terrasse des audiences du clair de lune," mm. 42–45.

from *Suite: Pour le piano*, "Mouvements" from the first book of *Images*, and several of the *Preludes*, among others. Also, however, there are numerous individual pieces that lie well within the capabilities of pianists of modest attainments. Not so with the *Douze études* (1915). All twelve of these studies, written with Debussy's pianistic idol, Chopin, in mind, require virtuosic agility and suppleness combined with extraordinary sensitivity of touch and the ability to control a musical line under any circumstances.

A comparison of these études with Debussy's other piano music suggests that, true to their title, these later works are more self-consciously concerned with the physical act of playing the piano and less involved with intuitive combination of sounds. A study "for thirds" or "for fourths" will, once the necessity for writing such a work has been established, focus the composer's imagination on certain physical possibilities and limitations that might not otherwise seem pertinent. Yet this can hardly explain the not inconsiderable change in style that takes place in the relatively short period between the *preludes* and these final keyboard works.

One can surmise that part of this change emanates from Debussy's increasing awareness of his own illness—he had an incurable cancer, which steadily weakened him and to which he succumbed in March 1918. Also, the war plunged him into deep depression; he referred to himself as "a poor atom buffeted by this terrible cataclysm; what I am doing seems to me so miserably small."[5]

However, though enervated by illness and devastated by the war, Debussy was at the same time possessed by an overwhelming inner urge as a *musicien français*, as he frequently referred to himself, to return the music of his beloved and beleaguered country to the brilliance and *clarté* it had enjoyed with Rameau two hundred years earlier. Driven by the knowledge that his own life was soon to come to an end, and with his strong revulsion to German musical influence exacerbated by the war, he set about writing a new kind of music—sonatas and studies—that would kindle this compositional renaissance in France.

Thus we have the *Douze études*, for the most part more brilliant than atmospheric, as unpredictable and as full of color as Debussy's earlier music but more objective—the primary colors taking precedence over the previously favored pastels. Some of these studies seem a bit long: the composer possibly felt he had to be definitive rather than suggestive at this point in his life; perhaps he was taking his experiments with sound and form into more remote corners. But in any case, the collection is a major contribution to the genre.

The first study, "Pour les cinq doigts, d'après Monsieur Czerny" ("For the Five Fingers, after M. Czerny"), begins with the composer's tongue in his cheek but quickly changes into a good-natured exploration of a startling number of permutations of Czerny's most fundamental five-note exercise. The second, "Pour les tierces," is much different from Chopin's famous étude in thirds, Op. 25, No. 6, being in a more moderate tempo and treating the basic interval in every variety of diatonic and chromatic scale as well as arpeggiated figurations. A startling and unforgettable feature of the study, which for the most part flows along quietly in sixteenth notes, is the sudden appearance, just before the end, *fortissimo con fuoco*, of a broad, strongly accentuated triplet figure (example 1.22). This idea is presented briefly once before in the work, but this sudden outburst, leading directly to a *tutta forza* ending, is surprising in the otherwise gentle context.

Debussy told his publisher that he believed the next étude, "Pour les quartes," was the most unusual of the twelve; certainly his handling of the interval of the perfect fourth was unprecedented. Any number of felicitous moments could be cited from this study, but the little *scherzandare* passage near the middle, with its suave right-hand chords (soon to be appropriated by all jazz pianists) interspersed with rising (m. 50) and falling (m. 54) pentatonic double arpeggios, will suffice (example 1.23).

The étude "Pour les sixtes" is, appropriately for the relatively soothing interval involved, the gentlest of the twelve. It is followed by an octave

EXAMPLE 1.22. Debussy, *Douze études*, "Pour les tierces," mm. 66–68. © 1916 Durand S.A. Used by Permission of the Publisher. Sole Representative U.S.A. Theodore Presser Company.

EXAMPLE 1.23. Debussy, *Douze études*, "Pour les quartes," mm. 49–54.

étude and then by a study "Pour les huit doigts" ("For the Eight Fingers"), which Debussy declared was best performed without the use of the thumbs, a suggestion neither agreed to nor followed by all. Number seven, "Pour les degrés chromatiques," is somewhat academic in its square rhythms; it requires unerringly quick lateral displacement of either hand as the performer sustains a four-note chromatic scale in a rhythmically calm and unruffled manner.

"Pour les agréments" ("For Ornaments") is one of the best of the collection, full of beautiful melodies and some of Debussy's lushest harmonies, as in the scintillating passage with its widespread thirteenth chords and cascading triads shown in example 1.24.

Following a study in repeated notes and another in opposed sonorities ("Pour les sonorités opposées"), there is the most popular of the études, "Pour les arpèges composés" ("For the Composite Arpeggios"). Kaleidoscopically colorful, this study is particularly well written for the instrument, containing passages of sly, finespun humor, and exhibiting a near-perfect balance of form and content.

Last of all is the étude "Pour les accords" ("For Chords"), taxing and vigorous, slightly reminiscent of the coda of the second movement of the

EXAMPLE 1.24. Debussy, *Douze études*, "Pour les agréments," mm. 33–38.

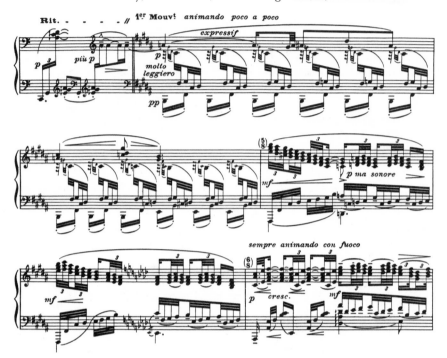

Schumann *Fantasie* in its challenge to the pianist's accuracy and tonal refinement (example 1.25). Loud, yes, says Debussy, but *sans lourdeur* (without heaviness). This, characteristically, is his final admonishment.

EXAMPLE 1.25. Debussy, *Douze études*, "Pour les accords," mm. 1–12.

CHAPTER TWO

Arnold Schoenberg

There is no question that the piano music of Claude Debussy has for many decades been considered part of the pianist's basic repertoire; surely Debussy appears more often on piano recitals than any other twentieth-century composer. Differences of opinion concerning his work do not question the intrinsic quality but, rather, address such matters of interpretation as tempo, pedaling, rubato, and touch. The music has found its place; arguments concerning how it is to be played only corroborate the esteem in which it is held, just as the passionate differences of opinion on the interpretation of Bach, Beethoven, or Chopin reinforce the high valuation placed on their music.

The same cannot be said of the piano music of Arnold Schoenberg (1874–1951). Although his final composition for piano solo was completed more than half a century ago, and although his stature as a seminal composer is universally accepted, the music itself is more often talked and written about than played, and the manner of its interpretation (though subject to as many points of view as the music of Debussy) has not often been the subject of debate.

There is irony in this, for Debussy was more the "rebel" of the two, not only vehemently rejecting the dominance of the Austro-German tradition but opposing what he perceived as the outmoded, stultifying compositional practices of the Paris Conservatoire. Though he was a highly trained musician, much of Debussy's most original music was accomplished instinctively. His desire to "revive" French music forced him to reject the immediate sources of his own training, which were entirely French. Schoenberg, almost wholly self-taught, was nevertheless steeped in the music of late German romanticism and believed his music resulted from inevitable historical and evolutionary forces, making it a logical, predictable continuation of the middle-European tradition he revered. Like Brahms, Schoenberg was suspicious of that which was subjective; ultimately he was at pains to keep intellectual control over his essentially passionate, fervent nature.

The eventual acceptance of a composer's work does not, of course, hinge on the composer's attitudes or sources of inspiration but lies in the nature of the music itself. Debussy's music sounds fresh and spontaneous, and it is necessary to isolate its radical aspects in order to point out how daring it actually was. On the other hand, though Schoenberg's music never loses its romantic, personal nature, many listeners and performers have difficulty seeing through the complex intellectual overlay to appreciate it. Unfortunately, contemporary studies of the music lead one to revere it rather than like it, to see the logic but not the underlying emotional message.

At issue here also is both composers' perception of the disintegration of traditional functional tonality. If in the first decade of the century a line was drawn somewhere between tonality and its absence, Debussy viewed it as a border of little importance and stepped easily across it in either direction. Schoenberg, on the other hand, was only too aware of the centuries-long role of tonality as a shaper of musical grammar and syntax; for him the line separating tonality from whatever lay beyond was clearly marked, and though it seemed impossible not to cross it eventually, its traversal was not only exhilarating but fearsome in its consequences, not only for the listener but for the composer himself.

Schoenberg lived in Vienna. There was no city in Europe more seriously dedicated to the status quo. As in Paris, artistic life in Vienna flourished in certain cafés such as the Café Landtmann, where Schoenberg often saw the poets Arthur Schnitzler and Hugo von Hofmannsthal, the satirist Karl Kraus, conductors Artur Bodanzky and Bruno Walter, and other adherents of new artistic trends. Unlike Paris, which even in the most bourgeois circles was secretly proud of its yeasty artistic life, Vienna had developed a deep enmity toward the sort that gathered at the Landtmann, a contempt that made the appearance of anything nontraditional the signal for battle. Thus, even as Debussy rebelled against tradition, he sought to win the hearts of his countrymen. Schoenberg, in his growing frustration, found it necessary to feel contempt for and ignore the Viennese public. Whatever else one may say of the temperamental or nationalistic differences between the two men, the effect of the underlying attitudes of their respective cities was profound.

Arnold Schoenberg was born on 13 September 1874 in Vienna. As with Debussy's parents, his mother and father had no apparent musical talent. Attracted to music at an early age, Schoenberg eventually taught himself to play the violin and cello rather badly and, throughout his youth, composed constantly, writing in the styles he heard around him — mostly light opera and the military music played by park bands.

In 1897 Schoenberg was introduced to the Viennese public with *String Quartet in D*, a romantic work clearly influenced by Brahms. It was a success, but another more ambitious work, a string sextet called *Verklaerte Nacht (Transfigured Night)*, written in 1899, was rejected. "It sounds as if someone had smeared the score of *Tristan* while it was still wet!" was one observation.[1]

In the ensuing years Schoenberg became more and more convinced that Vienna was dominated by philistines. A lengthy published statement[2] attributed to him, announcing the formation of the antiestablishment Society of Creative Musicians in 1904, vents these feelings. He lashes out at Vienna, where even works well proven elsewhere "meet with little interest, indeed with hostility." Performers prefer "for the most part to put on works of proven effectiveness, which the public has already taken to its heart." Finally, "the possibilities of performing modern music are still further reduced because the existing concert agents and promoters . . . influence the choice of programs as much as they can, with an eye to their own financial advantage." Calling these people "special enemies" of musical life, he remarks that "with their identical and never-changing programs, the general public has already begun to stop being interested in music at all."

In spite of this and the fact that the Society of Creative Musicians lasted only one season, Schoenberg continued to write. He became more and more aware that the language of his early string quartet and *Verklaerte Nacht*—in other words, the densely chromatic but still tonal music of late Romanticism—had been used up by Mahler, Richard Strauss, Hugo Wolf, and himself to such an extent that it could no longer adequately serve his purposes. So, in the final movements of his *Second String Quartet*, Op. 10 (1908), and more particularly in his first set of piano pieces, Schoenberg stepped over the line into atonality. Although he was to say that "this music was distinctly a product of evolution, and no more revolutionary than any other development in the history of music,"[3] the *Three Piano Pieces* (*Drei Klavierstücke*), Op. 11 (1909), are not only a strong musical statement, but they constitute a break with the past and were to have an indelible effect on the music of the remainder of the century.

"That I was the first to venture the decisive step [into atonality] will not be considered universally a merit—a fact I regret but have to ignore."[4] This uncharacteristically disingenuous statement by Schoenberg barely suggests the venomous attacks that were heaped upon him not only at the first appearances of his non-tonal works but for decades thereafter. Even Richard Strauss, that once-daring composer, exclaimed in 1913, "Only a psychiatrist can help poor Schoenberg now,"[5] a statement as much informed by fear of the unknown as by measured artistic judgment.

What about the *Three Piano Pieces* stirred up such uncontrollable disquietude, anger, and fear? In many ways, the music of the first piece is indistinguishable from other turn-of-the-century middle-European romantic music. The opening melody (example 2.1) could have been written by a composer such as Mahler or Wolf. This same melody, in octaves, returns near the end of the piece in a traditional recapitulation or reprise of the opening.

In addition, the rhythmic configuration of these three opening

EXAMPLE 2.1. Schoenberg, *Three Piano Pieces*, Op. 11, No. 1, mm. 1–3. Used by permission of Belmont Publishers.

measures is often heard, with different pitches, at important junctures in the work. Sometimes the sequence is complete (example 2.2); sometimes it is incomplete (example 2.3); and at other times it is compressed but still recognizable (example 2.4).

EXAMPLE 2.2. Schoenberg, *Three Piano Pieces*, Op. 11, No. 1, mm. 9–11.

EXAMPLE 2.3. Schoenberg, *Three Piano Pieces*, Op. 11, No. 1, mm. 31–32.

EXAMPLE 2.4. Schoenberg, *Three Piano Pieces*, Op. 11, No. 1, mm. 17–18.

One can say, then, that there is a traditional scheme of melodic and rhythmic relationships. Further, the essential nature of these recurring melodies is quite simple, and their transformations are clearly effected in the manner of Wagner and the postromantic symphonists, Mahler and Strauss.

Also, this music is metrically straightforward. All but a handful of the sixty-four measures in the piece are in $\frac{3}{4}$ time (one measure is in $\frac{2}{4}$ and four are in $\frac{4}{4}$). That meter retains its historical accentual function is evident from the opening phrase, in which the emphases are clearly on the downbeats of both the second and third measures.

One notes in addition that there are passages of traditional imitative writing; certain repeating figures exude the expressive rhetoric of late nineteenth-century music. Finally, the form emerges clearly as a traditional A-B-A, with the B section intimately related to A through development of the opening melody (example 2.5).

Again one asks, why the fearful reaction? The answer must inevitably lie in the harmony. The complaint was made that Schoenberg's music, "something in the nature of physical indisposition, transcribed for

EXAMPLE 2.5. Schoenberg, *Three Piano Pieces*, Op. 11, No. 1, mm. 34–36.

piano,"[6] was "too dissonant," a grievance that Debussy's professors held against his music and that those few souls who would agree to listen held against the music of Charles Ives in America.

In fact, Schoenberg's early atonal music is no more dissonant than much of Wagner, who had rather thoroughly exploited lingering fourths and spicy sevenths long before his final opus. With Schoenberg, however, those sounds that had come to be known as dissonances and were expected eventually to be resolved *were no longer resolved*. They were, rather, allowed to stand by themselves, unfettered by convention. To underline this "emancipation of the dissonance," as it has subsequently been called, Schoenberg assiduously avoided using two kinds of harmonic sound that had, by the early eighteenth century, developed a kind of monopoly in chordal priorities and what might be called indelible psychological functions: the dominant-seventh sonority and its partner, the resolving triad built of one major and one minor third.

From our vantage point one hundred years later it is clear that functional tonality as a viable harmonic system had lost its potency by the end of the nineteenth century. Non-chordal tones, ambiguous use of chromaticism, modulation by third relationships, and the constant employment of a host of deceptive cadences (which, eventually, are neither deceptive nor cadences in any real sense) had weakened tonality so much that it hardly functioned anymore (thus, for example, Wagner's need to employ leitmotifs in his later operas in order to hold his structures in place—the substitution of a literary device for a musical one). Debussy, Schoenberg, and Ives believed it was imperative to move on to something else. Each perceived the need independently and in his own way, but, significantly, at almost exactly the same time.

It has been demonstrated over and over that composers of genius in Western music history have been able to develop their talents to the full—find their "own voice"—only by defining their particular languages, which, while based on the music of their immediate heritage, must also challenge accepted principles. Schoenberg saw his technically small but philosophically giant step into complete atonality as a logical continuation of what had gone before, but his listeners took no cognizance of historical evolution or artistic necessity. Rather, they received his music as an affront. According to conventional Viennese and Western wisdom, tonality had always existed. Therefore, it would always continue to exist.

Indeed, tonality had seemingly become entrenched in Western mythology. It was something one could believe in. But in fact, the system had been developing for centuries, shaping and reshaping contrapuntal and harmonic thought long before the Baroque and presenting the composers of the First Viennese School—Haydn, Mozart, and Beethoven—with a fully developed, complex, interlocking set of protocols that were so imbedded in practice that they became unconscious assumptions (i. e., the perfect fourth *will* resolve to a third, the recapitulation *will* be in the tonic, and so forth). Surely Beethoven, as willing to break rules as anyone, never had to *decide* to write tonally. He could choose between major and minor with all the extramusical associations each had come to imply. But tonal or atonal? No. That was a choice his exploratory music pointed toward, but it was still too far over the horizon to be conceivable for Beethoven himself.

However, for the Viennese musical public seventy-five years after the death of Beethoven, the fact that a composer had at last been forced by inner necessity to face such a choice was meaningless. Tonality was, according to these listeners, God-given, a basic law of nature, or both. Far more important, the resolution of tension in this imperfect world was a deep emotional necessity. Schoenberg seemed to be challenging this with his non-resolving atonality, and so, not surprisingly, his music was greeted with overwhelming resentment.

The miracle is that in these extraordinarily hostile surroundings Schoenberg was able to move from the heavily chromatic but still functional harmonies of late romanticism into the realm of atonality with such conviction, authority, and consistency. It could be argued that the fact that so much of the first piece of Op. 11 is traditional made this transition easier. Quite the contrary: to use a new harmonic language in an older melodic, rhythmic, and formal context must have been a singular challenge. In addition, several passages in the piece are not as conventional as those alluded to above. For example, quick, fleeting passages in thirty-second notes featuring extreme octave displacement occur in measures 11–13 (example 2.6).

EXAMPLE 2.6. Schoenberg, *Three Piano Pieces*, Op. 11, No. 1, mm. 11–13.

Several unprecedented figurative passages are integrated into the music with surprising ease, due almost certainly to Schoenberg's ability to make them harmonically compatible with the adjoining material. More astonishingly, in the third piece the traditional melodic relationships described in the first movement disappear almost completely. In their place Schoenberg proceeds in a manner no longer depending on the presentation, development, and restatement of themes. Rather, he goes to the diverse psychological states that underlie such surface features. Although the essential harmonic languages of the first and third pieces of Op. 11 are the same, the third, avoiding melodic repetition, may be said to be the first musical statement of Germanic expressionism undisguised by previous formal conventions (example 2.7). It is often described, incorrectly, as being "formless." The violence of the emotions so generated, combined with the abandonment of tonality, aroused a tumultuous storm of protest in 1909. Even today this piece sounds strikingly "modern."

EXAMPLE 2.7. Schoenberg, *Three Piano Pieces*, Op. 11, No. 3, mm. 1–4.

From 1909 through 1913, Schoenberg composed at a furious pace. Following *Three Piano Pieces* he wrote the *Five Pieces for Orchestra*, Op. 16 (1909), the one-act monodrama *Erwartung* (1909), *Six Little Piano Pieces*, Op. 19 (1911), *Pierrot Lunaire* (his most famous work), Op. 21 (1912), and several other compositions.

On the one hand all this music was astonishingly radical, though Schoenberg repeatedly asserted that he did not mean it as such. His stated goal was to allow music to follow its logical evolutionary path, which for him had been leading away from tonality and its related forms ever since the chromaticism of Bach and the expanding structures of Beethoven. On the other hand, however, the music could be said to reflect the end of an era. World War I lay on the horizon. It would profoundly change every aspect of life in Europe, certainly creative life.

There was, in what Charles Rosen calls "the intense and morbid expressivity" that seemed to "breathe the stuffy atmosphere of that enclosed nightmare world,"[7] a strong intimation of approaching catastrophe in the works of the German expressionist writers, painters, and composers, of which Schoenberg was one of the leaders.

Vilified by the Viennese public, Schoenberg seems always to have been, on the conscious level, sure of what he was doing. Yet, at the same time, he was disturbed by the nature of what resulted, a feeling that was undoubtedly exacerbated by the negative responses he received. His "logical" move into atonality gave him the feeling, he was to write, that "I had fallen into an ocean of boiling water . . . it burned not only my skin, it burned internally."[8]

The principal problem seemed to be that he could not *explain* the music that poured out of his inner being in these fertile years before the war. Having put aside some of the previously sacrosanct rules of composition, he was at a loss to invent new rules to take their place. He was a dedicated, demanding composer and pedagogue, and this problem haunted him, particularly in the period following this astonishing outburst of creative activity. He was eventually to find some answers, but not for a long time—not until the war was over and a new decade was well begun.

In the third and most radical of the *Three Piano Pieces*, Schoenberg explores not only the possibilities of non-tonal harmonies but also the concept of the nonrecurrence of themes. Returning to this latter idea in some of the *Six Little Piano Pieces*, he avoids any kind of melodic repetition. In so doing, in eschewing all rhetoric, he found continuation beyond a few phrases difficult; a piece was soon over, its message compressed. Not surprisingly, then, five of the six pieces are only one page long, and the total performance time is about five minutes.

The dynamic level, also, is reduced in these small pieces, as if to correspond to their temporal dimensions. There are brief fortes in three of the pieces, but the music dwells more characteristically in the range of double, triple, and even (on the final page) quadruple piano. One of Schoenberg's many written indications, occurring three measures before the end, *mit sehr zartem Ausdruck* (with very delicate expression), might well serve as an overall injunction for performance of the entire set.

By far the most complicated of the pieces is the first, with its flowing counterpoint and delicate *flüchtig* figures. The second, with barest wisps of melody intervening, is based entirely on a metronomically repeated, staccato third.

The third piece has directions that in the first four measures the right hand is to play forte, the left pianissimo. This unprecedented "two musics" idea is not found elsewhere in Schoenberg's piano music; one must look to the work of Charles Ives for more of this sort of thing. Played with conviction (particularly the pianissimo in the left hand, which must be extremely soft), this becomes one of the most striking passages in the set (example 2.8).

EXAMPLE 2.8. Schoenberg, *Six Little Piano Pieces*, Op. 19, No. 3, mm. 1–4. Used by permission of Belmont Music Publishers.

The next-to-last piece, though not labelled as such, is a waltz. Amusingly enough, Schoenberg, who heard waltzes every day of his life as a young man, only dared call a piece a waltz much later, after he had devised his "method for composing with twelve tones." Perhaps he felt, a dozen years later, that he could relax a bit and indulge himself in one of his favorite dance rhythms and call it just what it was. In any case, he uses that rhythm, consciously or otherwise, here in Op. 19, no. 5, and the turn-of-the-century Viennese manner is clearly evident.

The bell-like sounds of the final piece summon to mind a pastoral mountain landscape (example 2.9). Many of the works of Anton Webern, Schoenberg's student and friend, find their genesis in this haunting, exquisite piece, which was written in memory of Gustav Mahler, who had died thirty days before in June 1911. One measure in particular, the next-to-last, is unlike any other measure in this piece or those preceding it. Interrupting the static melancholy of the rest of the piece, these complex, unresolved sounds—played "exactly in time" and then disappearing coldly and abruptly—presage the shape and feel of another new kind of music forty-five years later: that of the postwar avant-garde. It is uncanny that the impersonal character of this single measure, a singular denial of feeling in an otherwise ethereally expressive piece, could so effectively predict similar gestures in the music of a Stockhausen or a Boulez two generations later.

Schoenberg wrote more piano music, but only after a long period of contemplation, during which he devised an entirely new way of com-

EXAMPLE 2.9. Schoenberg, *Six Little Piano Pieces*, Op. 19, No. 6, complete.

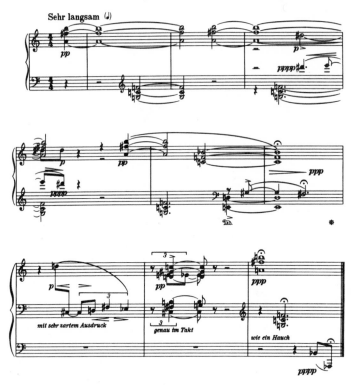

posing. We shall return to him, but first we will look at the last of the three great composers of piano music at the beginning of the century, Charles Ives.

CHAPTER THREE

Charles Ives

In the lives and music of Debussy and Schoenberg, identification with place was a matter of extraordinary importance. Debussy absorbed and reflected the cultural milieu of Paris; unhappy away from the city, he prided himself on being a *musicien français*. Schoenberg grew up with the waltzes of Vienna in his soul, and, while his relationship with the musical public was of the love-hate variety, he never wavered in his belief in the preeminence of the Austro-German musical tradition, which he sought to further in his own work.

Neither composer, however, could be said to have a more deeply rooted identification with place than their American contemporary, Charles Ives (1874–1954). Ives, now acknowledged as the most profoundly original American composer, was born in Danbury, Connecticut. Living there for twenty years, he absorbed completely the provincial attitudes and mores of the small New England town: its religious beliefs, social etiquette, and views on the place of art in everyday life. He later recognized the homespun nature of some of these attitudes and placed them in a perspective based on the cosmopolitan nature of his adult life. But that made them no less powerful a molding and motivating force in his music and a source of reflection and inspiration in his thinking.

Unlike Debussy and Schoenberg, whose parents were neither musical nor interested in music, Ives was blessed with a father, George Ives, who was a fine, intelligent musician and, equally important, an extraordinarily communicative teacher. Later in life Ives often spoke of his father, surely his most important influence, with particularly warm remembrances of "his remarkable understanding of the ways of a boy's heart and mind." In lessons that began when Charles was five and continued for almost fifteen years, the elder Ives not only passed on the basic skills of music theory he himself had mastered, but imparted to his son a devotion to music coupled with a spirit of openmindedness that was to inform all his mature works.

According to Ives, his father loved to experiment, and when his son was old enough he included his son in his "speculations." Some of these were pedagogical, as when young Charles allegedly had to sing "Suwannee River" in E-flat while George played the accompaniment in C. Others were just matters of sonic curiosity, as when they built an instrument with microtones in order to try to reproduce exactly the sound of a church bell. Then there was the fun of making up strange, widely spaced melodies on the "Humanophone," in which each member of a group of singers would be assigned a single pitch, to be sung on the conductor's cue and whim.

George Ives made it clear that these were private experiments not to be confused with the civic music making with which he, as town bandmaster, and Charles, who rather early on became a church organist, were regularly involved. The difference between private and public music translated, in Charles Ives's later work, into a clear distinction between an experimental piece, which was usually short and served to investigate the possibilities of a single new idea, and the large concert works, which often incorporated, with necessary transformations, what had been worked out in the speculative study.

The music Ives absorbed in his first twenty years was that of his father's band (for which Charles himself wrote a number of pieces and arrangements), church hymns, the sentimental ballads of the day, and the experimental pieces he and his father would improvise in private.

A totally different kind of music was brought to his attention when, as a student at Yale University in 1894, he attended classes given by the newly appointed music professor, Horatio Parker. Parker, a well-schooled, traditional composer, introduced Ives to European classical music and the idealistic philosophy that prevailed in late romanticism. Uninterested in Ives's experiments, toward which he was cool and unsupportive according to Ives's later testimony, Parker instead deepened his technical command of traditional composition and taught him to respect music not just as functional or entertaining, as it had been in Danbury, but as an end in itself and as a statement embodying the composer's personality. It is clear that Parker's influence was an important counterweight to the somewhat limited concepts Ives had developed earlier.

Ives attempted for some years to become a successful performer-composer. Moving to New York after finishing his work at Yale, he began work in the insurance business but also held a succession of church organ jobs. Writing large romantic works, following the teachings of Parker, his success with publishers and the musical public was slight. Finally, in 1902, he decided to take quite another direction. Abruptly terminating his latest organ position (he was never to perform, except privately, again), he began to divide his days between his insurance business, at which he became extremely successful, and composing. He set about writing in a new way, abandoning all thought of immediate success, composing in a personal, private manner. He devoted himself to this "after-hours" composing with enormous energy, and new works streamed out of him, especially after he met and married Harmony Twitchell, who was to become his greatest inspiration and most dependable support during the remainder of his life.

The music that Charles Ives brought out of his soul was a summation of his thought, feeling, and experience. Passionate, massive, confusing at times, heartrending, humorous, and intimate, the music did away with every possible compositional convention. In a determined and immensely ambitious attempt to capture the deep emotions that lay beneath the hymn tunes, popular ballads, and band music of his youth, Ives cast these feelings onto larger frameworks that originate with, but do not copy, the forms of the great classic composers he had studied with Parker.

Ives worked so hard at his insurance and so feverishly at his composing that, inevitably, his health suffered. An immensely positive person who came increasingly to identify with the thinking of the American Transcendentalists, especially Ralph Waldo Emerson and Henry David Thoreau, he fervently believed in progress and in humanity's ability to better itself. The destruction and cruelty of World War I seemed to him to mock these beliefs and created an inner despair, which, coupled with weakened health due to overwork, resulted in a heart attack in October 1918. From that time on Ives's ability to compose diminished. Although he lived until 1954 he wrote very little during the final three decades of his life.

Rejected and ridiculed by the musical community during his years as an active composer, Ives was sixty-five when he finally heard his great *Concord Sonata* played for the first time in 1939 by John Kirkpatrick. Ironically, as his compositional powers faded away, he slowly became recognized as America's greatest and most original composer, first through the efforts of Kirkpatrick and composers Henry Cowell, Nicolas Slonimsky, and Lou Harrison, and later through a legion of performers and conductors who came to recognize the power and wonder of his music.

Charles Ives wrote forty works for solo piano, of which a number have been lost or remain unpublished as of this writing. Most of the pieces are short experiments, but at least two, the *First Sonata* (1901–1909) and the *Second Sonata* ("Concord") (1910–1915), are massive, richly expressive masterworks, unparalleled in twentieth-century piano literature.

The *First Sonata*, a thirty-minute work in five movements, was first performed by the American pianist William Masselos in a recital in Town Hall, New York City, 17 February 1949, forty years after its completion. With composer Lou Harrison, Masselos co-edited the Peer International edition of the work. The project involved immense labor over a long period of time. The manuscripts were conflicting and often impenetrable, and the aging composer, though enthusiastic about the project, was not always helpful in reaching a definitive version of a passage or movement, for reasons discussed below. In his preface to the edition, Masselos writes, "This sonata has become very much a part of my life. . . . For me it has a very strong mystique. It is not just harmonies and form, but an emotion—a vision. . . . Its unpolished grandeur and intensely American spirit say something new to me every time. It always seems like an inspired improvisation."

With these words in mind, it is pertinent to compare Ives's most important piano music with that of his two great European contemporaries, Debussy and Schoenberg. Debussy's music, for all its freshness, color, and élan, exhibits complete polish; one feels, with his piano music, that it is the ultimate version, containing everything, be it structural breadth or detailed innuendo, as succinctly developed and as clearly portrayed as could be imagined. Schoenberg, his treatment of the instrument somewhat less polished than Debussy's, also decided on the definitive form of each piece. The unprecedented care with which he notated articulations leaves little doubt as to the exactitude and finality of his decisions.

Ives, on the other hand, presents us with music in which there is a genuine sense of indefiniteness, as though the succession of phrases given on paper is just one of several possibilities. Ives was determined to wring from his soul the secret essences of his response to life and to the mysteries of being. Thinking back to his youth in Danbury, he attempted to capture every aspect of that early existence, good and bad, in a kind of stream of consciousness. Included would be the raw emotions involved with the never-ending struggle with sin and self-negation that dominated the socio-religious thinking of New England life, a struggle that lay, barely disguised, under the seemly, proper hymns Ives knew so well, with their decorous, edifying texts.

To achieve this nearly impossible end, knowing that such emotions are too volatile to be captured and permanently mounted once and for all, Ives had to be the kind of composer for whom there need not be final and definitive versions of pieces, only close approximations or "inspired improvisations." In his *Memos* he exclaims that some passages he himself played "haven't been written out . . . and I don't know as I shall ever write them out, as it may take away the daily pleasure of playing this music and seeing it grow and feeling that it is not finished. (I may always have the pleasure of not finishing it.)"[1] It is a rare composer who finds pleasure in an unfinished or unfinishable piece!

A glance at the first movement of the *First Sonata* illustrates something of this aspect of Ives's nature; one might first conclude, in fact, that he was either negligent or lacking in compositional craft. While some passages are carefully notated, others are not; measure bars appear and disappear; dynamic markings congregate together in one passage, then do not appear for several pages; marks of articulation are altogether absent in a number of places. However, more familiarity with the score reveals that these discrepancies in detail are of little importance. In fact, in the performer's search for the central focus of the piece these problems tend to vanish. Every pianist who has seen through to the core of this music has eventually understood Masselos's words and has made his or her own personal accommodations, allowing each performance to become another version of the "inspired improvisation" of which Masselos writes.

This much said, a few words concerning Ives's ability to shape a piece are in order. Continuing with the same movement, one discovers that the principal melody is a hymn tune called "Lebanon," better known by the text of its first phrase, "I Was a Wandering Sheep" (example 3.1).

EXAMPLE 3.1. *Lebanon*, mm. 1–8.

This simple hymn had, for Ives, a rich collection of youthful associations including guilt and joy, sin and salvation, communal conformity and family warmth. The melody is completely diatonic, and although Ives occasionally makes chromatic alterations in it, he is primarily concerned not with distorting it but rather with *imbedding* it in the texture of the music (see example 3.2). For this reason he retains its essential shape, thereby encompassing the conscious and unconscious emotions he associated with it, but uses only fragments of the whole tune, sometimes rather long, but often short—short to the point that it becomes difficult to perceive (example 3.3).

In this example, near the beginning of the movement, Ives quotes the first two-measure phrase almost verbatim, but then repeats the opening perfect fifth of the second two measures and, instead of continuing the hymn tune, extends the melodic use of perfect fifths considerably in the next measure. In fact, the use of melodic perfect fifths becomes more and more important as one of the two counterweights to the basically

EXAMPLE 3.2. Ives, *First Sonata*, first movement, m. 101. Copyright 1954 by Peer International Corporation. Used by permission.

EXAMPLE 3.3. Ives, *First Sonata*, first movement, mm. 8–10.

diatonic hymn tune as the movement progresses. The other, logically enough, is the chromatic scale. One might graphically depict Ives's choice of materials in this movement as shown in figure 3.1:

FIGURE 3.1.

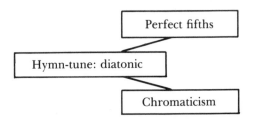

Lest this seem too simplistic or artificial an observation, I hasten to point out that the use of all three of these possibilities becomes more pronounced as the movement progresses, implying that Ives was completely aware of the use and development of these three markedly different kinds of material. Phrases taken directly from "Lebanon" are longest at the end of the movement; the unspecific chromaticism of the opening pages yields later to long and completely chromatic bass lines (example 3.4) and to undulating harmonies that appear on the final page of the movement (example 3.5).

Also, the occasional open fifths near the beginning of the movement later establish themselves more firmly (example 3.6) and more

EXAMPLE 3.4. Ives, *First Sonata*, first movement, mm. 86–89.

EXAMPLE 3.5. Ives, *First Sonata*, first movement, m. 101.

EXAMPLE 3.6. Ives, *First Sonata*, first movement, m. 98.

forcefully in the next passage just a few seconds before the movement closes (example 3.7).

Whether this piece is an "inspired improvisation" or not, Ives is very much in control of what may seem completely spontaneous. Beginning with a diffuse and even confusing contrapuntal texture in which the listener may only *think* he hears fragments of a tune, the composer gradually presents more complete phrases from the emotion-laden hymn,

EXAMPLE 3.7. Ives, *First Sonata*, first movement, m. 101.

surrounding it eventually with chains of clear, open fifths on the one hand and chromatic passages on the other, thereby placing it in a well-defined psychological-harmonic context. The rhythm, too, sometimes free, sometimes strict, gives the music a malleable, subjective quality in keeping with Ives's restless exploration of the metamorphoses of life's deepest feelings.

The structure of the *First Sonata* is symmetrical. There are five movements: the first and last are large fantasies, the second and fourth are ragtime movements, and the third is not only central to the work as a whole but is itself a symmetrical slow-fast-slow movement.

The sonata's arch form is clear (see figure 3.2): In addition, the hymn tunes used in the various movements underscore the overall symmetry. For example, the tune most often heard in the first movement, "I Was a Wandering Sheep," appears again only in the final movement. "Bringing in the Sheaves" and "Welcome Voice" both play an exuberant part in the two ragtime movements, whereas the middle movement makes exclusive use of "What a Friend We Have in Jesus."

FIGURE 3.2.

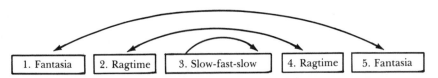

Far more important, however, than the organization or distribution of hymn tunes throughout the sonata is Ives's immensely imaginative use of his materials. This is music unlike anything written before; the strength of Ives's unshackled musical personality sweeps one into a new world of sound in which emotions of every sort are laid bare. This is accomplished in a musical language that defies every convention while, in its own way, making use of every convention.

Recent scholarship[2] has questioned the dates of composition of some of Ives's works and his own insistence, later in life, that because he had little or no knowledge of the music of his contemporaries he was uninfluenced by it. The suggestion has been made that, in their enthusiasm, such strong advocates of Ives's music as Henry Cowell emphasized the originality of his work to the extent that Ives himself exaggerated and falsified certain aspects of his musical background, including the closeness of his musical relationship with his father and the dates of works. One is sorry to be informed of spots on the image of a hero, of course, but setting the record straight in these matters, while important, does nothing to diminish Ives's actual compositional accomplishments. Whatever its dating and derivation may be, one must remember that the *First Sonata* was, at least for the most part, written some time in the first decade or so of this century, in a milieu that could hardly have been more conservative. What James Joyce was able to accomplish several decades later in literature—by spelling a single "word" several different ways he could simultaneously refer to three, four, or five different layers of experience or trains of thought—Ives was able to do in music through a kind of "rhetoric of interruption" for which one would be hard pressed to find a precedent. Ideas are announced, broken off, interpolated into other ideas, combined in new ways, and repunctuated abruptly; the harmonic language is impenetrably dissonant, innocently consonant, richly allusive, or bluntly bare; and all—whether marked *fff* or *ppp*—is insistent, urgent, and constantly assertive. Even had the work been written twenty-five years later, it would still have been astonishing.

Listeners and performers who are put off by the complexity or seemingly arbitrary nature of some of Ives's music often suggest that he must have written things down without knowing how they would sound. This is not true. Ives was a good pianist and was capable, at least in private, of playing his own difficult scores. Lou Harrison, who did an enormous amount of work to put some of Ives's music into readable shape after Ives was no longer able to do so, reported that the composer, late in life and with failing eyesight, "had memory of every page he'd ever written."[3] Indeed, Ives's early experiences writing for his father's band and choir, and his later work as a professional organist, made him a practical musician, at least in some respects. As a carefully prepared and deeply felt performance of his music makes clear, he meant what he wrote. That he might, on a given day, decide on a different version of a certain passage does not detract from this in the least.

Much more has been written about the *Second Sonata*, subtitled "Concord, Mass., 1840–1860," than about the *First Sonata*. In part this is due to Ives's own *Essays before a Sonata*,[4] a collection of six essays related to the sonata that Ives published himself in 1920. These essays are, not surprisingly, fascinating and important; also, they have focused the attention of many commentators on the *Second Sonata* to the neglect of the other.

The two works differ in approach and manner, yet it would be futile to claim that one or the other is the more substantial, convincing, radical, American, or anything else. Both stand at the pinnacle of Ives's achievements and, as has already been suggested, have no peers in the rich repertoire of piano music by American composers.

The *First Sonata* focuses on the inner revelations Ives associated with the hymn tunes of his youth; the *Concord Sonata* is an extraordinary series of meditations on four American literary figures associated with the Transcendental movement: Ralph Waldo Emerson, Nathaniel Hawthorne, Amos Bronson Alcott, and Henry David Thoreau. All lived in Concord, Massachusetts, in the years just before the Civil War. Each wrote about the philosophical, ethical, and religious issues of the day. Thus, one can say that both of these sonatas are concerned with spiritual values. In fact, Ives goes to great lengths in his essays to show how deeply involved in such values each of these writers was. For example, "It must be remembered that 'truth' was what Emerson was after—not strength of outline, or even beauty, . . ." and, "any comprehensive conception of Hawthorne, either in words or music, must have for its basic theme something that has to do with the influence of sin upon the conscience."

To hold together the vast collection of diverse musical ideas found in the four-movement *Concord Sonata*, Ives makes use of several motives that appear in each movement. The most obvious is the four-note motive that opens Beethoven's *Fifth Symphony*, a motive Ives associated with the strength of character he found in the Transcendentalist writers. (One can only wonder what irony the aging Ives felt, he whose vision of the basic goodness of humanity left no room for war, in the appropriation during World War II of this same motive—translated into the dot-dot-dot-dash Morse code signal for the letter "V" and the consequent "V for Victory"—as a rallying cry in the fight against Beethoven's homeland!)

Less obvious is the recurrence of a gentle, lyric melody that Ives called his "human faith melody" (example 3.8). This simple tune appears at least once in each of the four movements. In the "Alcotts" movement it is followed immediately by the "Beethoven motive" (example 3.9).

EXAMPLE 3.8. "Human Faith Melody."

Upon examination of the massive first movement, "Emerson," one sees that, just as in the *First Sonata*, Ives is concerned with specific melodic figures, which he manipulates, develops, and expands in pursuit of his larger goal. That goal has little to do with traditional musical forms. Rather, it is a musical representation of an idea or a belief, in this case Emerson's characteristically vigorous and variegated philosophical discourse. Ives seeks to achieve this by first bringing several different idea-motives together quickly in a texture so disconcertingly thick that one can

EXAMPLE 3.9. Ives, *Second Sonata*, "The Alcotts," "Beethoven motive," lines 2–3 of first page (there are no measures). Used by Permission of G. Schirmer, Inc.

scarcely discern individual strands. Then, as the movement progresses, he examines each in more leisurely fashion from various points of view. As in an essay by Emerson, repeated readings are necessary for full appreciation.

The "human faith" and "Beethoven" motives are, of course, present in "Emerson." In addition there are several other recurring motives, unidentified and unnamed by Ives. One we shall call a "contemplation motive" (example 3.10). A second, "hope" motive (example 3.11) is often used in connection with the first, but also may appear alone. A final "declamatory motive" (example 3.12) asserts itself fully only as the long movement draws to a close.

EXAMPLE 3.10. "Contemplation motive."

EXAMPLE 3.11. "Hope motive."

In example 3.13, the first three lines of "Emerson" are reprinted (the first two lines have been strung together). Directly below is the motivic skeleton of the same music with the various fragments labeled as above. All of these ideas are audible, yet the density of information is so

EXAMPLE 3.12. "Declamatory motive."

great that most listeners would probably admit that they were unaware of all or most of them as the music surges by. Perhaps this was Ives's intent. In any case, later sections of the movement develop these motives in more extended and detectable fashion. Nevertheless, it is fascinating to discover that all of the generating musical material in this gigantic movement is present in its opening moments.

A full study tracing the diverse settings of these motives is beyond the scope of this book. In fact, such a study is most valuable if done by the pianist at the keyboard or by the interested listener with score and recording in hand. In either case, one emerges with a heightened appreciation and sense of wonder at Ives's insight into the possibilities of musical discourse and at his bold yet sensitive concepts of the many shades and colors of beauty.

These two sonatas stand as Charles Ives's greatest musical accomplishments. For those interested in the composer's other, shorter works for keyboard, there are a host of studies and miniatures. Chief among these are the *Three-Page Sonata* (1905), the *Étude No. 22* (1912; the number is that of the page in Ives's notebook on which it was written—he composed twenty-seven "studies," of which about a dozen still exist), *The Anti-Abolitionist Riots in Boston in the 1850s* (1908), *Some Southpaw Pitching* (1908), and *Varied Air and Variations* (1914–23). Although the scope of these works can hardly be compared with that of the sonatas, they are full of Ives's characteristic humor, audacity, and ingenuity, and will brighten the repertoire of any pianist.

EXAMPLE 3.13. Ives, *Second Sonata*, "Emerson," mm. 1–6.

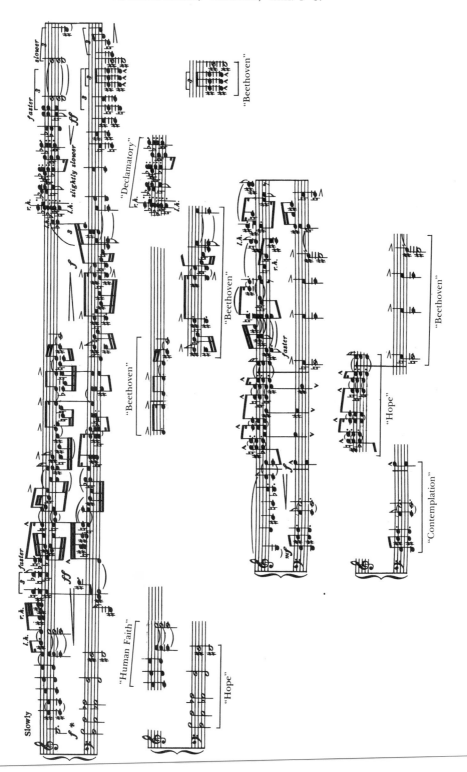

CHAPTER FOUR

Maurice Ravel

Although *Jeux d'eau* (1901) was not his first composition for the piano, the French composer Maurice Ravel (1875–1937) considered it to be the real starting point for the "pianistic novelties," as he called them, of his considerable output for the instrument. The single-movement work is, indeed, startlingly original. Ravel was a great admirer of the piano music of Liszt, and there is no question that *Jeux d'eau* is informed by the virtuosity of the nineteenth century's foremost keyboard artist. As Roger Nichols points out, Ravel's title "invites comparison with Liszt's *Jeux d'eau à la ville d'Este*."[1] However, Ravel succeeded in finding a new kind of pianistic sonority with a sparkle and glitter that was all his own.

To achieve this, he exploited the high register of the instrument with successive seventh and ninth chords in widespread, rhythmically precise arpeggiation. Here, as in the best of his later work, he demonstrates the combination of instrumental imagination and compositional control that were among his greatest attributes. An exceptionally fastidious man in all his habits, he was deeply committed to the craft of composition, so much so that the act of preparing the final score of a work was almost more important than its eventual realization in performance. And when his music was performed, he tolerated no deviations from what he had written, especially with regard to rhythmic accuracy. Indeed, if one were to mark the manner in which Ravel's music diverges most sharply from that of his compatriot, Debussy, it would be in its classic approach to meter, tempo, and rhythm.

Ravel often looked to the past, in fact, for musical models. The charming *Sonatine* (1905) is distinctly classical in structure. The *Valses nobles et sentimentales* (1911) take the listener directly to the nineteenth-century Viennese waltz. The titles of the six movements of *Le tombeau de Couperin* (1917) all reach back to the days of the great French harpsichordists of the seventeenth and eighteenth centuries. That Ravel and the young Russian composer, Igor Stravinsky (1882–1971), who was to be credited with the initiation of the neoclassic movement after World War I, were close friends and great admirers of one another's work is no surprise.

Ravel's most original piano music written after *Jeux d'eau* is found in the five pieces that constitute the *Miroirs* set (1905) and in the three-movement *Gaspard de la nuit* (1908). In these eight pieces, each of which has a pictorial or literary title, the composer's powers of evocation are at their zenith. *Miroirs* consist of portraits in sound of (1) "Noctuelles," the fluttering of moths at night, (2) "Oiseaux tristes," the songs of sad birds, (3) "Une barque sur l'océan," a ship sailing on the ocean, (4) "Alborada del gracioso," the strumming of a Spanish guitar, and (5) "La vallée des cloches," the chiming of distant bells.

The first, "Noctuelles," is particularly interesting for its rhythmic and harmonic complexity, both of which are evident in the first four measures (example 4.1). Note in particular the hemiola in the third measure. Ravel switches from the preceding $\frac{3}{4}$ to an inferred $\frac{6}{8}$ as indicated by the slurs and accents, a rhythmic jump made unusually tricky by the concurrent change in the division of the beat from three-against-four to sextuplets.

EXAMPLE 4.1. Ravel, *Miroirs*, "Noctuelles," mm. 1–4.

"Une barque sur l'océan" is less complex musically but more difficult technically. The marvelously effective arpeggiation not only conjures up the swell of the sea but also recalls the earlier water piece, *Jeux d'eau*, now set lower on the instrument (an ocean has more bass than a fountain!). Throughout, the writing style is again reminiscent of Liszt but also presages the keyboard-enveloping figural technique Ravel was soon to employ in "Ondine" from *Gaspard de la nuit* and later in the astonishing cadenza of the *Concerto for the Left Hand* (1930).

The "Alborada del gracioso" is the best-known piece from *Miroirs*. Its biting dissonances evoke both the slashing chords of the Spanish folk guitar and the bizarre *acciaccature* employed by Domenico Scarlatti in his harpsichord *esercizi* written during the mid-eighteenth century in Spain. This is a wild Spanish dance with brilliant harmonic coloration and rhythmic excitement. It is briefly interrupted in the middle section by the florid melody of the *cantaor*, a song that becomes quite elaborate before the dance returns in a concatenation of double glissandi, quickly repeated notes, and brilliant harmonies.

"La vallée des cloches" and "Oiseaux tristes" have about them the kind of treatment of "found-object" sounds—distant bells and bird calls, respectively—which, had they been written half a century later, might have caused them to be labeled "sound pieces." In the opening measures of "La vallée" the seemingly artless arrangement of different types of bell sounds is particularly remarkable, though the very boldness of the idea, with its suspension of harmonic and melodic activity, makes the subsequent, more conventional melody seem cloying (example 4.2).

EXAMPLE 4.2. Ravel, *Miroirs*, "La vallée des cloches," mm. 1–7.

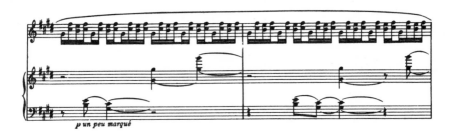

Ravel was never more consistently brilliant and inspired than in *Gaspard de la nuit*. He wished, he later commented, "to write piano pieces of transcendental virtuosity." That he was able to produce a work as technically challenging as Liszt's *B-Minor Sonata* or Balakirev's *Islamey* (which he used as a technical model) is only of passing interest. It is rather the musical achievement—colorful evocations of three diabolical poems by Aloysius Bertrand—that impresses today. Indeed, most performers and listeners would agree with the pianist Alfred Cortot that "these poems enrich the repertory of our time by one of the most astonishing examples of instrumental ingenuity ever contrived by the industry of composers."[2]

"Ondine," the first piece, begins with a murmuring ostinato figuration in the treble (example 4.3). Again, as in *Jeux d'eau* and "Une barque sur l'océan," this is water music, for Ondine is a water sprite. In the third measure the sprite's cajoling song begins, and one can almost hear the opening lines of Bertrand's poem: "Ecoute!—Ecoute!—C'est moi, c'est Ondine" ("Listen!—Listen!—It is I, it is Ondine.")

EXAMPLE 4.3. Ravel, *Gaspard de la nuit*, "Ondine," mm. 1–4.

This beautiful, quiet melody continues, briefly becoming octaves as the ostinato also becomes more wide-ranging, moving on in setting after setting, each more ravishing than the one before. Ravel's ingenuity in finding ways to divide melody and accompaniment between the hands is demonstrated again and again (example 4.4).

This same melody eventually serves as the foundation for the climax of the piece, perhaps the most memorable single passage in all of Ravel's piano music (example 4.5). Here the composer's harmonic language is extended to the utmost, yet he never allows the listener to lose track of the functional nature of the complex chords he employs: the progression is replete with shifting dominant-tonic resolutions. At the same time, in a passage of enormous virtuosity, he is able to maintain exactly the right spacing between notes, particularly in the bass, allowing

EXAMPLE 4.4. Ravel, *Gaspard de la nuit*, "Ondine," m. 52–53.

EXAMPLE 4.5. Ravel, *Gaspard de la nuit*, "Ondine," mm. 67–68.

the piano to develop a maximum richness without muddiness, to ring dazzlingly without being forced.

"Le gibet," the second piece, evokes the haunted vision, described in Bertrand's poem, of "la carcasse d'un pendu que rougit le soleil couchant" ("the carcass of a hanged man reddening in the sunset"), the only sound being that of "la cloche qui tinte aux murs d'une ville sous l'horizon" ("the clock that rings on the walls of a town on the horizon"). The sound of the distant bell and the macabre aura of the hangman's gibbet are captured immediately by Ravel's singular, hypnotic use of a pedal point—an octave B-flat—that continues unabated from the beginning to the end of the piece. Set against it, at first, is a mournful figure in open fifths (example 4.6).

Ravel notes at the outset that the "very slow" tempo should continue steadily, "without rushing or slowing until the end." The work becomes more complex but never loses its mesmerizing, inevitable nature. For the pianist, timbral and dynamic problems abound, as in that shown in example 4.7.

EXAMPLE 4.6. Ravel, *Gaspard de la nuit*, "Le Gibet," mm. 1–7.

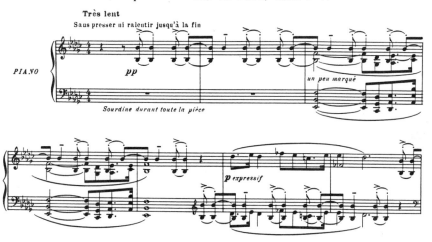

EXAMPLE 4.7. Ravel, *Gaspard de la nuit*, "Le Gibet," mm. 19–21.

Ravel described the final piece in *Gaspard de la nuit*, "Scarbo," as an "orchestral transcription for piano." Again the composer evokes an other-worldly being, in this instance a macabre goblin, through the use of an entire catalogue of colors and pianistic figurations, all tied together with one simple motive, first heard as five quick staccato notes, and, much later and in a slower tempo, enveloped in a soft, chromatically undulating figuration (examples 4.8 and 4.9). From this single figure Ravel extracts innumerable varied melodic and figural possibilities, some (for example, the famous passage in consecutive major seconds) unprecedented in the literature of the piano.

Today, Ravel's piano music is often performed in a romantic manner involving considerable use of *tenuti*, agogic accents of an exaggerated nature, and other forms of rubato. As mentioned earlier, Ravel was insistent on scrupulous adherence to the details of his scores, especially with regard to rhythm. He was not afraid, for example, to take conductor Arturo Toscanini to task for taking a wrong tempo in a performance of

EXAMPLE 4.8. Ravel, *Gaspard de la nuit*, "Scarbo," m. 52.

EXAMPLE 4.9. Ravel, *Gaspard de la nuit*, "Scarbo," m. 428–29.

the *Bolero*. Vlado Perlemuter, a distinguished pianist who studied Ravel's music under the composer and later became professor of piano at the Paris Conservatoire, writes that Ravel "let nothing slip by either in the notes or, just as much, in its interpretation." He adds, significantly, "through this passion for perfection in the letter, one found oneself in tune with the spirit."[3]

CHAPTER FIVE

Alexander Scriabin and Sergei Rachmaninoff

Alexander Scriabin (1872–1915) was the son of an aristocratic Russian family. His mother, a piano student of Leschetizsky, died when he was only two, passing on to her son not only a brilliant talent but a great love for the piano, the instrument for which Scriabin was to write ten sonatas and dozens of preludes , études, and other short works. As a small child the composer displayed a musical memory reminiscent of the young Mozart, reproducing entire compositions at the keyboard after only one hearing. This astonishing facility, coupled with a strong and sometimes bizarre creative imagination, enabled him later to compose at incredible speed: the *Fourth Sonata* and *Fifth Sonata*, certainly among his best works, were completed in two and three days, respectively.

Like his compatriot, Sergei Rachmaninoff (1873–1943), he combined a career as a concert pianist with that of a composer. Unlike the younger man, however, Scriabin showed little or no interest in the music of others, performing only his own works. Notwithstanding this extremely specialized repertoire, he was welcomed again and again in the major musical centers of Eastern and Western Europe as a pianist of consummate gifts.

It is a commonplace to state that Scriabin's early piano music is strongly influenced by Chopin. All composers begin to write more or less in the style or styles of the music around them in their youth. Scriabin, as a young piano student, would have had maximum exposure to the music of the Polish composer. Thus, many of Chopin's musical characteristics are found in his early works: the strong right-hand melodies with chromatic accompaniment and occasional secondary voices in the same hand, the combinations of marked, slow bass lines and extended left-hand arpeggiation, and the mournful sadness and melancholy cry. The real surprise is that the Russian composer was able, without artificial stylistic leaps, to move away from this consuming influence and arrive at a kind of music that, while somewhat rarified and not always convincing in its balance of form and content, remains totally pianistic, ecstatically romantic, and unlike that of any other composer. (One wonders what kinship Chopin would have felt could he have heard a performance of the *Ninth Sonata*, Op. 68, or the *Poème vers la flamme*, Op. 72.)

The linking together of an entire work through the cyclic use of a single motive or theme is a characteristic of all of Scriabin's mature music. His manner of doing so lies somewhere between Berlioz's occasionally forced or artificial *idée fixe* and Liszt's "thematic transformation," in which a melody is often times recast in so strikingly different a manner as to be nearly unrecognizable. The creation of an integral whole was of the utmost importance to Scriabin's esthetic; the unifying idea was for him the crux of the work, and therefore its reappearances had to seem both immediately intelligible and completely inevitable. In some cases (such as the theme-poor *Third Sonata*, Op. 23, or the much too long *Eighth Sonata*, Op. 66), the result is unfortunate, but in his best works, given the harmonic complexity marking each successive major composition, he succeeds admirably in avoiding formal ambiguity.

This is certainly the case with the *Fourth Sonata*, Op. 30 (1903), written when Scriabin was thirty-one years old. This sonata, the first consistently to demonstrate Scriabin's mature style, is in two connected movements of unequal length. The first acts as a relatively brief, lyric prelude to the second, a fast movement in sonata-allegro form. The sonata begins with a melody that completely dominates the short first movement (example 5.1), while the second movement begins with thematic material of a totally different nature (example 5.2). At the climax of the second movement's development section, the opening melody of the first, with a new accompaniment, suddenly shines forth (example 5.3). To tie things even more firmly together, Scriabin closes the recapitulation and ends the sonata with another return of this first-movement idea, this time in a typically ecstatic setting designed to bring forth the maximum sonorousness from the instrument (example 5.4).

EXAMPLE 5.1. Scriabin, *Fourth Sonata*, first movement, mm. 1–5. With permission of International Music Company, New York City.

Op. 30 (1903)

The *Fifth Sonata*, Op. 53 (1908), was written just a few years later. Here again, after an opening flourish, there is a short, lyric section of considerable harmonic ambiguity followed by a much faster section. In this sonata, however, there is only one movement, not two, and the tempo change referred to is just the first of many. Throughout the so-

EXAMPLE 5.2. Scriabin, *Fourth Sonata*, second movement, mm. 1–2.

EXAMPLE 5.3. Scriabin, *Fourth Sonata*, second movement, mm. 66–69.

EXAMPLE 5.4. Scriabin, *Fourth Sonata*, second movement, mm. 144–45.

nata tempos change restlessly from one extreme to another, each having its own specific motivic material. Nothing remains in place; the composer is constantly interrupting himself to move to another of the four or five tempo-motives from which the work is constructed. Still, though the form is more irregular and quirky than in the *Fourth Sonata*, it is still possible to follow the composer's design because of the clear use of motivic relationships.

The next several sonatas, as well as the preludes, études, and other short pieces written at the same time, push further into the realms of atonality than any Russian composer had dared to go, though Stravinsky was soon to go much further. It is interesting to note that Scriabin's tritone-dominated *Seventh Sonata*, Op. 64 (1911) (example 5.5), was com-

pleted just a few years after Schoenberg's epoch-making *Three Piano
Pieces*, Op. 11, of which Scriabin almost certainly had no knowledge, and
one year before Stravinsky's *Rite of Spring* (1913). This is not to imply that
Scriabin's *Seventh Sonata* is as significant as either of these works; rather,
it indicates that he was, at least in some ways, moving in the same direction as the other composers, especially from a harmonic point of view.

EXAMPLE 5.5. Scriabin, *Seventh Sonata*, mm. 12–14. With permission of International Music Company, New York City.

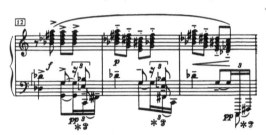

Perhaps Scriabin felt that his harmonic-contrapuntal language was
becoming a bit too thick and abstruse in the *Seventh Sonata* and the *Eighth
Sonata* (1913). The final two sonatas, Op. 68 (1913), called the "Black
Mass" (the *Seventh* had been called the "White Mass"), and Op. 70 (1913),
while still fundamentally chromatic, are leaner in texture than their immediate predecessors. Witness the beautiful opening of the *Ninth Sonata*
with its simple, transparent, yet almost completely non-tonal antiphony
(example 5.6).

EXAMPLE 5.6. Scriabin, *Ninth Sonata*, mm. 1–4. With permission of International
Music Company, New York City.

With all that can be said about Scriabin's harmonic boldness, certain
qualifications must be admitted in other areas, rendering his music something of a paradox. Though enraptured by increasingly complex sonorities throughout his career, he remained surprisingly uninquisitive from
a rhythmic point of view, relying too heavily on long cycles of four-
measure phrases. Becoming more deeply involved with his own kind of
philosophical mysticism, which led him, just before his untimely death in
1915, to the creation of pan-sensory works of the most extraordinary

nature, he was nevertheless at pains to maintain what he considered to be a convincing formal order in most of his compositions, sometimes to the detriment of their enigmatic content.

Scriabin was a fascinating composer, and his unique piano music, rooted in the romantic tradition and evolving into a world of its own, remains a challenge today.

In 1912 and 1913 there was a concerted effort on the part of the Moscow press to depict Alexander Scriabin and Sergei Rachmaninoff (1873–1943), the two leading Russian composer-pianists of the day, as rivals. Reminiscent of the famous Wagner-Brahms "feud" a few decades earlier, which was also fueled more by newspaper commentary than actual personal animosity, Scriabin and Rachmaninoff had in reality a healthy respect for one another's work and a genuine liking for one another despite their esthetic differences as composers. In fact, after the sudden death of Scriabin, Rachmaninoff organized and played a series of concerts devoted exclusively to the late composer's music, for which he continued to profess the highest admiration.

Notwithstanding his respect for Scriabin's music, Rachmaninoff remained essentially a traditionalist in his long and immensely successful career as a pianist, conductor, and composer. A man of the deepest sensitivity, he escaped from the Russian revolution late in 1917 and spent much of the remaining twenty-five years of his life in the United States. Despite receiving the adulation of the entire musical world, he never ceased to mourn the loss of his native country. His hundreds of recitals, always received as musical events of the first magnitude wherever they were presented, consisted exclusively (except for the brief Scriabin series) of the masterworks of the past and selections from his own compositions and arrangements. Today his ample discography attests to the fact that he was one of the great pianists of all time, possessing a transcendent facility in every aspect of his art.

Like Scriabin, Rachmaninoff was deeply affected by Chopin's harmonic and melodic style and by the extraordinary manner in which he wrote for the piano. He was never as much under the spell of Chopin, however, as was Scriabin in his early music. Rather, he may be said to have translated Chopin's lyric chromaticism into an essentially Russian idiom. Highly gifted as a composer and rigorously trained in the formal techniques of the art, Rachmaninoff not only brought Chopin's work to a logical conclusion, but added his own deep sense of spirituality, brooding melancholy, and, when the occasion demanded it, a soaring spontaneity that was to capture the imagination of thousands of pianists and listeners.

Unlike Scriabin and later Russian composers such as Stravinsky and Shostakovich, Rachmaninoff was not an innovator. He was to state many times with characteristic candor that he did not understand the new music of the twentieth century and had no interest in it. For him the harmonic and melodic path set forth by the great nineteenth-century romantic composers—Berlioz, Liszt, Tchaikovsky, and Mussorgsky—was the only road to travel.

Although Rachmaninoff remained active as a pianist well into his sixties, almost all of his music was written before he left Russia. The *Ten Preludes*, Op. 23, were completed in 1904, and the *Thirteen Preludes*, Op. 32, in 1910. The famous "inescapable" *Prelude in C-Sharp Minor*, Op. 3, No. 2, which is now combined with Opp. 23 and 32 to make a total set of twenty-four, was written much earlier, in 1892. In addition, the first version of the *Second Sonata*, Op. 36, was completed in 1913, and the nine *Études-tableaux*, Op. 39, in 1917. After this time he wrote only one more work for solo piano, the *Variations on a Theme of Corelli*, Op. 42, which he completed in the summer of 1931. Thus, his compositional career superficially (and ironically) resembles that of Charles Ives, who stopped composing almost entirely, because of his health, at the end of World War I. Rachmaninoff's compositional career was also contemporaneous with that of Debussy and Scriabin, whose compositional efforts were cut short by death. For his part, Rachmaninoff insisted that it was virtually impossible for him to compose away from his native country. This sentiment dominated his increasingly melancholy nature during what might have appeared to be a happy, successful, and rewarding artistic and personal life.

Not surprisingly, the melancholy that tinged his life even before he left Russia is everywhere present in his music. The opening of the much-loved *Prelude in B Minor*, Op. 32, No. 10, expresses in simple diatonic language the kind of desolation and grief so characteristic of the composer's music (example 5.7). This phrase is harmonically simple, consisting almost entirely of unaltered triads.

EXAMPLE 5.7. Rachmaninoff, *Prelude in B minor*, Op. 32, No. 10. mm. 1–6. With permission of International Music Company, New York City.

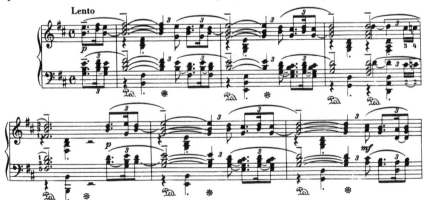

The same dotted-triplet rhythm appears in a much different context, the opening of the second theme of the first movement of the *Second Sonata* (example 5.8). Here the figure is somewhat more chromatic and the modality somewhat brighter, but the basic melancholic character remains pervasive.

EXAMPLE 5.8. Rachmaninoff, *Second Sonata*, first movement, mm. 37–38. With permission of International Music Company, New York City.

Rachmaninoff's extraordinary figural techniques and the demands he makes on the pianist's flexibility are found in passage after passage of both his solo music and the solo parts of the well-known piano concerti. Example 5.9, from the *Prelude in B-flat Major*, Op. 23, No. 2, is ample evidence of both. The wide-ranging left hand is entrusted with the principal melodic line as well as the sonorous, open accompaniment; the right hand moves with great speed through a counter-melody in octaves and chordal reinforcements. With its sweeping inner melody and shimmering, sonorous accompaniment, this passage provides a wonderful contrast to the blazing virtuosity of the opening and closing sections of the Prelude.

EXAMPLE 5.9. Rachmaninoff, *Prelude in B flat major*, Op. 23, No. 2, mm. 21–24. With permission of International Music Company, New York City.

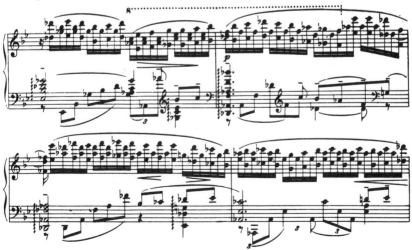

Rachmaninoff's music has not been treated kindly by composers of the twentieth century, most of whom find it anachronistic and superficial. That it is immensely popular is also cause for suspicion, at least among those for whom popularity is equated with lack of quality. It is true that he ignored virtually all twentieth-century musical trends. It is also true that his music is uneven in quality and that in some instances his skill at writing for the piano seems to become a mask for passages of fragile substance. However, as time gives perspective to his accomplishments, it is possible to see that the best of his work exhibits not only compositional craft of a high order but also an emotional message that is becoming increasingly meaningful. And the challenge to the pianist's resources remains incomparable.

CHAPTER SIX

Other Composers

As these initial discussions of piano music from 1900 to 1920 indicate, the present century began with a period of richness and diversity. While some composers set off on new paths, others developed more traditional styles. As for the instrument itself, the piano remained central to the thinking and compositional procedures of most composers, just as it had been throughout the nineteenth century. Worthy of note is the fact that the dissemination and study of the important orchestral scores written in these decades were accomplished through the medium of four-hand piano transcriptions. Thus the composer was, as a matter of course, a pianist. But the piano was not just a vital tool for the composer, it was an important fixture in the homes of tens of thousands of amateur musicians, and the piano recital was an institution integral to the musical life of every major city.

In addition to Debussy, Schoenberg, Ives, Ravel, Scriabin, and Rachmaninoff, hundreds of other composers contributed to the repertoire, several of whom should be mentioned before passing on to the next period.

Carl Nielsen

The eccentric, iconoclastic Carl Nielsen (1865–1931) has long been considered Denmark's most significant composer. His numerous works for the piano were written over four decades, thus giving an interesting picture of the compositional development of an unusually imaginative man.

Of particular interest is the *Chaconne* (1916), which is modelled on the baroque variation form of the same name, specifically the "Chaconne" from the Partita in D minor for unaccompanied violin by J. S. Bach. The twenty variations all reach back to the eight-measure bass line heard at the outset. Though the work is tonal throughout (like its model, it is in D minor), Nielsen's characteristically quirky harmonic turns and twists, handled here with convincing assurance, are clearly evident. Each variation introduces and develops a new pianistic figuration, reminding one of Beethoven's *Thirty-two Variations in C minor* (which is also a chaconne with an eight-measure theme).

Later works, such as the *Three Piano Pieces* (1928), juxtapose atonal and tonal sections for reasons that are not immediately apparent. Passages of the most diverse styles succeed one another, not for the purpose of achieving a species of Ivesian stream of consciousness but simply, it would seem, for the sheer sake of boldness. Unfortunately, too, the piano writing is not as gratifying as in the earlier work. Despite these reservations, it must be said that Nielsen's music is strong and unusual; it deserves more of a hearing than it presently receives.

Ferruccio Busoni

The great Italian-born and German-trained pianist-composer Ferruccio Busoni (1866–1924) produced most of his significant piano music between 1910 and 1920. During this period, particularly in his six *Sonatinas*, he experimented with the fusion of baroque contrapuntal practices, classical formal procedures, and contemporaneous developments in harmonic and rhythmic freedom.

Of particular interest is his correspondence with Arnold Schoenberg concerning the latter's *Three Piano Pieces*, Op. 11, which were sent to Busoni for his perusal.[1] Twelve years younger, Schoenberg remained always polite and deferential in his response to the older man's comments and suggestions, but it is obvious that he soon became extremely disturbed over Busoni's somewhat cavalier revisions of his pieces. Busoni explained, "Although I have become completely at one with the content [of the piano pieces], the form of expressing it on the piano has remained inadequate to me,"[2] a statement that could hardly have endeared him to Schoenberg.

Busoni was, of course, a great pianist, and his musical thinking was focused in pianistic terms. This is evident in his wonderful use of the instrument's resources in the transcriptions of Bach's organ works, the violin *Chaconne*, and chorale preludes. The long correspondence with Schoenberg illustrates clearly the difference between the priorities and sense of self-worth in two strong-minded personalities who embodied irreconcilable perspectives.

As a composer Busoni presents stubborn problems. For someone so enamored of the piano his original music for the instrument seems to be primarily based on intellectual concerns, eschewing the sensuous to a fault. For example, in the fourth of the *Sonatinas*, the little *Sonatina in Diem Navitatis Christi* (1917), one can easily hear the various themes and the clearly demarcated sections as they occur and recur. Everything is logical. However, the strange, quasi-Bach counterpoint, uninspired accompaniment figures, and arbitrary chordal progressions tend to leave one unmoved. Perhaps, in striving for a new kind of music, Busoni envisaged a basically unemotional style. If so, it is difficult to be convinced by the results.

The dauntingly challenging *Fantasia Contrapuntistica* (1910), of which there are four versions, certainly demonstrates the workings of an intellect of a high order. In this extended work Busoni brings together his thoughts about the music of Bach. However, the lack of differentiation in the writing style, ironically enough, eventually becomes overbearing, and again there is a sense of emotional disappointment.

Busoni was one of the most famous musicians in Europe throughout his lifetime. His influence was enormous. The conflicts between his dual roles as performer and composer are of particular interest in a study of his music for the piano.

Erik Satie

The French composer Erik Satie (1866–1925) has been credited by some commentators with such feats as initiating the neoclassic movement or, at least, of fathering an entirely new kind of music, elegant, cool, and supremely un-Wagnerian. One of the most eccentric composers of the century, he wrote short, simple pieces with a kind of outrageous harmonic boldness that is considered artlessly childlike by some, craftily prescient by others. Eric Salzman calls him "a remarkable innovator who displayed more genius than talent."[3] Salzman goes on to admit that though his music is trivial, his use of "disconnected, static, objectified sound . . . divorced from the organizational and structural principles of tonal form and development"[4] had far-reaching effects not just in his own time but decades later. Thus his influence may be said to have been felt equally by some of his contemporaries—Stravinsky, Milhaud, Poulenc, and others—as well as composers of more recent times such as the American John Cage.

This influence, however noteworthy, may be more literary and philosophical than musical. The ingenuous parallel chords of Satie's first piano pieces, *Ogives* (1886), and the static over-simplicity of the *Trois gymnopédies* (1888) are hardly improved upon in his later music. The eventual adoption of titles such as *Véritables préludes flasques* (1912) ("Flabby Preludes"), with ridiculous directions in Latin, demonstrates the composer's mordant sense of linguistic wit and satire but do very little to add to one's opinion of him as a musician.

A rather typical example of this sort of thing is the second of the three *Valses distinguées du précieux dégoûté* (Distinguished Waltzes of a Jaded Dandy, 1914), which is short enough to be reprinted in its entirety (example 6.1). The music, taken alone, is extremely simple. Despite the absence of barlines, the waltz rhythm is clear throughout. The relationship between the quotation from Cicero under the title, Satie's own text above and around the staves, and the music itself is, at best, in the realm of the surreal. (The English translations are not in the original; they have been added to the American edition by Salabert.)

EXAMPLE 6.1. Satie, *Valses distinguées du précieux dégoûté*, "Son Binocle." Used by Permission of G. Schirmer, Inc., on behalf of Copyright Owner Editions Salabert.

à Mademoiselle Linette CHALUPT
II. SON BINOCLE
(HIS MONOCLE)

A young man was forbidden by our ancient mores to appear naked in the bath, and modesty began to take root in the soul of the people.
(CICERO: "On the Republic" translated by Victor POUPIN).

Nos vieilles mœurs interdisaient au jeune homme pubère de se montrer nu dans le bain, et la pudeur jetait ainsi de profondes racines dans les âmes.
(CICERON: "De la République", traduction Victor POUPIN).

In a footnote to a similar piano piece, Satie wrote the following (in French): "To whom it may concern: I forbid anyone to read the text aloud during the performance. Ignorance of my instructions will bring my righteous indignation against the audacious culprit (*l'outrecuidant*).

No exceptions will be allowed." Whether or not this injunction is to be taken seriously is, naturally, unknowable.

Satie's most convincing piano music is probably found in the twenty wispy pieces of *Sports et divertissements* (1914), which, in the beautifully engraved original edition, include drawings in addition to titles and running commentary. Even here, however, it is possible to say only that at its best the music is innocently charming.

Manuel de Falla

Manuel de Falla (1876–1946) is among Spain's most distinguished composers. He wrote two works for solo piano. The first, *Pièces espagnoles* (1908), is a delightful collection of four characteristic dances in Spanish rhythms. Much more ambitious is the virtuoso work entitled *Fantasía baetica* (1918). Falla, who was much enamored of the music of his homeland, filled the pages of this unique composition with the colorful sounds of the Spanish guitar, as in the *molto ritmico* passage found in example 6.2.

EXAMPLE 6.2. Falla, *Fantasía Baetica*, mm. 9–11. Reprinted with permission of J & W Chester Music, New York.

Falla also successfully transcribed to the keyboard the singing style so characteristic of Andalusia; (the word "Baetica" in the title is the old Roman word for that part of southern Spain which is now called Andalusia). This strong, declamatory vocal tradition, relying heavily on constant chromatic inflections, is translated by the composer into octaves with what might be termed "doubly dissonant" grace notes (example 6.3).

Béla Bartók and Zoltán Kodály

Because his best known works for piano solo were written during the 1920s, the music of Béla Bartók (1881–1945) will be discussed in chapter 7. For the moment it should be at least mentioned that some of his most original works for the piano were written in the earliest decades of the century. His compatriot, Zoltán Kodály (1882–1967), made his principal musical contributions in areas other than for the piano. Nevertheless, his evocative *Seven Piano Pieces*, Op. 11 (1910–18), and *Dances of Marosszek* (1930) demonstrate a fresh, improvisatory approach to the setting of folk music.

EXAMPLE 6.3. Falla, *Fantasía Baetica*, mm. 135–41.

Karol Szymanowski

Karol Szymanowski (1882–1937) was in his day considered the greatest Polish composer since Chopin. Not surprisingly his first works for the piano, written while he was a student at the Warsaw Conservatory, are very much influenced by the earlier composer. Szymanowski's *Sonata No. 1*, Op. 8 (1905), which won top honors in the 1910 Chopin Centenary Competition in Lwów, demonstrates his abilities as a composer of sonorous virtuoso piano music, but the strictures of sonata form, as he perceived them, seem to have been more a barrier to expression than an aid.

More suited to his abilities are the *Four Études*, Op. 4 (1903), which are beautifully balanced formally and have a nice sense of pianistic sound and flow. Technically challenging, as is all his music, these are probably Szymanowski's best known pieces.

He returned to the challenge of the piano sonata on two occasions. The *Sonata No. 3*, Op. 36 (1916–1919), indicates that Szymanowski's musical development led beyond Chopin toward the mystic works of Scriabin's late period, the sprawling tone poems of Richard Strauss, and the labyrinthine chromaticism of Max Reger. The sonata is in one long movement, and again the writing is fiercely difficult. Unfortunately the busy, opaque texture of most of the piece makes it difficult to follow.

Again, his smaller works are more successful. The *Twenty Mazurkas*, Op. 50 (1923–1929), are well worth investigation. The composer himself called the mazurkas "a pure, undisturbed expression of the Polish race."

Alban Berg

Alban Berg's (1885–1935) youthful *Sonata*, Op. 1 (1908), is well known. Though it is completely tonal, the one-movement work, completed while Berg was a student of Schoenberg, is so heavily inflected chromatically that it is not difficult to trace the path that led the composer from it to such later serial works as the *Lyric Suite* (1926) for string quartet, the operas *Wozzeck* (1921) and *Lulu* (1934), and the *Violin Concerto* (1935). The sonata is often called a "modern" work by pianists, probably because of its composer's later accomplishments. More properly, as is the case with Scriabin's early music and all of the oeuvre of Rachmaninoff, it is a fine example of romanticism, redolent of late nineteenth-century compositional thought and practice.

Berg adheres to the basic procedures of sonata-allegro form in this extended movement, even providing a repeat of the exposition. Because of the music's hyper-romantic nature, fluctuations in tempi are a constant feature. These are carefully indicated by the composer; in fact, relatively few measures do not include a *ritard* or an *accelerando*. Careful attention to the composer's specified tempo relationships is important in order to project the structure of the large work convincingly. Indeed, a fault of many performances is that important points of arrival are ill-defined through excessive rubato, which the rich harmonic diet makes tempting. Note, for example, that the second idea in the first group of themes (m. 11) is *Rascher als Tempo I* (faster than tempo I), the second theme (m. 29) begins *Langsamer als Tempo I* (slower than Tempo I), and the closing idea (m. 49) is marked *Viel langsamer* (much slower). Adherence to these relationships is essential. However, between each of these important structural moments in the exposition are other tempo shifts; it is therefore imperative to gauge every change with considerable care so that one arrives at these key points with a sense of inevitability. And, of course, the kind of "rubato on rubato" that can creep into the performance of any romantic work after long familiarity must be carefully guarded against.

Though the opening statement of the principal theme is homophonic (melody with chordal accompaniment), (example 6.4), the sonata is full of beautifully written contrapuntal passages, lifting up to the first big climax on the way to the second theme (example 6.5). Such passages abound throughout the sonata, giving the performer rich opportunities for color and voicing. One only wishes Berg had been able to contribute more than this one impassioned work to the repertoire.

Charles Tomlinson Griffes

In the United States the most original composer of piano music at this time, other than Charles Ives, was Charles Tomlinson Griffes (1884–1920). Griffes's music pales in comparison to his Transcenden-

EXAMPLE 6.4. Berg, *Sonata*, Op. 1, mm. 1–4. Reprinted by permission of C. F. Peters Corporation on behalf of Robert Lienau, Berlin (Lichterfelde).

EXAMPLE 6.5. Berg, *Sonata*, Op. 1, mm. 17–24.

talist contemporary in New England, nor does it have the strength nor the individuality of his great successor, Aaron Copland (b. 1900). Nevertheless, the *Roman Sketches* (1916), especially "The White Peacock" and "The Fountains of the Acqua Paola," show that Griffes understood better than most of his contemporaries what Debussy and Ravel were accomplishing in Europe. His *Sonata* (1918) is structurally flawed but not without moments of grandeur and beauty.

By 1920 what had previously remained of the traditional nineteenth-century European way of life had been violently laid to rest. The Great War, the "War to End All Wars," had seen to that. In music the break with nineteenth-century traditions was also thoroughly accomplished during the first two decades of the century. By 1920 the music of Debussy, who had freed sound from the last strictures of functional tonality, was tremendously influential everywhere, so much so that anti-Debussy movements were already afoot. Schoenberg, having put tonality completely behind him, was slowly becoming a powerful force on the international scene, though the full effect of what he had achieved would only become apparent in later years. Charles Ives, perhaps the greatest innovator of them all, would have to wait half a lifetime to see his music receive the recognition it deserved. The younger Stravinsky had rocketed to fame with his colorful, explosively rhythmic ballets, and now he was confusing everyone by setting off in new directions.

The intense seriousness and complexity of much of the music of the first two decades of the century was now rejected by a society exhausted by war. The Dadaist movement allowed people to have a good laugh; Cocteau and Satie championed the music of the café and music hall; the study of folk idioms by Bartók and others helped composers to develop truly indigenous styles; Stravinsky began to write for small, economical ensembles using clear, objective sonorities in pieces that were the progenitors of the neoclassic movement; such diverse composers as Hindemith and Copland would soon recognize, each in his own way, that the composer must consciously reach out to his audience, even if it meant simplifying his style; American jazz was blooming, and, as it began to influence Europeans, thereby reversing what had been previously a one-way cultural flow, so independent-minded composers such as Henry Cowell began to call for music that was completely free from the dictates of the conservatory traditions of Europe.

As before, many of the finest composers of the new era saved their most innovative and personal thoughts for the piano. Bartók, Stravinsky, Prokofiev, Shostakovich, Enesco, Casella, Poulenc, Copland, and Cowell all spent at least a portion of their careers as concert artists. Each developed a personal approach to the instrument as composer-pianist, leaving a rich and varied legacy.

PART 2

Between the Two World Wars

CHAPTER SEVEN

Béla Bartók

The piano music of Béla Bartók (1881–1945) is significant in a number of ways. In particular, his unique compositional style, involving both tonal and atonal elements, incorporates classical formal procedures with deeper understanding than does the music of almost any other twentieth-century composer; also, his keyboard writing extended the technical development of the instrument in a manner virtually unrivalled; in addition, his pedagogical works enriched the repertoire immeasurably at every level; finally, his music in all genres demonstrated to a generation or more of composers what could be gained from the study of indigenous folk idioms.

This extraordinary man was born 25 March 1881 in the Hungarian town of Nagyszentmiklós (since the Treaty of Trianon in 1920 the town has been part of Romania and is called Sânmiclăuşulmare). His parents were musical and, consequently, there was a great deal of music in the home. Bartók's development as a musician would probably have proceeded quickly and happily had he not himself contracted a number of childhood illnesses and, even more unfortunate, had his father not died suddenly when the boy was only seven, leaving the mother in severe financial circumstances. Bartók's extraordinary talent grew despite these problems. When he was eleven he gave his first performance: a movement from Beethoven's *Waldstein Sonata*, Op. 53, and a composition of his own called *The River Danube*.

Bartók was, apparently, an exemplary student. He was constantly studying, practicing, rehearsing, and composing, and, in addition, he took every opportunity to hear concerts. In his autobiography he states that by the time he was eighteen he knew music literature—solo music, chamber music, orchestral literature, and opera—from Bach to Brahms, "pretty well." At that time, in 1899, he was accepted into the Budapest Academy of Music, where the professors were so impressed with his audition as a pianist that all fees and other examinations were instantly waived.

His days as a student at the Academy were active and, for the most part, encouragingly successful. His principal problem, in addition to a constant lack of money, was his insistence on the fact that as a composer he wanted to develop a specifically Hungarian kind of music. This was an ideal for which his German-trained teachers had little sympathy. It is difficult to know exactly how or where he received, much less maintained, the tremendous inner impetus to achieve this goal, one that he shared with virtually no one else in the conservative musical environment of Budapest at the turn of the century. But maintain it he did, and there is no question that his eventual researches into the folk music of the Hungarian countryside gave him the means with which to achieve it.

"I was seized with the desire to travel," he wrote concerning his activities during his twenty-fourth year. "So I began to explore Hungary. As I went from village to village I heard the true music of my race—folk music. This was just the stimulus I needed . . . I wanted to do two things: to bring back the spirit of folksong, and to harmonize the melodies in modern style."[1] Meticulously transcribing hundreds of Hungarian, Slovakian, and Romanian folksongs, Bartók became the quintessential ethnomusicologist long before that term was invented. He and his close friend Zoltán Kodály published their first volume of folksongs in 1906, and Bartók himself published his first arrangements of folksongs, *Three Folk Songs from Csík County*, for piano, in 1907.

It should be noted that the composer's earlier piano music—of particular interest are the *Four Piano Pieces* (1903) and the *Rhapsody*, Op. 1 (1904)—is in a decidedly nineteenth-century romantic style reminiscent of Brahms and Liszt. The forward-looking harmonic practices for which Bartók later became famous are not to be expected in this music. It was only with the discovery and gradual integration of folk music that he was able to free his talents from the heavy influence of middle-European traditions.

Bartók was not just interested, then, in making settings for or arrangements of the folksongs he studied. That was only the first step. Far more important was the fact that the study of folk music could be the starting point for what he referred to as a "musical renaissance." He wished to internalize peasant music to such an extent that it would be like a musical mother tongue. Amplifying this, Kodály wrote that "a German musician will be able to find in Bach and Beethoven what we had to search for in our villages: the continuity of a national musical tradition."[2]

Having been trained in the classical tradition and knowing that repertoire intimately, Bartók was now superbly prepared to investigate his own "national musical tradition." Music poured from him. There was orchestral music, a string quartet (1908), and an opera (*Duke Bluebeard's Castle*, 1911), but the majority of his works at this time are for solo piano. There are the *Fourteen Bagatelles*, Op. 6 (1908), *Ten Easy Pieces* (1908), *Two Elegies*, Op. 8b (1909), *For Children* (1909)—eighty-five arrangements of folksongs—*Two Romanian Dances*, Op. 8a (1910), *Sketches*, Op. 9 (1910), *Four Dirges* (1910), *Three Burlesques*, Op. 8c (1910), and the famous *Allegro Barbaro* (1911). All demonstrate the extraordinary effects on his compositional imagination of his investigations into the music of Hungary and the surrounding countries. It is also evident that Bartók was a pianist as well as a composer, and that his keenly sought "musical renaissance" was worked out, more often than not, at his favorite instrument.

The *Fourteen Bagatelles*, in particular, show clearly that Bartók's musical language was taking definitive form. The first bagatelle, only one page long, astonishes; the folk-like melody in the right hand, in four sharps, is accompanied by descending scales in the left, in four flats (example 7.1).

EXAMPLE 7.1. Bartók, *Fourteen Bagatelles*, Op. 6, No. 1, mm. 1–9. New version © copyright 1950 by Boosey & Hawkes, Inc. Reprinted by permission.

Among the various notational experiments to be found is the following from the opening of the twelfth bagatelle (example 7.2), to which the composer affixes the following note: "a gradual acceleration, without a fixed number of repeated notes."

EXAMPLE 7.2. Bartók, *Fourteen Bagatelles*, Op. 6, No. 12, mm. 1–3.

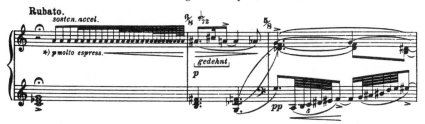

In the years from 1916 to 1926 Bartók wrote his finest works for the piano, beginning with the *Suite*, Op. 14 (1916). The *Fifteen Hungarian Folksongs* are from the following year, and the *Three Études* from the year after that. Then came the piano compositions for which he is best known: the *Improvisations on Hungarian Peasant Songs*, Op. 20 (1920), the *Sonata* (1926), and the *Out of Doors* suite (1926). With the notable exception of the six volumes of *Mikrokosmos*, 153 progressive studies completed in 1937, Bartók wrote no more for piano alone. He became absorbed primarily with chamber and orchestral music: the string quartets, the *Sonata for Two Pianos and Percussion* (1937), the three piano concerti and two violin concerti, *Music for Strings, Percussion and Celeste* (1936), the *Concerto for Orchestra* (1944), and other ensemble works.

By the time of the *Suite*, Op. 14, the classical and folk elements had been completely fused in Bartók's work. The piece is in four movements, of which the first, a dancing "Allegretto," is the most folk-like. Though not a long piece—only four pages in the printed score—one becomes aware during its short span of the composer's mastery of form and shape as he moves the simple melodic material through his special kind of continuous development. Characteristically, the music seems constantly to be evolving. Bartók was later to write concerning all of his mature work, "I do not like to repeat a musical thought unchanged, and I never repeat a detail unchanged. This practice of mine arises from my inclination for variety and for transforming themes."[3] Clearly in this little piece there is the progression from statement to development and climax to return, but by the end one also has the impression that the opening tune has been developed out of existence.

As elsewhere, Bartók's penchant for tritone relationships is much in evidence. Ostensibly a piece in B-flat, the secondary key center is E, and the alternation between the two centers is usually abrupt, as is shown in example 7.3. The lighthearted second movement is a rapidly moving scherzo that makes use of interlocking augmented triads in the initial statement (example 7.4). Much of the movement extends and varies this basic idea.

EXAMPLE 7.3. Bartók, *Suite*, Op. 14, first movement, mm. 1–12. © Copyright 1918 by Universal Editions; Copyright Renewed. Copyright and Renewal assigned to Boosey & Hawkes, Inc. Reprinted by permission.

EXAMPLE 7.4. Bartók, *Suite*, Op. 14, second movement, mm. 1–16.

The third movement, "Allegro molto," is considerably darker in mood than the "Scherzo." Over a constantly moving ostinato, Bartók introduces the simplest possible motive (example 7.5), adds its tritone counterparts, A and G-sharp, develops the motive with continuously rising excitement, and drives to a climactic close.

EXAMPLE 7.5. Bartók, *Suite*, Op. 14, third movement, motive.

Of all the movements, the slow "Sostenuto" that ends the work demonstrates Bartók's mastery of variation, sensitivity to musical shape, and extraordinary emotional intensity. Enigmatic to many pianists at first, the movement repays close study, revealing the somber, introspective side of the composer in a manner seldom surpassed in his other piano music. Again the principal melodic idea is of the utmost simplicity and brevity, yet by the end it has been stretched, turned, and otherwise examined from all sides, disclosing an emotional pathos one would not expect possible using such transparent means.

If the *Suite* is the easiest of Bartók's major works to play, the *Three Études*, Op. 18, are the most difficult. Perhaps because of their specific nature as études, they show less of the influence of folk music than his other mature piano music. Here Bartók, the concert pianist and pedagogue, concerns himself with those technical problems that he felt needed to be addressed in new ways, ways that nineteenth-century études could not have done.

If one were to characterize the overall intentions of these studies in two words, they might be "asymmetrical extensions." For example, the first étude keeps both hands stretched further than an octave almost all the time, but the precise interval is subject to constant change. The music shown in example 7.6, for instance, never repeats the same interval immediately. Add to this the ever-changing black-white keyboard relationships, and one has a passage in which the position of the extended hand and wrist will always be shifting.

EXAMPLE 7.6. Bartók, *Three Studies*, Op. 18, No. 1, mm. 19–22. © Copyright 1920 by Universal Editions; Copyright Renewed. Copyright and Renewal assigned to Boosey & Hawkes, Inc. Reprinted by permission.

The second étude deals in somewhat similar fashion with wide-ranging arpeggios that often follow asymmetrical, nonrepetitive patterns, thereby causing the hand to extend in a rapidly changing manner while moving laterally about the keyboard.

The third étude, most difficult of all, requires the left hand to move rapidly through constantly fluctuating patterns while the right hand punctuates with staccato chords. This may well be Bartók's most atonal piece for the piano. It is also extremely complex metrically, as example 7.7, with its succession of time signatures, $\frac{6}{8}, \frac{15}{16}, \frac{6}{8}, \frac{4}{8}, \frac{10}{16}, \frac{11}{16}$, illustrates.

EXAMPLE 7.7. Bartók, *Three Studies*, Op. 18, No. 3, mm. 19–23.

The *Improvisations on Hungarian Peasant Songs*, Op. 20 (1920), consists of eight movements, each devoted to a single folktune. Altogether they form a lively textbook of Bartók's skill at harmonizing tunes and creating variations. Most of the movements are short; altogether the eight settings take about thirteen minutes to play. Usually the tune is introduced immediately, though there may be a short introduction. The first statement is already a "variation" of sorts, and it is followed by two or three more, each of which, in characteristic fashion, develops further a specific approach to the harmonization of the tune. For example, the second folksong is first set to chromatically expanding harmonies; each of three succeeding variations seems quite different from the first, but in every case small intervals expand to large. On the other hand, the seventh piece, ("À la memoire de Claude Debussy"), is a fascinating and affecting study of harmonies that seem to collapse on themselves.

The pieces are arranged in an admirable succession, and it is highly recommended that the work be done as a whole with movements in the original order. Performers will do well to note carefully the presence or absence of "attacca" directions by the composer. These tend to link slow pieces with fast in characteristically Hungarian fashion.

The *Out of Doors* suite (1926) is in five movements, each with a title. The first, "With Drums and Pipes," begins with percussive sounds, major and minor seconds, played low on the instrument in imitation of drums. Little by little the music ascends into the middle range and treble, becoming more melodic and contrapuntal but never losing the rhythmic drive of the opening. The piece concludes by returning to the drum sounds, which now accelerate, becoming quite wild just before being interrupted by a brief coda.

The second and third pieces, "Barcarolla" and "Musettes," have many interesting features. Both suffer from being somewhat overlong, a fault quite uncharacteristic of most of Bartók's writing. In "Barcarolla" the composer takes the basic $\frac{6}{8}$ meter associated with Venetian boatsongs and plays with it, expanding to $\frac{7}{8}$ and contracting to $\frac{5}{8}$ or $\frac{4}{8}$. In so doing he makes many subtle changes on the basic underlying motive, which nevertheless seems to wear out its welcome before it is heard for the last time. "Musette," based on drone or bagpipe folkmusic, fascinating in detail, also seems a bit overextended.

The most famous of the movements is the fourth, "Musiques nocturnes," or "Night Music(s)." Bartók was a lover of nature and always enjoyed walking in wooded areas in the country. In this piece he has tried to capture the feeling of being alone in the forest at night, not necessarily by trying to transcribe exactly the kinds of sounds one might hear, though some of them are there, but by replicating the emotional atmosphere of the cool darkness and that tinge of anxiety or unease that can underline such an experience. In example 7.8, the left hand, written on two staves, plays a quiet, broken-cluster ostinato while the right hand skitters about with sudden and unpredictable calls and echoes.

In "La vallée des cloches" from *Miroirs* Maurice Ravel had already done something like this, creating a sense of landscape and distance with bell sounds reproduced on the piano. Bartók carries the idea of transplanting natural sounds and the feel of the forest much further in "Musiques nocturnes." Fascinating in conception, this movement had an indelible influence on composers of succeeding generations. One thinks, for example, of the second movement of Leon Kirchner's fine *Piano*

EXAMPLE 7.8. Bartók, *Out of Doors*, "Musiques nocturnes," mm. 9–12. © Copyright 1927 by Universal Editions. Copyright Renewed. Copyright and Renewal assigned to Boosey & Hawkes, Inc. Reprinted by permission.

Sonata (1948) and the two haunting "Night-Spell" movements in George Crumb's two-volume *Makrokosmos* (1972–1973) for solo piano.

The final movement, "The Chase," is an exciting, driving study requiring strength and endurance from the left hand. The intensity never lets up from beginning to end.

Bartók's greatest contribution to the solo repertoire is surely the *Sonata* (1926). In this relatively short three-movement work he brought together the two principal currents of his compositional life, a deeply rooted understanding of the manner in which central European classical formal procedures could be used in the twentieth century, and a completely digested synthesis of folk idioms originating outside the classical tradition.

The Viennese sonata procedure, as Haydn, Mozart, and their predecessors had developed it from various baroque antecedents, was notably concerned with key centers: establishment of a home key, departure from it and temporary affirmation of a secondary key, and reestablishment of the original home key. Melodic themes were not insignificant, nor was a rather loosely defined structural procedure, but while these could be subject to manipulation and rearrangement, basic key relationships were almost never tampered with in early sonata movements.

As tonality evolved, expanded, and eventually weakened in the sonatas of Beethoven, Schubert, Chopin, and their successors, the importance of key relationships lessened as well. Contrast between themes became much more sharply marked, episodes with a harmonic life of their own were introduced, and the basic, functional dominant-tonic structures gave way to more exotic, mobile key relationships in increasingly lengthy compositions.

By the mid-1920s, of course, this was all a matter of history, yet it was of great concern to Bartók. His goal was not to step backwards but to extract the essence of the early sonata procedure, which he felt exhibited the highest artistic balance between form and substance, and translate it into modern terms usable to him. In so doing he rejected the idea expressed by Stravinsky in reference to his own *Piano Sonata* (1924, see chapter 8) that the word *sonata* meant only a piece "sounded" on an instrument or instruments and that no formal or tonal procedures need be invoked. And because of his involvement with folk music he could not, for his own work, accept Schoenberg's premise that a piece of music could be non-tonal, though it was clear to him that many rules of functional tonality had been rendered inoperative.

The first movement of Bartók's *Sonata for Piano*, not surprisingly, is in a sonata-allegro structure that, while of his own devising, owes much to essential aspects of early sonata form. Immediately, one hears that the opening measure serves as a dominant to E, and the remainder of the first two pages, in addition to developing the opening rhythmic and melodic motives, essentially confirms E as the tonic center of the piece (example 7.9).

A transition follows, leading to the folklike second theme. Having passed through several temporary key centers on the way, Bartók sees less need to preserve the late eighteenth-century tonic-up-to-dominant arrangement than eventually to return to the home key, and so the second theme travels elsewhere, as does the brief development that follows. But when it is time to recapitulate, the composer again returns to E by way of the dominant, though in a variant of the manner in which it was introduced at the outset (example 7.10).

Equally conclusive in this discussion is the fact that the coda, which, following numerous excursions into foreign harmonic territory, reiterates E as tonic and B as dominant in the strongest manner (example 7.11), then holds the B as a pedal point until finally resolving it through a long *glissando* to the last note, E (example 7.12).

These seem to be small details, and one may not see that they dem-

EXAMPLE 7.9. Bartók, *Sonata for Piano*, first movement, mm. 1–12. © Copyright 1927 by Universal Editions; Copyright Renewed. Copyright and Renewal assigned to Boosey & Hawkes, Inc. Reprinted by permission.

EXAMPLE 7.10. Bartók, *Sonata for Piano*, mm. 186–87.

EXAMPLE 7.11. Bartók, *Sonata for Piano*, mm. 247–50.

onstrate anything important concerning Bartók's skill as a composer or his deep affinity for the essence of classical sonata procedures. But in fact these dominant-tonic relationships occur in a composition that is probably noted more for its seething rhythmic energy and driving force than for its tonal coherence, and they occur in those same places—the opening, the retransition to the recapitulation, and the closing—that were of such importance to the composers who did so much to define the sonata a century and a half earlier.

EXAMPLE 7.12. Bartók, *Sonata for Piano*, mm. 267–68.

B———E
(V———I)

Of equal fascination is a study of motivic development throughout the movement. Bartók's craft and sense of timing are particularly evident in his manner of varying the simplest figure, little by little, until there is nothing more to do with it.

The second movement is still enigmatic to some, though not so much as it used to be.[4] It is now recognized that the slow reiteration of a single tone—again, it is E—at the opening and at several important junctures in the piece recalls a kind of mourning chant that Bartók often heard among Hungarian, Romanian, and other Slavic peasants when he did his painstaking ethnomusicological fieldwork. Many earlier compositions show his interest in this kind of chant: elegies, *nenies*, and the like.

In fact, the second movement of the sonata is one of the composer's most affecting, poignant works for the piano. In A-A'-B-A" form, it is particularly interesting to see how the two returns of the A section are varied, each time deepening the pathos and sense of grief that envelops the piece. Thematically, Bartók chooses the simplest materials: the single-note chant, a four-note diatonic scale, and a chain of perfect fourths harmonized with characteristic open sonorities. These are linked together in expanding yet recognizable ways as the movement proceeds to its trenchant close.

The last movement is a delightful rondo, bumptious and even impudent at times, but always smiling (example 7.13). As in so many of Mozart's keyboard finales, the principal theme, again in E, is set twice at each appearance, the second time (also as with Mozart) in an expanded timbre. This theme is also used in thinly disguised variations in the several digressions, so the movement, for all its whirling energy, is held together tightly.

Pianistically, the sonata is demanding, but not overbearingly so. The biggest danger is overplaying, a sin Bartók himself almost never committed as a pianist. The old myth that he is a "percussive" composer is dying, if not quite dead. Anyone who writes for the piano, after all, may justifiably be called a percussive composer, since sound is created on the instrument by striking strings with felt-covered hammers. The fact that Bartók often employs repeated notes, large chords, and reiterated ostinati should not define his music as more percussive than, for example, that of Beethoven, Liszt, or Rachmaninoff, who also use the same devices. Voicings, balance, tonal control, and supple command of coun-

EXAMPLE 7.13. Bartók, *Sonata for Piano*, third movement, mm. 1–19.

terpoint: all have as much a place in the performance of Bartók's music as with that of any other composer for the piano.

Bartók began writing the pieces to be included in the *Mikrokosmos* collection during the same year in which he wrote the *Sonata*, completing the six volumes eleven years later, in 1937. The 153 pieces progress from easy to intermediate to difficult. More importantly, they demonstrate at every stage a wide range of idioms and musical concepts in a comprehensive and imaginative manner still unrivaled in the pedagogical literature. In addition, the pieces provide excellent stimulation to creative work, demonstrating at the outset how one can work imaginatively with simple material and, in the later volumes, that it is possible to maintain discipline and control while addressing unfamiliar rhythmic, contrapuntal, and stylistic problems.

Although *Mikrokosmos* is rightly considered a collection designed for teaching, there is plenty of material in the last two volumes suitable for concert use, such as "Boating," "Merry Andrew," "From the Diary of a Fly," and the challenging "Six Dances in Bulgarian Rhythm," which concludes Book VI. That these and other pieces from the collection have been transcribed for various instrumental combinations over and over again is surely a tribute to their musical effectiveness and, therefore, to the uniquely gifted composer who conceived them.

CHAPTER EIGHT

Igor Stravinsky

In all the volumes that have been written about Igor Stravinsky (1882–1971), mention is unfailingly made of his sensational success with Sergei Diaghilev and the Ballet Russe. For them he wrote *L'oiseau de feu* (*The Firebird*) in 1910, *Petrouchka* in 1911, and, best known of all, *Le sacre du printemps* (*The Rite of Spring*) in 1912. The furor and scandal surrounding the first Paris performance of *Le sacre* in 1913 is legendary.

Following these works, however, Stravinsky confounded everyone by setting off in a new direction. Putting aside the huge orchestral sonorities and crashing rhythms of *Le sacre*, he began to employ thinner textures, smaller forms, and a kind of neo-tonality which established tonal centers through reiteration rather than functional gravity. With a generally spare and more objective musical language he wrote for small ensembles, sometimes just a few instruments of contrasting timbre as in *L'histoire du soldat* (*The Soldier's Tale*) from 1918. He looked to the music of the past for formal models and even for stylistic characteristics, though his musical personality was so strong that he was able to transform whatever model he chose into his own specific and incomparable style, full of wit and vigor. One could say that he used the music of the past as Bartók used folk music: assimilating, synthesizing, and transmuting it to his own purposes. More than anyone he was responsible for the establishment of the neoclassic movement in the 1920s, not a "school" per se but rather a point of view that found unacceptable the blurred pastels of impressionism and the anguished gloom of expressionism, neither of which seemed appropriate to those who had just lived through the agonies of World War I. All the principal composers between the two world wars were affected by and, in some way, contributed to the neoclassic movement, as shall be seen in the chapters ahead.

One could term the neoclassic period a time in which composers remained in a holding pattern after the explosive changes that had taken place during the first fifteen years of the century. But that does the period an injustice, or at best it is only a partial truth, for strong, enduring music came from a host of pens during this time.

Stravinsky was a fine pianist and wrote a number of extended works for piano and orchestra: one thinks of *Petrouchka*, which started as a piano concerto and ended as a ballet, as well as the two piano concerti and *Mouvements* (1959) for piano and orchestra. However, the list of his solo piano music, containing a number of minor or youthful works such as the uncharacteristic *Sonata in F-sharp Minor* (1903), the *Four Études* (1908), the over-refined *Piano Rag Music* (1919), and the *Tango* (1940), includes only three works that are clearly of major importance. Completed within five years of one another in the early 1920s, when the composer was most active himself as a pianist, they are the *Three Movements from Petrouchka* (1921), the *Piano Sonata* (1924), and the *Sérénade en la* (1925). Of these, the last two perfectly illustrate, in quite different ways, the essence of neoclassicism at its best.

The *Three Movements* are virtuosic transcriptions of portions of the first, second, and fourth scenes from the ballet *Petrouchka*, which was first produced by Diaghilev in 1911. Earlier that year by chance Stravinsky had mentioned to Diaghilev that he was working on a concert piece for piano and orchestra. Hearing some of it, the ballet director set about convincing Stravinsky to recast it as a ballet. In the final version of the work, therefore, the piano's dominant role is not surprising. The success of the score and the appealing, individualistic nature of the piano writing in it made the work a natural for transcription.

In fact, however, all of the Stravinsky ballets were transcribed for piano four-hands as a matter of practical necessity: ballet rehearsals could take place only if the music could be repeatedly played at the keyboard. But a two-handed concert version of a work for piano and orchestra, a work that was already taxing for the pianist? Obviously Stravinsky was intrigued and challenged with the idea and, in 1921, came up with not only one of the great virtuoso piano pieces of the century but also an engrossing lesson in keyboard transcription that is virtually without peer.

It is, unfortunately, not possible to reproduce here the orchestral score from which an excerpt from the beginning of the "Danse russe," the first of the *Three Movements*, is taken (example 8.1). Those who have access to the full score can compare this passage and see how Stravinsky managed to encapsulate a diverse and complex ensemble sound and produce its essential attributes at a single keyboard.

The next two works, the *Piano Sonata* and *Sérénade en la*, are considerably less showy than the *Three Movements*, but just as individualistic and personal as the famous transcription. The sonata is an elegant work of modest scope in three movements, arranged in conventional fast-slow-fast order. In the outer movements, Stravinsky eschews traditional Italian tempo indications (both could have been labeled simply "Allegro") in favor of a metronomic value for the quarter note ($\quarternote$ = 112) and nothing more. This seeming inflexibility is consistent with Stravinsky's distaste at the practice of many performers who took constant, sometimes extraordinary liberties with the tempos and rhythms of pieces they played in order to make them "expressive." The composer's comments on "non-

EXAMPLE 8.1. Stravinsky, *Three Movements*, "Danse russe," mm. 1–17. © Copyright 1948 by Boosey & Hawkes, Inc.; Copyright Renewed. Reprinted by permission of Boosey & Hawkes, Inc.

expression" in music have been given wide currency, but it is enough to suggest now that he wished his music to receive the same rhythmic respect accorded that of Mozart, which is to say that rhythmic liberties should be both extremely discreet and musically justified. Stravinsky's son, Soulima, a pianist, composer, and pedagogue of considerable insight and acclaim, repeatedly said that his father's views on musical expression were far from inflexible, and that, in fact, he was quite put off by a cold, "objective" performance.

There is a great deal of quasi-baroque two-voiced counterpoint in the outer movements of the *Piano Sonata*, whereas the slow middle movement is a beautifully sculpted arioso, not too dissimilar in approach, if not harmonic style, from the middle movement of J. S. Bach's *Italian Concerto* with its steady left-hand pulse and florid, melismatic right hand (example 8.2).

EXAMPLE 8.2. Stravinsky, *Sonata for Piano*, second movement, mm. 1–3. © Copyright 1925 by Edition Russe de Musique. Copyright assigned to Boosey & Hawkes, Inc. Copyright Renewed. Reprinted by permission.

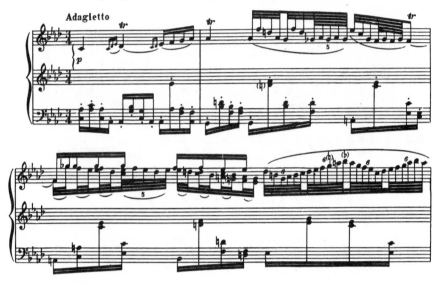

Stravinsky's creative approach to rhythmic groupings, so fiercely evident in *Le sacre* (indeed, many composers consider his greatest genius and, therefore, his most pervading influence, to lie in the area of rhythmic imagination), is equally apparent, if more subtly, in the sonata. The final movement features a particularly delicious use of $\frac{5}{16}$ and $\frac{3}{8}$ bars interspersed into a basically $\frac{2}{4}$ and $\frac{3}{4}$ context, keeping the overall flow alive and unpredictable (example 8.3).

In the previous chapter reference was made to Stravinsky's and Bartók's differing approaches to sonata form. Within two years of one another, each wrote a single piano sonata. Each piece is in three movements, fast-slow-fast, and each is relatively short. Both are tonal. But while Bartók took pains to employ the principal structural outlines and developmental procedures of the classical sonata-allegro and rondo forms, Stravinsky's compositional manner makes it difficult to assign traditional designations such as transition, development, and so forth, to any of the three movements. Not that Stravinsky was arbitrary or athematic; quite the contrary, principal ideas are repeated, often verbatim, at important junctures. But his procedure is modular rather than developmental, and one senses that while his arrangement of sections in a movement *might* be the best one, other orderings are also possible and would produce little loss of effect. With Bartók this is impossible; for him a piece of music is a logical discourse moving steadily from premise to conclusion rather than a collection of rhythmically related but distinct musical complexes that may be viewed, so to speak, from many directions

EXAMPLE 8.3. Stravinsky, *Sonata for Piano*, third movement, mm. 94–104.

without losing identity, like a Calder mobile. The juxtaposition of two such different works is fascinating, and if the above comparison errs on the side of oversimplification, nevertheless an essential difference between two composers of superabundant talents is illustrated.

The *Sérénade en la* is a fascinating suite of four movements unified by their mutual relationship to the pitch "La" or A, which serves as a point of convergence in each. Each of the four movements, entitled "Hymne," "Romanza," "Rondoletto," and "Cadenza Finala," was designed to fit on one side of a ten-inch, 78 rpm recording, so that the entire suite could occupy two complete discs. This rather novel restriction is nowhere evident in this splendid work, which may well be the most varied of any of Stravinsky's compositions for the piano.

Not surprisingly, there are some similarities to the *Piano Sonata* written the previous year. The "Rondoletto" is a kind of perpetual motion piece resembling the two-voiced outer movements of the earlier work, and the "Romanza" has echoes of the *Sonata's* slow movement. But the majestic "Hymne," with its grand and portentous sweep, has no predecessor among his solo piano works (example 8.4). Also, the flowing "Cadenza Finala," with its reminiscences of the "planed" triads found in some of Debussy's music, is a unique movement of great simplicity and beauty coupled with an extraordinarily sophisticated harmonic palette (example 8.5).

EXAMPLE 8.4. Stravinsky, *Serenade en la*, first movement, mm. 1–6. © Copyright 1927 by Edition Russe de Musique. Copyright assigned to Boosey & Hawkes, Inc. Copyright Renewed. Reprinted by permission.

EXAMPLE 8.5. Stravinsky, *Serenade en la*, fourth movement, mm. 1–6.

CHAPTER NINE

Arnold Schoenberg and Anton Webern

Of the three composers discussed in the first chapters of this book, only Schoenberg was able to continue to be musically productive after World War I. Debussy died of cancer in 1918, and Ives suffered a physical breakdown about the same time, leaving him unable to compose.

Even Schoenberg was forced to pause in his work. This was in part because of the anguish and devastation of the war, of course, but he had also come to a creative impasse, the solution for which was not easy. He knew that the music he had produced up to that time was well-written, deeply felt, and even praiseworthy—Schoenberg was never lacking in feelings of self-worth. But he was dissatisfied with the intellectual underpinnings of his work. He could not fulfill that very typical German need to explain what he had done. Yes, he knew it had been, historically and artistically, a logical and necessary step to reject functional tonality. In the early piano pieces, Op. 11, and the works that followed, he had done so. But music that was simply non-tonal with no organizing principles beyond the composer's pleasure was too irrational and subjective, he felt. Above all it was *too negative* to carry on the central European tradition that he revered and of which he felt an essential part. It was of the utmost importance that a logical, intellectually satisfying organizing principle be developed to replace the all-embracing authority of tonality. That principle would have to allow for personal flexibility just as tonality had done over the centuries. It must be a procedural guide to the composition of music and a consolidating system that would serve as an aid in its comprehension.

What emerged from Schoenberg's deliberations was, eventually, the twelve-tone method, a technique for organizing total chromaticism.[1] Though I shall not go over the techniques of twelve-tone composition again, a few words are necessary to attempt to dispel the stigma that is still attached, in the minds of many performers and listeners, to twelve-tone music. I cite, for example, a small portion of a review, written in the mid-1980s, sixty years after Schoenberg published his first twelve-tone compositions. The review is of the recording of a recent work for piano, but that is not important. It is the patronizing attitude of the critic, even in praising the work, that is the problem. "Most remarkable is the fact that though the work sounds so poetical and personal, some of the [movements] *actually contain passages of strict dodecaphonic writing*" (emphasis added). The implication is that the twelve-tone technique is so coldly mechanical that most music employing it can by definition be neither poetical nor personal.

Unfortunately, this is not an uncommon point of view. As a consequence I have found myself, over the several decades during which I have been performing, teaching, lecturing, and writing about twentieth-century music, avoiding reference to the fact that such-and-such a piece "is twelve-tone." Rather, I have tried to bring out those aspects of the piece that demonstrate its basic musicality and inner expressiveness. This expressiveness *is in no way dependent* on the compositional technique involved. Eighteenth- and nineteenth-century composers did not guarantee success of their works by writing in this key or that and employing the strictures of tonality. In like manner, the twelve-tone composer uses the technique as an aid to the realization of the musical discourse and to the achievement of his or her musical goals. But it is just that: a compositional technique that may help but that guarantees nothing. Twelve-tone music can be beautiful or ugly, poetic or academic, enthralling or tedious. In this it is like music written in any style, at any time, with any ground rules.

This much stated, it is fair to add that Schoenberg's discovery became, by mid-century, the most important and influential compositional procedure of the century. It spawned the many theories and sub-theories associated with what is called serialism. Composers who were at first repelled by the method—Stravinsky, Copland, Sessions, Carter, Britten, and many others—eventually adopted some aspects of it for their own purposes. That this technique should become the most compelling source of basic compositional techniques for so many decades is surely proof of its flexibility and artistic usefulness.

Of the three multi-movement compositions by Arnold Schoenberg in which the basic procedures of the twelve-tone technique are worked out, two are for solo piano. The *Five Piano Pieces* were published as Op. 23 and the *Suite for Piano* as Op. 25 (the third work, the *Serenade* for voice and seven instruments, was designated Op. 24). The opus numbers do not really indicate the order of composition; the works were all written during the same years. "Each work is made up of at least five pieces, written and reworked at various times between 1920 and 1923."[2]

One of the most remarkable things about the two sets of piano pieces, Op. 23 and Op. 25, given that they were written more or less within the same time period, is that each set is stylistically consistent within itself and at the same time strikingly different from the other.

The *Five Piano Pieces*, Op. 23, can hardly fail to remind the sensitive listener of the postromantic ardor of Schoenberg's earlier works. Though they are sparer in texture than the sometimes dense sonorities of the Op. 11 pieces from fifteen years before, the fervency of the expression is similar. Compare, for example, the intensity of the opening of Op. 23, No. 2 (example 9.1) with the much thicker but equally ecstatic opening of Op. 11, No. 3, quoted in chapter 2 (example 2.7). As in the earlier pieces (and this is profoundly important for the performer to recognize) the composer introduces a motive at the outset of every piece and then proceeds to investigate its subconscious emotional potential. One could say that for Schoenberg the act of composition in these works consisted of entering into the affective content of a living motivic idea, tunneling into its most sensitive areas, and finding a means to illuminate it in sound. No movements illustrate this better than the first pieces of both Op. 23 and the much earlier Op. 11. Yet while in Op. 11 Schoenberg was, for the first time, exploring the new world of atonality, in Op. 23, stymied by the anarchy he himself had unleashed, he was painstakingly seeking a basic organizing principle in order to be able to continue to write at all.

EXAMPLE 9.1. Schoenberg, *Five Piano Pieces*, Op. 23, no. 2, mm. 1–5.

If the *Five Piano Pieces* are hyper-romantic, the *Suite for Piano*, Op. 25, invokes a different, more classic kind of expression (example 9.2). Though there are moments of considerable warmth in the outer movements and of lyric ardor in the central "Intermezzo," the work as a whole exhibits discretion insofar as feelings are concerned and in its formal arrangement. At no time does one feel that Schoenberg is concerned with penetrating the secrets of a particular melodic cell; rather, he is balancing phrases with scrupulous counterpoint and well-designed cadences, very much as baroque composers for the harpsichord did in their suites and partitas.

EXAMPLE 9.2. Schoenberg, *Suite*, Op. 25, "Gavotte," mm. 1–4. Used by permission of Belmont Music Publishers.

These are two extraordinary compositions. The *Five Piano Pieces*, Op. 23, are romantic, impassioned, and searching—searching in a technical as well as an expressive sense, since only in the fifth movement does the composer "find" the twelve-tone technique; the previous movements, with shorter row forms, are "on the way." In contrast, the *Suite for Piano*, Op. 25, reaches back to the baroque for its charming "Gavotte-Musette," "Menuett and Trio," and "Gigue." These dances are preceded by a "Praeludium" and interspersed by a more romantic "Intermezzo." Unlike the pieces in Op. 23, all of these movements are based on the same row. It is of particular interest that just at the moment when Schoenberg stabilized his compositional method, he found it possible to return to older forms. Even in Op. 23 the only movement using the twelve-tone technique is the only piece with a title, "Waltz." No movements in his previous music had been given such titles.

The implications of this are not obvious, but certainly Schoenberg was not regressing, as has been inferred by some. Rather, he may have been suggesting, consciously or otherwise, that the "method of composing with twelve tones," as he called it, is only an aid in systematizing his employment of the total chromatic. In addition, Schoenberg's use of titles and old forms suggests that the twelve-tone technique does not relieve the composer of the task of choosing and constructing forms. Implied, finally, is that the emotional substance of the music is still as much the task of the composer to realize as always, and if the method *might* help unify a composition (as it does in Op. 25) there is no guarantee that it *will*.

That Schoenberg felt it was possible to create a link between row techniques and formal procedures, as tonality had united harmonic and constructive practices, is clear from the nature of subsequent compositions. In the *Klavierstück*, Op. 33a (1928), Schoenberg convincingly constructs a sonata-allegro movement in which the generating row materials also are heard in contrasting thematic forms and developmental procedures. His final work for the piano, continuing these experiments, is the *Klavierstück*, Op. 33b (1931) which was published in California by Henry Cowell (see chapter 14), an irony not lost on Schoenberg when he was forced to flee Europe by the Nazis just a few years later, eventually to take up residence in Los Angeles where he remained for the rest of his life.

Of all the pupils and successors of Schoenberg, the one who most immediately carried forward the development of twelve-tone methods was another Austrian, Anton Webern (1883–1945). It is not known exactly how he came to study with Schoenberg. In 1902, at the age of nineteen, he moved with his parents from the small town of Klagenfurt, Austria, to Vienna, where he entered the university, and it is likely that Professor Guido Adler, with whom he studied musicology, recommended him to Schoenberg for instruction in composition.

In any case, Webern immediately became a devoted disciple of the fiery, demanding Schoenberg, studying with him from 1904 until 1908 and remaining his faithful friend thereafter. From him he received a greatly enhanced perspective in many areas, since Schoenberg did not confine his lessons to music but spoke at length of literary and philosophical matters. Above all, Webern's contact with the older composer enabled him to come to the esthetic conclusions that led quickly to what was to become his characteristic style, a style that left an indelible imprint on the music of the generation of composers who came of age after World War II.

Schoenberg's important works during the time Webern was his student included the *Second String Quartet*, Op. 10, and the *Three Piano Pieces*, Op. 11, discussed in chapter 2. These works served as catalysts to Webern, opening completely new compositional possibilities. Schoenberg's *Six Little Piano Pieces*, Op. 19, were of particular consequence to Webern; the condensation of expression and focused intensity were like magic keys to a new world. He was so taken with the Op. 19 pieces that he wrote of them, "Whatever one says, no words can do justice to this music."[3] Webern's own *Five Movements for String Quartet*, Op. 5 (1909), *Four Pieces for Violin and Piano*, Op. 7 (1910), and the even more diminutive *Three Short Pieces for Cello and Piano*, Op. 11 (1914), demonstrate not only the influence of Schoenberg's teaching and music, but also show that Webern found it possible to carry his teacher's ideas concerning brevity and motivic concentration still further.

Schoenberg's twelve-tone formulations in the early 1920s were, if anything, more congenial to Webern than to their originator. He immediately adopted the principles set forth by Schoenberg, adapting them to his own purposes. His compositions thereafter continued to be unusually brief and concerned with the balance of tiny motives and canonically related row forms. His scores took on a spare, almost hygenic aspect, which contributed to some unfortunate misunderstandings concerning their interpretation. This is particularly true of the only really important work for solo piano he wrote, the *Piano Variations*, Op. 27 (1936).

The *Piano Variations* are in three movements, of which only the last is actually a set of variations (example 9.3). The first movement is in a clear A-B-A form, and the second is a quick binary movement in which each of the two sections is repeated. The entire work lasts barely five minutes.

EXAMPLE 9.3. Webern, *Piano Variations*, Op. 27, third movement, mm. 1–12. Copyright 1937 Universal Edition. Copyright renewed 1965. All Rights Reserved. Used by permission of European American Music Distributors, sole U.S. and Canadian agent for Universal Edition.

At the time of his tragic death in 1945,[4] Webern was not widely known. He would have been astounded to learn that in 1953, less than a decade later, a memorial concert of music would be given at Darmstadt, and that he would be proclaimed the principal inspiration for a new generation of composers and the springboard to the serial techniques developed in Europe and America shortly after the close of World War II. Webern became the patron saint of the postwar avant-garde; this is most succinctly demonstrated by the fact that the "in" music of the period was given the appellation "post-Webern."[5]

It is possible that if a composer is deified shortly after his death a misreading (purposeful or otherwise) may be at work. This seems true of Webern in his posthumous ascendancy. Moreover, no Webern piece was more thoroughly misread than the *Piano Variations*. For this the composer is, at least partially, at fault. As mentioned earlier, Webern's music, consisting essentially of miniscule motives arranged with geometric precision, was notated in the most austere, spare manner. One might imagine, glancing at the primly meticulous score, that the music was to be played without feeling of any kind. To the leaders of the postwar avant-garde, anxious to avoid traditional expression and determined (at least for a brief period) to do away with all vestiges of subjective inspiration, this reading of Webern's music was consistent with their cause. In the sterile appearance of his scores they found it possible to conclude that not only had he achieved an objectivity surpassing anything accomplished by Schoenberg, Stravinsky, or anyone else, but that he had also arranged in series musical parameters other than pitch, thereby giving a reassuring precedent for the "total serialism" then being developed. In particular they seized upon the tiny second movement of the *Piano Variations;* they attributed to it a precompositional serial scheme that would have left Webern wide-eyed with astonishment.[6]

Webern, in fact, thought of his music as standing squarely in the mainstream of the expressive Austro-German romantic tradition. While at work on the *Piano Variations* he had referred to the piece as sounding "like Brahms." And though he was willing to discuss row techniques, palindromes, and the like with other composers,[7] he refused to concede that these matters had anything to do with performance.

Why Webern chose to notate his music as he did is a moot point. Luckily, there exists an edition of the *Piano Variations* that puts to rest the possibility that it is a cold, expressionless piece.[8] The editor of this unusual publication is Peter Stadlen who, on 20 October 1937, gave the first performance of the work after having numerous detailed coaching sessions from the composer himself. In these sessions, according to Stadlen, Webern "was in the habit, while standing next to me and discussing a passage, to complement his remarks with casually pencilled entries."[9]

In this edition each left-hand page contains photostat of a page from Stadlen's score (the original Universal edition, which is still available today) with these pencilled remarks intact. These alone are illuminating. On each right-hand page the same page is reprinted, this time with Webern's written remarks printed in red, and further recollections by the pianist of things Webern said but did not write down printed in green.

What emerges is a fervently emotional conception which, without changing any of Webern's original score, throws a fascinating light on the manner in which the composer meant it to be interpreted. Each section of the music, each phrase, each figure has its own mood and character. The tempo is to move ahead at times, hold back at others. There is always a sense of drama, shape, and line. "And indeed," writes Stadlen, "he never tired of conveying to me the poetics of the work down to the minutest, most delicate detail—conducting, gesticulating, singing."[10]

It is interesting to note Webern's assumption of a specific *Aufführungspraxis* (performance practice) for his music, another indication that he was confident that it belonged to the mainstream of the Austro-German tradition. Obviously he felt his music would be played in a certain "meaningful" way without his having to indicate as much in the notation. That this belief was incorrect was something he did not live to see.

CHAPTER TEN

Paul Hindemith

Although Webern's status as a musical demigod has reduced since the early 1960s, the continuing influence of his music is assured in the chronicle of the twentieth century. The fate of the music of Paul Hindemith (1895–1963), however, is a different matter. It is now difficult to imagine the commanding place he occupied in the 1940s and early 1950s; therefore it is equally hard to recall how rapidly his prestige subsequently evaporated. Of course no composer's influence remains precisely constant from one generation to the next, but Hindemith is a special case. No other composer of this century had such a dominating position in the minds of so many composers, both in Europe and America, only to see it wane and virtually disappear while he was still alive. It is of more than passing interest to consider something of how this came about.

Hindemith was the eldest child of a poverty-stricken Silesian family. Precocious, he learned to play the violin at an early age. After his father was killed in France during World War I he helped sustain his mother by playing in small orchestras and chamber groups of various kinds. He composed prolifically and, though he was circumspect in his dealings with most people, demonstrated to those closest to him that he was a "veritable volcano of opinions, convictions and feelings"[1] even as a young man. Certainly his early experiences as a practical musician, coupled with an all-pervading enthusiasm for music and a highly developed belief in his own opinions, had much to do with his later success and the single-mindedness with which he developed and disseminated his compositional creed.

A basic tenet of that creed was that it is the composer's duty to write music for practical, immediate use and to be able to participate in its performance. He rejected the nineteenth-century concept of musical composition as the consequence of creative inspiration, preferring to regard it as a skilled craft that one learns and perfects by practicing regularly and methodically.

Another of his strong beliefs, one that became even stronger as he matured, was that music had to be tonal to be comprehensible. He rejected out of hand the viability of atonal music, and was vehement in his opposition to Schoenberg's twelve-tone technique, which he viewed as a restrictive set of rules rather than a method that had evolved naturally.

The time between the two world wars was, at least in part, a period of retrenchment and reevaluation following the explosive musical discoveries of the first years of the century. Many composers felt a great need to find ways to organize tones, chords, rhythms, and formal procedures. Schoenberg organized the chromatic spectrum into row forms. Stravinsky looked to the past for models and brought about the neoclassic movement. Bartók incorporated folk elements, and Webern examined the molecular structure of music. Composers grouped together at small festivals at Donaueschingen and pooled their thoughts; Hindemith played an important part there, though he found a danger in too much talk about music and not enough performance. The composer, he declared, was not well served by "cackling over eggs just laid or crowing over others about to be laid."[2]

Little by little Hindemith formulated his thoughts on how musical composition could be brought out of the anarchy in which he found it. Working with his pupils at the Berlin Hochschule in the 1920s, he slowly built up a theory concerning the relationship between chords, not just the triads and seventh chords of the past but sound complexes built on seconds, fourths, and other combinations of intervals. At first the theory was strictly intuitive: he and his pupils discussed which progressions "worked" aurally and which did not, and then he tried by himself to find the logic that made it so. He found he could measure the tension of chords through their combined interval structure. He confirmed the importance of good contrapuntal writing, especially in the outer two parts, in any progression. He discovered justification for his convictions in the natural harmonic series. Above all, he continued to write—operas, orchestral scores, chamber music, vocal music, piano music—always with an immediate performance in mind (sometimes on the day the work was completed) in which he nearly always performed. These two double activities—teaching/searching and composing/performing—worked together. Wanting to perfect his own craft, he searched for a theory that would assure him that he would not have to rely too much on intuition and inspiration; wanting to formulate such a theory, he composed work after work, scrutinizing his own compositional processes to try to discover the criteria that made them function.

In 1937 he published his *Unterweisung im Tonsatz*. With the Nazis in power and world conquest on the horizon, there was little sympathy for or interest in new compositional theories in Germany. But the appearance in 1942 of Arthur Mendel's English translation, *The Craft of Musical Composition*,[3] combined with Hindemith's appointment to the post of Visiting Professor at Yale University, created something of a sensation.

Even in wartime America, interest in musical composition grew rapidly, an interest that increased many times over after 1945. There was, however, considerable confusion as to which direction to take. Still in awe of cultural matters emanating from Europe, young composers in the United States seized upon this unprecedented guidebook by a famous German composer. Those who could went to Yale to study with him; those that could not read *The Craft of Musical Composition*, did the two-part counterpoint exercises from one volume, and carefully examined the foldout chart in the other, which concentrated onto a single page the composer's discoveries and conclusions concerning the relative tensions of all possible chords, the determination of their roots, and how they should progress in logical fashion toward a final, satisfying tonal resolution.

Hindemith's popularity was immense. His music was played with great frequency, and the book was known to all composers. His star as a composer-pedagogue, at least for a few years, outshone all others.

The problem that eventually surfaced was not that Hindemith had too much influence. Rather, it was that the influence was too specific. His students began to complain that it was nearly impossible to develop their own individuality under his strict guidance. Elsewhere, composers became aware that the neat solutions to contrapuntal and harmonic problems found in *The Craft of Musical Composition* led, ironically, to the composition of music that almost inevitably sounded like Hindemith.

What does Hindemith sound like? His early music is full of romantic fervor and displays both imagination and (not surprising for someone who so often played in performances of his own works) idiomatic mastery. Stylistically, youthful works such as the four fine string-piano sonatas, Op. 11 (1918 and 1919), and the impassioned *Third String Quartet*, Op. 22 (1921), show kinship to the music of Brahms and Reger with some influence from Richard Strauss. But Hindemith seemed not to trust these ardent outpourings as time went on and, just as Schoenberg, Bartók, Stravinsky, and others before him had moved from youthfully strong but derivative music to more mature, individual modes of expression, so Hindemith strove for a leaner, more rational, and technically polished style.

At its best, in works such as the opera *Mathis der Maler* (1934), his later music is excellent—impeccably constructed and emotionally exciting. But much of his huge output is something less than inspired, possibly a result of his view of composition as a routine craft. The quality of the large number of "workaday" sonatas for seemingly every possible instrument and piano rarely rises above the predictable and the prosaic. The music is "usable," just as he intended, but has little of the passion and intensity of the earlier works. With the formalizing of his later manner in *The Craft of Musical Composition*, which led him to go so far as to rewrite some of his earlier compositions so they would conform more precisely to his theories, what at first appeared to be a boon to composition at mid-century came to be regarded as stultifying, and Hindemith looked on with ill-concealed bitterness and dismay in the late fifties as serial and aleatoric techniques eclipsed his orderly, pedagogically sound, but musically uninteresting compositional postulates.

Of Hindemith's considerable output for the piano, the principal works are the three sonatas (1936) and the collection of interludes and fugues called *Ludus Tonalis* (1942). Of the other pieces the early *Suite "1922,"* Op. 26 (1922), is the most appealing, though it is not among his better works from that time; his approach to ragtime and other popular dances of the day is heavy-handed.

Of the sonatas, the second, completed in 1936, is a gem. It is much shorter than the other two and is appropriately modest in its content. Nothing loses its attractiveness for being too long or overwrought, and the felicities—such as the rhythmically exciting recapitulation of the first theme in the first movement, the melodic integration of the slow and fast sections of the finale, and the splendid and sonorous chords that bring the work to a close—are many.

The five-movement *First Sonata* (1936) contains an abundance of the composer's worst attributes. Most of the movements are too long, and the material, with the exception of the opening of the first movement, is unfailingly unattractive. The *Third Sonata* (1936) is a big virtuoso piece, the pretentiousness of which can be overcome in a sensitive, variegated performance. It contains a scintillating scherzo and, for a finale, a powerful double fugue.

Ludus Tonalis: Studies in Counterpoint, Tonal Organization and Piano Playing was completed the same year the English translation of *The Craft of Musical Composition* was published and was hailed at the time as the "Well-Tempered Clavier of the Twentieth Century." There are some clever and attractive pieces among the twenty-five movements. "Fuga 2" is a lighthearted study made more diverting because of its $\frac{5}{8}$ meter, and "Fuga 9," the best of the fugues, maintains rhythmic and contrapuntal interest from beginning to end. Of the "interludia," the fourth and eighth are brilliant showpieces, well worth study. Most of the other movements, however, show Hindemith making pedagogical points rather than emotional statements, and one can only wish that his sense of fantasy had been more consistently up to the level of his craftsmanship.

CHAPTER ELEVEN

Sergei Prokofiev

The unsettling effect of the Soviet revolution on Russian composers during the first half of this century is common knowledge. For some it became impossible to remain safely in the country; permanent self-exile became a necessity. Others were able to stay, attempting as best they could to adapt themselves to the artistic requirements of the new regime. These requirements, more often than not closely entangled with political ones, could be devastating in their consequences. No one remained unaffected.

By 1917 Stravinsky was in his mid-thirties and well established. Settling permanently in the West after the 1917 revolution, he often wrote on Russian themes and admitted to intense feelings of homesickness throughout the remainder of his extraordinary career. Nevertheless he returned to visit his native country only once, late in life.

As we have seen, Rachmaninoff also fled the revolution, and though he had thereafter a long and extremely successful career as a pianist in Europe and America, his temperament, so different from Stravinsky's, made it impossible for him to write new works outside his homeland, which he missed grievously but to which he never returned.

The career of Sergei Prokofiev (1891–1953) differs from either of these. Ten years younger than Stravinsky, he was just beginning to make a name for himself when the revolution made it seem best for him to leave his country. After living in the United States for four years and in Paris for twelve, he could not bear his self-exile and returned to Russia just before the outset of World War II. There he had to face the bizarre and often crushing dictates of a political regime that demanded "socialist realism" in all the arts and severely condemned whomever and whatever did not conform to its baffling ideological boundaries. Prokofiev, suspect on many counts because of his years outside the border, was often to feel the sting of official denouncement.

Nevertheless, in exile and back at home, Prokofiev continued to compose his impressive array of symphonies, operas, cantatas, chamber music, concerti, film scores, and piano music. Among the Russian composers of his generation his achievements are rivaled only by those of Dmitri Shostakovich (1906–1975) and Dmitri Kabalevsky (b. 1904), and even here, at least for pianists, there is no contest. Shostakovich was primarily a symphonist; neither his strange, angry *First Piano Sonata* (1926), a dissonant, one-movement work, nor the over-extended, rhetorical *Second Sonata* (1943), nor the academic sounding *Twenty-four Preludes and Fugues* (1951) can compare with Prokofiev's nine piano sonatas and dozens of imaginative smaller pieces. Some of Kabalevsky's piano muisic has a certain innocent charm about it. Many of the *Twenty-four Preludes* (1947) are pleasant enough, though hardly challenging from a musical point of view, and the two well-known *Sonatinas* (1930; 1933) make fine teaching material. The *Third Piano Sonata* (1946), usually considered his most important concert work for the instrument, has too much that is in embarrassingly poor taste (witness the tawdry second theme of the first movement, for example). In short, it is Prokofiev's immense contribution to the literature of the piano, which still appears on recital programs with greater frequency than the music of any other composer since Debussy, that must be considered in some detail.

Prokofiev began his career as a radical, avant-garde composer and ended it as a conservative. It would be fascinating to know the unknowable: how would he have developed had there been no revolution or had he stayed in the West? That these are unanswerable questions does not make them frivolous, and it is intriguing to speculate what a composer of Prokofiev's talent might have done in other circumstances.

As with all the best composers of his day in and out of Russia, Prokofiev was thoroughly grounded in the traditional compositional practices of the classical period. He could not have proven this more brilliantly than he did in the marvelously lighthearted *Classical Symphony* (1917), in which his stated aim was to demonstrate what Haydn might have written had he still been alive. On the other hand, he had already convincingly demonstrated in other more characteristic works that he was fascinated by and determined to employ the most biting dissonances and radically unconventional forms. One sees this immediately in the five *Sarcasms* (1913) for solo piano and in the only slightly milder group of twenty short pieces titled *Visions fugitives* (1917). These works were written before the composer left Russia and, with the popular *Third Piano Sonata* (rewritten in 1917 from much earlier sketches) and orchestral works such as the *Scythian Suite* and *First Violin Concerto* (1914 and 1917, respectively), indicated a forward-looking, daring compositional career by someone who was willing to challenge his audience in every way. Consider, for example, the crashing chords and rapidly changing meters that open the final piece of *Sarcasms*, reminiscent of the just completed *Rite of Spring* and similar to some of Bartók's early piano music, the *Allegro Barbaro* in particular (example 11.1).

Not everyone took kindly to this sort of thing, of course, but there was, in pre-revolutionary Russia, a distinct interest in what was innovative in the arts, and Prokofiev would seem to have received a great deal

EXAMPLE 11.1. Prokofiev, *Sarcasms*, fifth movement, mm. 1–11. Used by permission of G. Schirmer, Inc. on behalf of Copyright Owner VAAP.

of encouragement from a number of sources. His *First Piano Concerto* (1911) was received very well by audiences when it was first performed in 1912, though the press was sharply divided.[1] Successful or not, Prokofiev eventually chose to leave Russia. Once abroad, he was soon in contact with the leading composers of Western Europe.

He seems to have been greatly influenced by the neoclassical trends of the 1920s. His textures became leaner, his forms became more traditional, his lyric gifts increased, and his wildness was tempered. The *Fifth Piano Sonata* (1925) is a particularly good example of this. Relatively little known, coming as it does between the popular (and much-abused) *Third Sonata* and the massive *Sixth* (1940), *Seventh* (1942), and *Eighth* (1944) sonatas, this three-movement work has moments of great charm and effectiveness. It begins in a pastoral manner, sounding almost Haydnesque (example 11.2). For those who know Prokofiev's style, there is much in this work that will sound characteristic, but the essentially diatonic lyricism seems to have left behind much of the raw vigor and trenchant whimsy of the early works. Certainly it does not follow the directions pursued by Bartók and Stravinsky in their piano sonatas, written at the same time. Rather, it confirms the fact that Prokofiev, despite his early adventures into atonality and formal experimentation, was moving toward the use of clearly defined, traditional structures with relatively straightforward metric groupings and a harmonic language which was very close to functional tonality. During the next phase of his career this shift in style became much more evident.

Prokofiev's return to the Soviet Union coincided with Stalin's rise to power and the accompanying terrors. Writing of Prokofiev's career, John Ogden refers to the effects of these "changes of environment which must have shaped his thought in unexpected ways."[2] This shaping of thought involved, of course, adherence to socialist realism as defined and

EXAMPLE 11.2. Prokofiev, *Fifth Piano Sonata*, Op. 38, first movement, mm. 1–8. Copyright by Boosey & Hawkes, Inc. Used by permission.

redefined by Premier Stalin and his poliburo. Simple, direct work was demanded of creative artists. Music that the masses could easily understand and appreciate and that, not incidentally, glorified the new Soviet state, was not only encouraged but required of all composers. Scrutiny was increased by the onset of World War II, during which there was no higher emotion possible than love of country nor no act more treasonous than reversion to Western "decadence."

Prokofiev, whatever the external pressures, remained intensely active as a composer, literally until the day of his death (ironically, he died on the same day as Stalin). Many of his most impressive works were written during this final Russian period, works of such diversity as *Peter and the Wolf* (1936) and the *Fifth Symphony* (1944).

It is difficult, however, to come to terms with the unevenness of the three "war" sonatas for the piano—the sixth, seventh, and eighth—all written between 1939 and 1944. There are, certainly, splendid ideas in all of them. The opening motive of the *Sixth Sonata*, for example, the descending interlocking major-minor thirds, is as individualistic as the unprecedented repeated chords with which Beethoven began the *Waldstein Sonata*, Op. 53, more than a century before; the interlocking motive dominates the entire first movement of Prokofiev's work as much as the repeated chords do in Beethoven's (example 11.3). There is, however, a certain squareness about the opening and what follows, as though Prokofiev, repentant over past obscurities, was determined that everything be as obvious as possible, even to the point of being blatant. How

EXAMPLE 11.3. Prokofiev, *Sixth Piano Sonata*, Op. 82, first movement, mm. 1–6. Used by permission of G. Schirmer, Inc. on behalf of Copyright Owner VAAP.

else to explain the inelegance of the fifth and sixth measures in the example just given?

Then, shortly later, when the opening motive-in-thirds is spread out over the entire keyboard and surrounds clangorous, bare octaves (starting in m. 12, not shown), the obviousness of the music becomes apparent. Perhaps Prokofiev felt this was an appropriate way to depict heroism; it now seems slightly ostentatious.

The second theme of the same movement has a decidedly stripped-down setting (example 11.4). It is possible that this is the result of Prokofiev's striving for a simple, naive style, but such writing is a trifle gauche on the piano. It works better if other instruments are involved: one thinks of similarly scored passages in the openings of both the *Violin Sonata* in F Minor and the *Fifth Symphony*, which are much more effective.

EXAMPLE 11.4. Prokofiev, *Sixth Piano Sonata*, Op. 82, first movement, mm. 40–43.

The second movement is another matter. It is an altogether charming scherzo and trio with a principal idea in which all elements blend in an ingratiating way (example 11.5). Simply stated at first, the theme is subjected to a startling accompaniment the next time around, the left hand leaping back and forth in a blithe and effective pianissimo (exam-

EXAMPLE 11.5. Prokofiev, *Sixth Piano Sonata*, Op. 82, second movement, mm. 1–6.

EXAMPLE 11.6. Prokofiev, *Sixth Piano Sonata*, Op. 82, second movement, mm. 36–38.

ple 11.6). Although the trio section is not one of Prokofiev's most inspired creations, this is still the best movement in the sonata.

In the third movement, "Tempo di valzer lentissimo," matters of taste arise that are impossible to dismiss. True, Prokofiev had always claimed that he was a lyric composer, and one needs only to listen to the beautiful melodies of such a work as the *Second Violin Concerto* to know this is undeniable. But poetic lyricism should not be confused with cloying sentimentality. This slow movement (as well as that of the *Seventh Sonata*) falls into the latter category (example 11.7). It is hard to imagine what he was thinking that caused him to decide that such oversweet music had a place in this, his biggest piano sonata, which otherwise aims so high, whatever its faults.

The fourth and last movement, in Prokofiev's vaunted toccata style, is effective, as is the stormy return of the opening movement's motive-in-thirds during the virtuosic conclusion.

For virtuosity, however, the final movement of the *Seventh Sonata* remains unexcelled (example 11.8). One suspects that more than a few pianists have decided to learn the entire sonata solely out of desire to perform this exciting finale. In $\frac{7}{8}$ time from beginning to end, it is (in a carefully gauged, non-bangy performance) hair-raisingly effective.

The first movement of the *Seventh Sonata* has moments of great power; there are also several passages of aimless meandering, especially in the too-long presentation of the second theme. Also, transitions often seem to have been roughly glued in, as if between sketches of ideas meant for different pieces. The middle movement has already been alluded to.

EXAMPLE 11.7. Prokofiev, *Sixth Piano Sonata*, Op. 82, third movement, mm. 1–6.

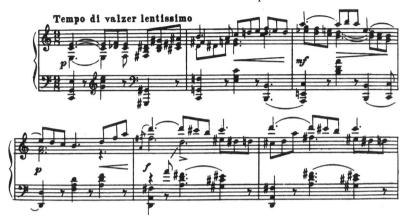

The *Eighth Sonata* is less bombastic overall than its two predecessors, but also has less individuality. There are long lyric lines, but again one has the impression that many of the ideas would have worked better in an ensemble rather than for solo piano.

EXAMPLE 11.8. Prokofiev, *Seventh Piano Sonata*, Op. 83, third movement, mm. 1–8. Used by permission of G. Schirmer, Inc. on behalf of Copyright Owner VAAP.

In spite of these qualifications concerning the late sonatas, Prokofiev remains among the three or four finest Russian composers of this century. An excellent pianist, he made substantial contributions to the piano repertory. As with many composers who are productive over a long period of time, his style of writing for the instrument went through several periods. How it would have developed had he been free of the "changes of environment which must have shaped his thought in unexpected ways" we shall, alas, never know.

CHAPTER TWELVE

"Les Six" and Others in Europe

The devastating effect of World War I on the lives and creative abilities of such composers as Debussy, Ives, Schoenberg, Ravel, and Rachmaninoff has already been noted. Though Debussy was the only one of these five who had died by the time of the war's conclusion, each of the others was profoundly shaken by the conflict. Only one, Schoenberg, was able to revive his creative activity afterwards to any great extent, and he could do so only after several years had passed.

Reactions to the war among composers of the following generation were many and varied. Not yet well established before the war began, their lives were affected in somewhat different ways. Of more than passing interest is the turn French music took in the decades between the death of Debussy in 1918 and the emergence of Olivier Messiaen and, subsequently, his illustrious pupils. A serious man, Debussy only occasionally attempted a humorous touch in his music—his jibes at the British ("Hommage à S. Pickwick, Esq., P.P.M.P.C.") and at Wagner (the brief *Tristan* quotes in "The Golliwog's Cakewalk") tend to be heavy-handed— nor, later in the century, could Messiaen be accused of frivolousness or lightheartedness. But the intervening generation of the 1920s and 1930s took a different view.

Inspired to a considerable extent by Erik Satie, whose titles are often hilarious even if the music is not, and by the writer Jean Cocteau, a group of French composers sought a new, clearer kind of music that would not rule out humor as a basic ingredient. In his manifesto, *Le Coq et l'Arlequin* (1918), Cocteau set out to define this new movement. Music should be simple, direct, objective, uninvolving, and light in spirit, he declared. He warned against the dreary complexities of Wagner's *Tristan*, Stravinsky's *The Rite of Spring*, and Debussy's *Pelléas*, claiming that such music was all-enveloping, too spellbinding, and, above all, dangerously lacking in humor. He declared that French music should communicate without artifice, allowing the listener to participate fully and enjoyably rather than being emotionally overwhelmed. And, he concluded, the music that best exemplified these criteria was that of the Parisian café and music hall with its clear rhythms, catchy melodies, and high good spirits.

That such music should come to the fore in the concert halls of Europe in the 1920s is hardly surprising. The length and brutishness of World War I left entire segments of society psychologically traumatized, unable to accept what had happened to their shattered convictions. Thus, relief from the contemplation of such matters was to be sought wherever it could be found, and what better avenue than music? In addition, the accelerating nationalistic movements caused artists of all kinds to look for inspiration within their own countries and to reject outside models, especially German!

No music from this movement could seriously rival that of Debussy or Ravel, and Messiaen and his pupils were later to behave as though the period had never existed. But Arthur Honegger (1892–1955), Darius Milhaud (1892–1974), and Francis Poulenc (1899–1963) wrote music of imagination, spirit, and individuality, some of which can move the listener considerably more than Cocteau's original statements might lead one to surmise. The best music of these three composers is rarely for solo piano, unfortunately, but each wrote at least one or two keyboard works that merit continuing attention.

Arthur Honegger

The *Sept pièces brèves* (1920) by Honegger are particularly attractive. These seven miniatures are extremely varied in nature: some are sardonically whimsical, others are dark and introspective. The outgoing, direct mood of the first piece is immediately apparent in the nonchalant first measures (example 12.1). The third piece, with its opaque harmo-

EXAMPLE 12.1. Honegger, *Sept pièces brèves*, No. 1, mm. 1–4. Used by Permission of G. Schirmer, Inc. on behalf of Copyright Owner Editions Max Eschig.

EXAMPLE 12.2. Honegger, *Sept pièces brèves*, No. 3, mm. 1–3.

nies, is pervaded with melancholy (example 12.2). The seventh and last-piece is an outrageously bawdy cancan, which brings the set to a lively conclusion.

Darius Milhaud

Milhaud was an extraordinarily prolific composer. He wrote quickly and did not have the temperament to take great pains with every phrase. Thus his work, which includes a substantial amount of piano music, varies greatly from piece to piece. Foremost among his compositions for the piano are the twelve dances of the *Saudades do Brazil* (1921), which are full of delights: interesting harmonic combinations, ingratiating rhythms, and challenging pianism. Although some of his other piano music seems awkward and strangely obtuse, the quasi-popular idiom of the *Saudades* enabled Milhaud to capture a special musical environment perfectly.

One of the most interesting aspects of these pieces is the consistent use of polytonality. Many composers in the 1920s experimented with writing in two keys at once—Bartók and Stravinsky, among others, had done so even earlier in the century. For the most part, polytonal techniques were employed in order to extend harmonic possibilities in a consistent and rational manner; rarely did one actually hear two keys at the same time. For a passage to be *audibly* polytonal the keys employed must first be simply and unambiguously presented and, second, be kept at a certain distance from one another with little or no overlapping. Most composers were not interested in this sort of simplicity, and so their ostensibly polytonal music tends to blend the two, three, or four keys together.

Milhaud's approach to polytonality, however, was different. The seventh of the *Saudades* is typical (example 12.3). He gives the left hand

EXAMPLE 12.3. Milhaud, Saudades do Brazil, No. 7, "Corcovado," mm. 1–8. Used by Permission of G. Schirmer on behalf of Copyright Owner Editions Max Eschig.

a simple tonic-dominant habanera figure in G major and the right hand, which stays well away from the accompaniment for the most part, a clear melody in D major. One can hear the two keys easily, and this adds a unique flavor to what is already colorful music.

Of course this music is not always as harmonically simple as this single example would indicate. The keys in either hand change often and unpredictably as the dance progresses. At times they flow together into a kind of "polykey," whereas, at other moments, polytonality may be completely abandoned as both hands come together at a cadence and agree on a single tonic.

Francis Poulenc

The spontaneous and unpretentious nature of Poulenc's music has been widely celebrated. Certainly he left a storehouse of delights for vocalists, both in his songs and operas. The latter, ranging from the madcap surrealism of *Les mamelles de Tirésias* (1947) to the somber religiosity of the *Dialogues des Carmélites* (1956), have won a deserved position in the relatively small operatic repertoire of the present century.

Like Milhaud, Poulenc wrote often and easily for the piano. Unlike Milhaud, he was an expert (if heavy-footed) pianist who loved to entertain his friends for hours with his improvisations. Many of his compositions are, in fact, written-out improvisations. All lie exceedingly well on the keyboard and invariably include certain basic sounds and gestures, which appear from piece to piece with only slight variations, giving a clear sense of what he liked to feel under his hand as he improvised.

The shorter pieces generally tend to be the more successful. Especially charming are the brief *Mouvements perpétuels* (1918) with their fluffy melodies and pleasantly appropriate "music hall" accompaniments. A much more extended work is *Les soirées de Nazelles* (1936), which consists of eight "variations" (actually separate pieces), originally improvised as portraits of friends, introduced by a "Préambule" and concluded with a "Finale." The work is full of attractive moments, but the allure tends to diminish as the length increases. However, for the pianist who is attracted by such voluptuous sequences as that from the second movement, Poulenc may be just the thing (example 12.4).

"Les Six"

Honegger, Milhaud, and Poulenc were for a short time associated with three other French composers in the early 1920s in a group christened "Les Six" by a newspaper reporter. The other members of the group, Georges Auric, Louis Durey, and Germaine Tailleferre, are now known at all only because of this ephemeral group. Their contributions to the piano repertoire may be passed over.

EXAMPLE 12.4. Poulenc, *Les Soirées de Nazelles*, second movement, mm. 33–40. © 1937 Durand S.A. Used by Permission of the Publisher. Sole Representative U.S.A., Theodore Presser Company.

Several other significant European composers of piano music who flourished during the period between the two wars should be mentioned.

Ernst Bloch

Although Swiss-born Ernst Bloch (1880–1959) resided in the United States from 1916 until the end of his life, he remained essentially a European composer who never lost sight of his traditional continental training. In his early piano music he reflects the influence of Debussy to some extent, as in the *Poems of the Sea* (1922). These three pieces seem naive to the point of artlessness, with the exception of portions of the first, called "Waves," which shows traces of the style developed by Bloch best described as a Jewish idiom. The rhapsodic, intense melancholy of this kind of music, with its improvisatory cantilena, oriental inflections, and endless iterations of quasi-programmatic chords and rhetorical figurations, is better displayed in a much later work for piano, *Visions et prophéties* (1940).

His major work for the piano, the *Sonata* (1935), combines the Jewish idiom with gestures derived from neoclassical models. The first of the three movements begins with a characteristic dotted rhythm, which wavers precariously between portentousness and pretentiousness with its repeated fanfare calls and sweeping arpeggios. Later, as the music gathers speed, it seems to remain constantly in a state of great agitation, searching over and over again for a climax. The *Sonata* is not without merit, containing moments of power and a certain beauty that was Bloch's special province, but the would-be performer must come to terms with the rhetoric and then work hard to shape the piece in a convincing manner.

Georges Enesco

Georges Enesco (1881–1955) is considered the spiritual father of the Romanian Union of Composers, a large group that uses his former palatial home in Bucharest as their headquarters. An internationally acclaimed violinist, he also appeared in concert as a pianist. As a young man he studied composition in Paris with Massenet and Fauré, and while there he became lifelong friends with such performing luminaries as the cellist Pablo Casals, violinists Jacques Thibaud and Eugène Ysaÿe, the pianist Alfred Cortot, and many others.

His several large-scale piano sonatas are well written for the instrument, reflecting his admiration for the chromatic harmonic practices of Franck and Wagner but also demonstrating his knowledge of the clearly defined textures of the neoclassical period, during which his compositional activity was at its height. This is particularly true of the *Third Piano Sonata*, Op. 24, No. 3 (1935), a lengthy, difficult work in three movements containing an interesting blend of dark Romanian emotionality and French neoclassic *clarté*.

Alfredo Casella

The Italian Alfredo Casella (1883–1947) was a very successful concert pianist, playing as many as one hundred and fifty concerts in a season, as well as being a prolific composer. His best-known work for the piano is the *Sinfonia, Arioso, and Toccata*, Op. 59 (1936), which is a fine example of clearly written, rhythmically straightforward keyboard music. In spite of occasional chromatic wanderings, it remains tonal throughout.

More adventuresome is the earlier *Sonatina* (1916) with its stylistic interplay between impressionist and classically contrapuntal passages. The third and last movement, which begins as a fast toccata, ends with a strange and forbidding march, *grave e solenne*, over which Casella has added a curious quotation from *Turandot:* "Al suono d'una marcia escono le guardie alla Chinese" ("At the sound of a march the guards go out to the Chinese").

Mention should also be made of Casella's atmospheric tone poem for piano, *A notte alta* (1917).

Nikos Skalkottas

Nikos Skalkottas (1904–1949) is considered Greece's finest composer before Iannis Xenakis (b. 1922). One of Schoenberg's most outstanding students, his later piano music, such as the *Suite No. 4* (1941), employs "free twelve-tone" writing, a curious contradiction in terms many composers indulged in (to no one's injury) before the reemergence of dodecaphonic composition and its further serial deployment on an international scale in the postwar period.

CHAPTER THIRTEEN

Aaron Copland

The closest "Les Six" ever came to actually working together (and even here Louis Durey declined to participate) was in the writing of the music for a ballet by Jean Cocteau, *Les mariés de la Tour Eiffel.* One member of the audience at the 1921 premiere of this bizarre work was a young American composer, Aaron Copland (b. 1900), who had arrived from New York only a few days before.

Paris had become the center of European musical culture, no longer rivaled by Vienna after the conclusion of World War I. Copland, eager to escape the conservative atmosphere of New York, was immediately delighted with the exuberance of the French capital, home of Satie, Stravinsky, and "Les Six." Though he did not know the name Nadia Boulanger when he left the United States, he was soon introduced to her and became the first of many American composers to profit from her astonishing abilities as a teacher. Staying in France for three years, Copland was able to study with Mlle. Boulanger and to hear and study much of the music then being written in Europe, not only by French composers but by Bartók, Schoenberg, Stravinsky, Prokofiev, Falla, Webern, Kodály, and many others. He also studied piano with Ricardo Viñes, one of the foremost performers of contemporary music of the day.

Returning to the United States in 1924, Copland found New York a different place from the city he had left three years earlier. An artistic rebellion had developed in the interim, transforming the thinking of many culturally minded people. America, which until World War I had been completely subservient to Europe in artistic matters, was beginning to develop a certain self-confidence and national pride. Beginning at first in painting and literature, this movement surfaced in music with the formation in 1924 of the League of Composers in New York. Its enthusiastic journal, *Modern Music,* was to continue for twenty-three years, providing a chronicle of the burgeoning musical activities around the country between the wars. Copland, fresh from his exhilarating Parisian experience, returned to this revitalized American scene and immediately became part of it.

He had already published two works for piano in Paris, the skittish, brief *The Cat and the Mouse* (1920—written before he went to Europe), and the *Passacaglia* (1922). The latter, dedicated to Mlle. Boulanger, shows her influence and that of French music (especially Franck) in general. His first completely original work for the piano, coming after the composition of such important works as the *Symphony for Organ and Orchestra* (1924) and the jazz-oriented *Concerto for Piano and Orchestra* (1926), was the *Piano Variations* (1930).

Copland has often said that this was the work in which he first felt secure that he had found his own personal style. Of the tremendous amount of music he had heard and absorbed in Paris and New York, he had been most drawn to that which used materials economically, was clearly shaped, and was serious in intent. He felt the new piano piece, the *Piano Variations*, accomplished all of these things convincingly.

Although the "theme" stated at the outset of the work is eleven measures long, it is evident that even this is the extension and working out of a much shorter unit, a motive of only four notes: E-C-D♯-C♯. These four notes are boldly stated at the beginning (example 13.1). In fact, these four notes, or rather the intervals they define, dominate virtually everything that happens in the remainder of the ten-minute piece. In some ways Copland's procedure resembles the row techniques then being developed by Schoenberg and Webern, techniques with which Copland was familiar, but the *Piano Variations* is by no means a serial work. It is, however, tightly organized and carefully shaped to an unprecedented degree.

EXAMPLE 13.1. Copland, *Piano Variations*, mm. 1–3. © 1932 by Aaron Copland; Copyright Renewed. Reprinted by permission of Aaron Copland, Copyright Owner, and Boosey & Hawkes, Inc., Sole Licensees.

The characteristic sound of the piece might be described as that of contrapuntally derived dissonance. Copland more often than not uses more than one version of the four-note motive at the same time, as in the second variation (example 13.2). Note that the middle staff in this example has the motive in its original order, 1-2-3-4, whereas the bottom staff changes the order to 3-4-1-2. Since the counterpoint between these two voices is note-against-note, minor ninths and major sevenths are the inevitable result. Similarly, in the sixth variation, almost every interval is either a major seventh or a minor ninth. This might be called a double variation, one in quarter notes and the other in sixteenths (example

EXAMPLE 13.2. Copland, *Piano Variations*, mm. 21–22.

EXAMPLE 13.3. Copland, *Piano Variations*, mm. 57–59.

EXAMPLE 13.4. Copland, *Piano Variations*, mm. 222–26.

13.3). This happens often later in the work—for example, in the difficult seventeenth variation (example 13.4).

Each variation introduces something new, either one strong idea or two contrasting ideas as just shown. The constantly recurring motivic material unifies the music melodically, harmonically, and contrapuntally. Finally, everything happens quickly: the Theme and twenty variations are over in about eight minutes, after which the Coda, slow and stately, fills out the final two minutes. No one figure or variant has time to linger too long. The music is constantly moving on to the next idea.

In an informal discussion a few years ago Copland remarked that when he was in the process of composing the *Piano Variations*, finding the proper sequence of variations so that this "moving on" could best be achieved was far more difficult to accomplish than the actual writing of the individual variations themselves. There was a great deal of experimentation until the most logical arrangement was found, he said.[1]

A few words concerning performance. At the bottom of the first page of the score, Copland assures the pianist that the metronome indications are only "approximate indications of correct tempi." What he does not say is that, approximate or not, the *relationship* of one metronomic speed to the next is critically important in projecting the structural growth of the piece. This is particularly true at the outset in which the increase in tempo from the Theme ($\downarrow$ = 48) to the first variation ($\downarrow$ = 54), second ($\downarrow$ = 72), and third ($\downarrow$ = 100) is most impressive if these relative increments, if not the exact numerical values, are carefully observed.

Second, tone quality. "He dwelt on every tone, as if to distil the last ounce of sonority out of it—which was as it should be, since there were so few tones," writes Arthur Berger[2] of an early performance of the *Piano Variations* by the composer. Implied is a certain deliberateness in approach and a sense that the composer was listening intensely to each sound he played. Today's performer needs in particular to listen carefully in order to avoid a too-percussive approach to this work, which has already proven its sinewy strength many times over. Warmth, clarity of line, and rhythmic accuracy serve this, one of the finest pieces in the repertoire of our century, to best advantage.

The three-movement *Piano Sonata* (1941) is also one of Copland's most serious works. As in the *Piano Variations*, motivic material plays an important part in creating and holding together the structure, but here the pace is broadened considerably (the work lasts over twenty minutes). The manner in which the performer makes audible the relationships that may be clear on the page is not always as apparent as in the earlier work.

There is no question about the importance of the two opening motives of the first movement (example 13.5). The first motive (mm. 1–2) is the more easily heard of the two. It sometimes reappears intact, sometimes is transposed or rearranged, but, as examples 13.6, 13.7, and 13.8 from the exposition show, it is always recognizable.

The second motive accounts for a great deal of the ongoing line, especially in the exposition, appearing in a variety of guises (example 13.9). The second theme, although it introduces a quieter mood, is really not a new idea. It, too, derives directly from the first motive of the opening (examples 13.10, 13.11).

The exposition is extended, consisting of more than half the playing time of the first movement. Because the entire exposition is based exclusively on the two motives heard in the first line, one is not surprised that when the development section arrives something unusual happens. Copland moves the tempo ahead from the opening *molto moderato* to *allegro* and presents a transformation of the second theme in the new tempo (examples 13.12, 13.13).

EXAMPLE 13.5. Copland, *Piano Sonata*, first movement, mm. 1–5. © 1942 by Aaron Copland; Copyright Renewed. Reprinted by permission of Aaron Copland, Copyright Owner, and Boosey & Hawkes, Inc., Sole Licensee.

EXAMPLE 13.6. Copland, *Piano Sonata*, first movement, mm. 50–51.

EXAMPLE 13.7. Copland, *Piano Sonata*, first movement, mm. 96–97.

EXAMPLE 13.8. Copland, *Piano Sonata*, first movement, mm.118–19.

EXAMPLE 13.9. Copland, *Piano Sonata*, first movement, mm. 11–18.

EXAMPLE 13.10. Copland, *Piano Sonata*, first movement, mm. 1–2.

EXAMPLE 13.11. Copland, *Piano Sonata*, first movement, mm. 58–59.

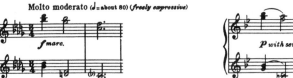

EXAMPLE 13.12. Copland, *Piano Sonata*, first movement, mm. 58–59.

EXAMPLE 13.13. Copland, *Piano Sonata*, first movement, mm. 133–35.

At the conclusion of this fast section the music builds to a climax and, after a brief pause, moves on to the recapitulation, much abbreviated, of the motives already presented and worked out in the exposition.

The second movement, a fast rondo, is worked out in a similarly economical manner. The first and second themes—the first light and angular and the second loud and chordal—turn out to be inseparably related to one another (examples 13.14, 13.15). In the middle of the movement a brief third theme appears (example 13.16). Strangely

EXAMPLE 13.14. Copland, *Piano Sonata*, second movement, mm. 1–3.

EXAMPLE 13.15. Copland, *Piano Sonata*, second movement, mm. 54–56.

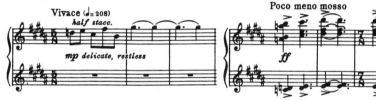

EXAMPLE 13.16. Copland, *Piano Sonata*, second movement, mm. 203–206.

enough, it is not a variant of what is heard in the first line of the piece. It is something quite new and apparently unrelated. However, this "free" melody is by no means allowed to exist only for itself, unconnected to the rest of the sonata. It appears again at the beginning of the third movement and subsequently serves as the melodic basis for the long, slow, fantasy-like finale (example 13.17).

Despite this thematic carryover, illustrating Copland's usual economy in the use of motivic materials, the third movement is freer and more improvisatory than the other two movements. With the music floating along on a series of chordal and rhythmic sequences, the composer seems intent upon avoiding too strong a melodic line during many parts

EXAMPLE 13.17. Copland, *Piano Sonata*, third movement, mm. 9–11.

of the finale. Perhaps this is done in order to prepare for the most dramatic moment in the entire work, the reintroduction of the opening motive of the first movement. This recall first appears with great passion and drama. Later it is heard again, quietly and with resignation, as the closing idea of the entire work.

The emotional effect of the reintroduction of this motive is stunning. It also may act to justify the shortness of the recapitulation in the first movement. That is, the reappearance of this germinal motive at the end of the piece seems, in fact, to move a portion of the recapitulation out of the first movement and into the third, thereby securely tying all three movements together.

The importance of these two works for solo piano in Copland's output can hardly be overemphasized. Clearly they contain some of the most deeply felt music of the first four decades of his life. In the ten years after his return from Paris–until about 1935–his principal works are essentially abstract and somewhat severe. He was, at that time, earnestly seeking a style of his own, and such compositions as the *Symphonic Ode* (1929), *Piano Variations* (1930), and the *Short Symphony* (1933) are, consequently, serious, weighty works. Of these three, the *Piano Variations* seems the strongest.

During the mid-thirties Copland, his musical langauge now well established, turned outward, becoming more concerned with the general state of music in this country. He was alarmed at the growing gulf he perceived between composer and listener. In an attempt to improve the situation he began to write music of a lighter, less complex nature. He wrote popular ballets—*Billy the Kid* (1938), *Rodeo* (1942), *Appalachian Spring* (1944)—sound tracks for movies and incidental music for plays—*Quiet City* (1939), *Of Mice and Men* (1939), *Our Town* (1940)—and, with the advent of World War II, patriotic music—*Lincoln Portrait* (1942) and *Fanfare for the Common Man* (1942). His concert music during this time consists largely of arrangements of portions of these ballets and movie and theater scores. Even the lovely *Violin Sonata* (1944) is on the light side. All of this music is well written and eminently listenable, and with it Copland did a great deal to win a large audience without ever compromising the high quality of his work. But his private world, the deeply serious musical nature that was strikingly revealed in the *Piano Variations*, was heard only in the telling sonorities of the *Piano Sonata* during this period. It would reappear later in his finest orchestral work, the *Third Symphony* (1946) and in the huge *Piano Fantasy* (1957).

CHAPTER FOURTEEN

Other Composers in America

Henry Cowell

One of the most prolific American composers of the century, Henry Cowell (1897–1965), was also the principal innovator in the generation after Ives. A man of endless energy and enthusiasm, he toured as a pianist in the United States and abroad. Beginning in 1923 he undertook several European tours and was the first American composer to be invited to Russia. Wherever he played he programmed his own music, which, with its novel pianistic techniques, provoked astonishment and, among at least some of his listeners, genuine enthusiasm.

With the launching of the New Music Society[1] in 1925 in Los Angeles, Cowell, still in his twenties, added entrepreneurship to his many other activities. He was to continue throughout his lifetime to support the cause of new music in tangible ways, by arranging concerts, publications, and recordings, and by promoting the music of American composers in general.

Cowell wrote many piano pieces, most of them quite short, in a variety of styles. The most interesting are those that are the most experimental. Just as the short piano pieces of Charles Ives are often vehicles for working out compositional problems, so Cowell's pieces often exploit a new kind of sound or an unusual combination of rhythmic figures.

He was only fifteen when he wrote his first tonecluster piece, *The Tides of Manaunaun* (1912). (According to a story by John Varian, Manaunaun was the god of motion who sent tremendous tides through the universe.) Clusters covering an octave, played with the flat of the left hand in accompaniment of the melody in the right, begin the piece. As the dynamics increase, the clusters grow to a two-octave span and are played with the forearm. At the work's *ffff* climax there are even larger, arpeggiated clusters (example 14.1). In 1912, this was indeed a new way to play the piano!

In 1923 Cowell began to experiment with sounds produced by playing directly on the strings inside the piano. *The Aeolian Harp*, written that

EXAMPLE 14.1. Cowell, *The Tides of Manaunaun*, mm. 24–25. Used by Permission of Associated Music Publishers, Inc.

year, involves strumming the mid-range strings with the fingers of one hand while the other hand silently presses down chords on the keys.

The music in these two pieces, *The Tides of Manaunaun* and *The Aeolian Harp*, is quite simple and straightforward. The novelty is in the kind of sound and the manner in which it is produced, rather than in the musical conception. This, however, is not the case with *The Banshee* (1925), certainly the most unusual piece Cowell wrote for the piano.

In *The Banshee* the performer stands at the crook of the piano. The damper pedal must be held down throughout, either with a wedge inserted under the back of the pedal or by a second person sitting at the keyboard. In his "Explanation of Sounds" accompanying the score, Cowell gives a dozen letter-coded ways of sweeping or plucking the strings. These letters are found throughout the score (example 14.2). Thoroughly original and quite sensational, the sound of *The Banshee* can hardly be imagined through an examination of its notation. Cowell's own recordings of this and other pieces[2] are instructive for the would-be performer, although the directions and score are clear and completely adequate.[3]

EXAMPLE 14.2. Cowell, *The Banshee*, mm. 6–11. Used by Permission of Associated Music Publishers, Inc.

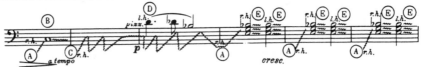

Cowell's zaniest, most ferocious piano piece is called *Tiger* (1928), which was first published in Russia. A facsimile of the original edition, with directions in Russian, German, and English, is included in the Associated Music Publishers' collection of nine of Cowell's pieces.[4] One of the composer's longest pieces, it treats the piano unmercifully with huge double-forearm clusters repeated at great length and extended passages played with both fists. At the outset it may remind the listener of the beginning of the last movement of Prokofiev's *Sarcasms* (see chapter 11), but while Prokofiev's jarring chords continue for only a few phrases and are set in a metrically interesting scheme, *Tiger* refuses to let up and, for all its frenetic activity, is not very interesting rhythmically, sticking close to $\frac{4}{4}$ too much of the time.

Cowell's contributions to music as a promoter of the works of others have rarely been equalled. He championed the music of Charles Ives, whom he admired tremendously, co-authoring with Sidney Cowell the excellent, if not always correct, study, *Charles Ives and His Music.*[5] He was a friend of Carl Ruggles (1876–1971), the long-lived, iconoclastic American whose *Evocations: Four Chants for Piano* (1937–1943, revised 1954) demonstrate a fervent, somewhat undisciplined search for expressive musical shapes in a highly chromatic, rhythmically inventive language. Cowell published the brief but notorious *Airplane Sonata* (1931) by George Antheil (1900–1959), even though he did not particularly like the piece and was suspicious of its composer, considering him an opportunist (the *Airplane Sonata* contains some very Cowellian toneclusters). He published four of Ruth Crawford Seeger's nine *Preludes* (1928), which are still available, from Merion Music, in the original 6 through 9 numbering. (The composer is listed variously as Ruth Crawford and Ruth Crawford Seeger in different publications; the score of the *Four Preludes* gives only her maiden name.) The pieces are strong and dissonant, projecting a wide emotional range and strong individuality. Cowell had harsh words for the young Aaron Copland, feeling that he had appropriated American folktunes and then run off to Paris to learn European ways of setting them (Cowell let his anti-European feelings get in the way of the succession of events in this case), but he published some of Copland's music nevertheless and saw to it that the *Piano Variations* appeared on New Music Society concerts. And, whatever his antipathy toward things European, he published Schoenberg's last work for the piano, *Klavierstück*, Op. 33b, though he first consulted with his friend and biggest financial supporter, Charles Ives, concerning the propriety (and expense—Schoenberg wanted one hundred dollars) of doing so.

Cowell's own music is of variable quality. The piano pieces have genuine historic importance, but their musical content, with the exception of the astonishing *Banshee*, is such that they can be considered more as curiosities than anything else. Nevertheless he is definitely an "American original" and an occasional revival of interest in his piano music will always be welcome.

Roger Sessions

Sessions (1896–1985) wrote five major works for solo piano, including three piano sonatas and two sets of smaller pieces. The *First Sonata* (1930) is of interest from many points of view, but primarily, in light of Sessions's later work, because of what it attempts to do stylistically. That it does not quite work can hardly diminish one's admiration for the endeavor. To begin, Sessions tries to stitch together a long-lined, romantic *cantabile* section and a Stravinskian allegro—the Stravinsky of the *Sérénade en la* rather than the *Piano Sonata*, but in any case heavier and without the Russian composer's sense of élan and detachment. The Chopinesque *cantabile* returns a second time, beautifully written, almost convincing one that it should be there, and leads to a second and concluding fast section in rondo form, again showing the composer reflecting the sounds and idiosyncracies of the neoclassic era. In this final section, in particular, the music resembles the kind of thing too many lesser American composers would be turning out in piece after piece a dozen or so years later, substituting frenetic activity for genuinely musical flow in what might be called the "allegro-energico" school of composition. That Sessions was to leave this somewhat faceless kind of writing behind as he developed his own mature style, based more on a Schoenbergian than a quasi-Stravinskian model, is to his credit.

From My Diary (1937–1940)—Sessions preferred his original title, *Pages from a Diary*—is a delightful set of four contrasting pieces, each dedicated to a friend. Though this is the easiest of his five major works for the piano, the second movement, "Allegro con brio," gives a foretaste of the kind of brilliant, driving pianistic style that he developed so well in the later works.

The *Second Sonata* (1946), *Third Sonata* (1965), and the *Five Pieces for Piano* (1975) rival the two massive sonatas by Charles Ives for profundity of statement. Ranging from exuberant joy and determination to resigned pathos, they project the widest possible spectrum of human emotions. These works will be examined in chapter 20.

John Cage

John Cage (b. 1912) will also be discussed later (chapter 19). Always regarding the piano as his primary instrument, he has written for it repeatedly. His wide-ranging and radically provocative ideas have made him one of the twentieth century's seminal figures. His fame as an experimenter had its first major breakthrough in 1938 when, possibly as a result of his association with Henry Cowell in California, he wrote his first piece for prepared piano, *Bacchanale* (1938), transforming the instrument into something that sounds like a Balinese gamelan. This and similar pieces, using few pitches and repeating them in small, circling figures at great length, are still influential today, prototypes of the long, mesmerizing productions of the minimalists.

Carlos Chávez

The most important works for piano by the Mexican composer Carlos Chávez (1899–1978) were written in the 1920s. Both the short

Sonatina (1924) and the slightly longer *Third Sonata* (1928) feature textures that can best be described as "lean." Chávez believed in strong, dissonant counterpoint. There is no concern with the niceties of foreground and background in this music; every note is bitingly important. Significantly, the rigorously ascetic *Third Sonata* is dedicated to Copland, whose tight, economical *Piano Variations* had not yet been written.

George Gershwin

One cannot leave this period in America without mention of the ebullient, immensely talented George Gershwin (1898–1937) whose short life—he lived exactly as long as Frédéric Chopin, but eighty-eight years later—was crammed with fame and success. He was happiest when seated at the keyboard playing his own music, whether in concert or at a party, in his hyper-energetic way. His published *Three Preludes* (1926), only a portion of a set of five or six short pieces that he wrote (improvised?) over a period of time, reflect his optimistic, convivial manner. They also demonstrate his genius as the composer best able to cross over from jazz and popular music into "classical", an ability he brought to near perfection in the famous *Rhapsody in Blue* (1924), *Concerto in F* (1925), and *American in Paris* (1928).[6]

CHAPTER FIFTEEN

Olivier Messiaen

The opening chapters of this book are concerned in part with the efforts by composers in the first decade of this century to break away from traditional functional tonality. The freeing of sounds from their old harmonic associations is one of the most striking characteristics of the music of Debussy; Schoenberg's plunge into atonality is the most radical aspect of his early piano pieces; Charles Ives employs traditional harmonic practices in moments of recollection and reminiscence only to shatter them completely and abruptly seconds later.

An integral aspect of functional tonality, in addition to characteristic harmonic progressions, is a regularly recurring pattern of strong and weak beats. Individual pieces written in the baroque and classical periods are, for the most part, in a single meter. The smallest melodic unit, the two-note slur, the second note a resolution of the first, presupposes strong beats arriving at regular intervals, as in example 15.1. Dissonance resolution on the two-note level is combined with functional chord progressions, as in the II–V⁷–I succession (example 15.1) or in the familiar passage from Beethoven's *Pathétique Sonata*, Op. 13 (example 15.2).

These passages are satisfying not only because they conform to the psychology of expectation associated with classical harmonic motion, but also because events follow the traditionally ordered metric parsing inextricably linked to such motion. (Is this really so? Play the version of the opening of Mozart's *Piano Sonata in B-flat Major*, K. 333 (example 15.3), and decide if it still feels Mozartian.)

EXAMPLE 15.1. Mozart, *Piano Sonata in B-flat major*, K. 333, mm. 1–4.

$$B\flat : \quad I \quad - \quad II \quad - \quad V^7 \quad - \quad I$$

EXAMPLE 15.2. Beethoven, *Piano Sonata in C*, Op. 13, second movement, mm. 6–8.

$$VI^7 \quad - \quad II \quad - \quad V^7 \quad - \quad I$$

EXAMPLE 15.3. Recomposed version of Example 15.1.

As functional tonality weakened throughout the nineteenth century, so did the need for regular meters. The fact that romantic music can be played with more rubato than the music of the classical period is to some extent due to its freer harmonic practices and the correspondingly weaker metric controls. Nevertheless, the barline in romantic music maintains its function as the signal of a downbeat, nor does this function disappear with Schoenberg; quite the contrary, the two-note slur still remains in all of the Op. 11 pieces with the first note almost always on a metrically determined strong beat and the second, whether or not it "resolves" anything, on a weak beat. Schoenberg confirms this by changing the meter several times in order to accommodate the accentuation of his phrases.

Stravinsky was the composer who seems to have been most conscious of the fact that meter and rhythm had now been completely emancipated and could be treated correspondingly. The famous $\frac{3}{16}-\frac{2}{16}-\frac{3}{16}-\frac{2}{8}-\frac{2}{16}-\frac{3}{16}-\frac{2}{8}$ . . . passage in the "Sacrificial Dance" from *Le sacre* (rehearsal no. 142 forward) is just one of dozens of examples of his creative use of the accentuating function of meter (see also example 8.3). In Stravinsky's hands what was once the least volatile element of the melody-harmony-rhythm triumvirate became an equal.

Bartók's use of meter, derived from his study of the irregular rhythms and asymmetrical phrase lengths of folk music, is certainly as inventive as Stravinsky's (see example 7.13, from the third movement of Bartók's *Piano Sonata*, with its irregular alternations between $\frac{3}{8}$, $\frac{2}{4}$, and $\frac{1}{4}$).

In the *Piano Variations* by Copland (see example 13.4), the changes of meter continue to reflect changes in pulse as the barline maintains its traditional accentuating function.

With Webern the measure line begins to lose this role. It becomes, instead, more of an organizing notational sign (a "visual aid," Boulez would soon call it) that demarcates a certain number of beats without real participation in the music itself, much as a ruler marks off inches or centimeters without affecting the object being measured. Thus in the theme of the final movement of Webern's *Piano Variations* (see example 9.3) the meter has considerably less to do with the rhythmic gestures of the piece than in the music mentioned above by Schoenberg, Stravinsky, Bartók, and Copland.

If by the 1930s rhythm and meter had been emancipated from a previously servile role, the next step was even more intriguing: the freeing of psychological time. Nearly impossible during the tonal period because of the almost constant presence of a repetitive beat, fast or slow, composers found it conceivable to experiment with music in which the rhythm was so free and so unmetrical that there would seem to be little or no relationship to ordinary clock time.

The manipulation of psychological time is only one of the many fascinating aspects of the music of French composer Olivier Messiaen (b. 1908), one of the unique composer-performer-pedagogues of the century. Always a devout Catholic, his life has been heavily influenced by the beliefs, liturgies, and mysteries of the church. What the music of Danbury, Connecticut, became for Ives and the folkmusic of Hungary for Bartók, the plainchant of the church and, strangely enough, the songs of birds have become for Messiaen: an internalized source of inspiration for the development of a singular musical style.

From the first, Messiaen was intent on capturing the essence of spiritual contemplation. *Le banquet céleste* (1926) for organ, written when he was only seventeen, moves with almost unbelievable slowness from beginning to end. The listener has very little sense of pulse, meter, or even of elapsed time. There is also the feeling that the harmonic language, rather than progressing from one chord to another, simply changes color but does not move.

Later, in *Vingt regards sur l'enfant-Jésus* (*Twenty Contemplations of the Infant Jesus*), a two-hour masterpiece for solo piano written in 1944, Messiaen carries slowness to audacious lengths. In the first movement, "Contemplation of the Father," triplets are heard throughout (example 15.4). Each sixteenth-note lasts one second, so the first measure will have a duration of twenty-one seconds. The same rhythmic figuration and tempo continue without change to the end of the movement seven and one-half minutes later.

Many of the other pieces are similarly slow. This is, of course, in the nature of contemplation. Unlike more traditional slow music, however,

EXAMPLE 15.4. Messiaen, *Vingt regards sur l'enfant-Jésus*, first movement, m. 1.
© 1947 Durand S.A. Used by Permission of the Publisher. Sole Representative
U.S.A., Theodore Presser Company.

this music does not depend on harmonic development or progression, even though one hears chords throughout. Messiaen's singular concept of harmony is that it serves only a decorative function. "Consonant" and "dissonant" chords do not exist in his vocabulary. Rather, different collections of notes produce different colorations or timbres. The traditional idea of the resolution of non-chordal tones gives way to the concept of timbre-chords, existing in and of themselves, and progressing only in the sense that they move on to other timbres.

The first piece of the *Vingt regards*, then, is rhythmically and metrically steady from beginning to end, thereby opening this vast collection of contemplative pieces in a hypnotic, spellbinding manner. Later movements, however, are rhythmically much different. In fact, Messiaen's genius comes through most effectively in the area of rhythmic variety and vitality, thereby energizing the timbre-chords he constructs. Example 15.5 shows a relatively simple example of this unusual rhythmic manipulation from the ninth piece, "Contemplation of Time." Particularly characteristic of the composer here is the "added" sixteenth in the first measure, the "extra" dots in the third and fourth measures, and the fact that the measures are unequal in length and subtly different in rhythmic accentuation. In this way the composer views his non-progressing harmonies from every possible angle, eventually capturing the listener with unexpected changes in emphasis.

Messiaen's principle of added values, derived to a great extent from a study of Indian *talas*, is discussed in his treatise, *Technique de mon langage musical* (1942). As a composer he has always felt the need to make detailed technical rules for himself, thereby formalizing as much as possible

EXAMPLE 15.5. Messiaen, *Vingt regards*, ninth movement, mm. 35–38.

his own intuitive inspiration. For an excellent summary of the composer's rhythmic ideas, as well as all other aspects of his style, Robert Sherlaw Johnson's book, *Messiaen*,[1] is highly recommended.

If Messiaen is audacious in stretching simple musical ideas over long periods of time, and if his slower contemplations seem to revolve endlessly around small adjustments in the rhythmic divisions of time, he is also quite able to storm the heavens in other movements. There are long, extraordinarily difficult passages in the *Vingt regards*, sometimes quite loud throughout, making full use of the complete range of sonority of the piano. Such a passage may circle around a short series of chords, as in the sixth piece, "By Him Were All Things Made" (example 15.6).

The composer whose music most influenced Messiaen is undoubtedly Debussy. A glance at the early *Preludes* (1929) confirms this initial debt. A second influence is Stravinsky, which is best seen in the manner in which Messiaen creates forms and achieves continuity. As is the case with Stravinsky, the primary concept in this area is juxtaposition. Like Stravinsky, Messiaen does not develop ideas; rather, he juxtaposes them. The order in which the pieces in *Vingt regards* is arranged to fill the enormous time span of the collection is very careful, of course. Within individual pieces there is also a building up of relationships. It is possible that there are no inner juxtapositions, no changes of tempo or figuration, as in the almost motionless opening piece, or there may be quick, unpredictable jumps in tempi, timbres, and dynamics. In addition, Messiaen will often juxtapose several layers of sound at the same time, each layer having its own dynamic level and rhythmic flow, each layer modifying the others in a specific way.

Mention should be made of the several themes that appear throughout the cycle, chiefly the "Thème de Dieu," a series of four so-

EXAMPLE 15.6. Messiaen, *Vingt regards*, sixth movement, mm. 124–25.

(Thème d'amour)

norities heard immediately at the beginning of the first piece and reappearing in various transformations, always recognizable, in six of the remaining movements. These themes not only unify the various movements but add appropriate extramusical connotations and connections to the music. In a preface to the score, Messiaen lists the themes and gives a brief summary of the spiritual nature of each of the twenty pieces.

The music of the *Vingt regards* is tonal; one of the unifying features of the cycle is the fact that so many of the pieces center on F-sharp. In Messiaen's next piano pieces, however, *Quatre études de rythme* (1949), he moves completely away from tonal centers in what he himself refers to as an "experiment." In one of the studies, "Mode de valeurs et d'intensités," the composer attempts something that, at least in part, has its genesis in the twelve-tone technique of Schoenberg. The piece uses three modes, each containing twelve notes. In each mode a specific range, length, and kind of attack is assigned to each pitch. The modes are not employed as tone rows in the Schoenbergian sense; it is not really a serial work. However, its unprecedented pre-compositional assumptions in the realms of durations, attack, and register made a lasting impression on several young composers who were or who had been students of Messiaen, among them Karlheinz Stockhausen and Pierre Boulez.

The "Mode de valeurs" is, frankly, a rather dry piece. It is more interesting for what it presages compositionally than for what it accomplishes musically. The other studies in the *Quatre études* are more spontaneous, though they are also working grounds for the composer's rhythmic theories. The most interesting is "Île de feu 1." Starting something like Bartók's "With Drums and Pipes" from *Out of Doors*, it soon surpasses it in terms of percussive declamation and virtuosic keyboard writing (example 15.7).

EXAMPLE 15.7. *Quatre Études* by Olivier Messiaen. © 1960 Durand S.A. Used by Permission of The Publisher. Sole Representative U.S.A., Theodore Presser Company.

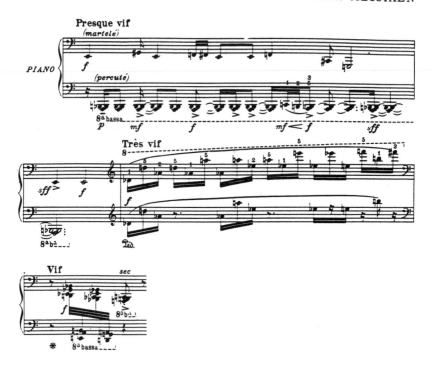

Olivier MESSIAEN

Following these experiments, Messiaen wrote a number of works using bird songs. The best known of these works is another long cycle of pieces for the piano, *Catalogue d'oiseaux* (1958). There are thirteen pieces in the set, which takes approximately two and one-half hours to play.

Each movement is preceded by a paragraph setting the scene. Underlying the music are explanations and identifications: here the raven sings, there the oriole. In the music itself the songs of the birds, in as close an approximation as the composer can achieve on the keyboard, appear in profusion. Again it is basically a work of contemplation, here concentrating on the joys of nature as well as the joys of the spirit.

In a more recent work, *Petites esquisses d'oiseaux* (1985), Messiaen again returned to his beloved bird songs in six colorful, imaginative pieces.

Musically and pianistically Messiaen's scores are different from anything previously written. Remembering Stravinsky's remarks concerning rhythmic strictness and Ravel's insistence on faithfulness to the score, one may say that in Messiaen's music rubato simply has no place, not because it would be unstylistic, as in Stravinsky or Ravel, but because it is literally impossible. The rhythms in fast passages are so precise and so complex with the sometimes microscopic "added values" that to play with rhythmic *espressivo* would do irreparable damage to the structure. In slow movements the tempi are such that rubato is again meaningless, since beats are too far apart to make it perceptible. Moreover, the removed, otherworldly quality of the music in which time is often suspended makes the addition of nuance on the part of the performer an unwanted intrusion.

These remarks concern rhythm only and hardly are meant to indicate there is nothing for the interpreter to do. Tone, timbre, line, sonority, dynamic control, and phrase shape are constant concerns, to say nothing of the considerable virtuosity often required. Above all, to perform Messiaen's mystical, devout music in the right spirit requires a certain personal peace and quietude.

Looking back on the period between the two world wars, one is struck with the fact that the most thoughtful composers were almost constantly concerned with setting compositional rules or restraints. In one of his lectures at Harvard University in 1940, Stravinsky declared, "My freedom consists in my moving about within the narrow frame that I have assigned myself for each one of my undertakings. . . . My freedom will be so much greater and more meaningful the more narrowly I limit my field of action and the more I surround myself with obstacles."[2]

Stravinsky's contemporary in Vienna, Arnold Schoenberg, was greatly occupied with his own search for a way to systematize musical composition. His way of limiting his field of action was to explore the ramifications of the twelve-tone technique. Hindemith formulated the harmonic and contrapuntal concepts of *The Craft of Musical Composition* over several decades. Messiaen felt it necessary to organize his personal compositional style in the *Technique de mon langage musical.*

This kind of codifying is hardly surprising. Composers in the hinge periods of music history are always more conscious of the need for rules of procedure than are composers in periods in which a style has matured to the point where it can be accepted and used without question.

What happened soon after World War II, however, is unprecedented in Western music history. Composers not only continued the search for compositional restraints but also began to feel it necessary to explain what they were going to do or had already done in a piece of music. These explanations, beginning at first as extended program notes, soon took on a life of their own, perhaps in response to the psychic needs of an increasingly technological society. For many, a comprehensive, exhaustive explication of every aspect of a piece of music was necessary in order to justify its existence.

The extent to which these explanations were to go, to say nothing of the language that was developed to accommodate them, provides a clear picture of the enormous degree to which the collapse of tonality and the concomitant developments in harmony, rhythm, timbre, and structural processes had changed music in the first years of the century, completely dismantling its traditional compositional processes. If the shock had been too much for most composers in the period between the wars, putting them in a "holding pattern," for those after World War II it was not. The young composers of the postwar period had grown up with *Pelléas*, *Le sacre*, *Pierrot*, *Wozzeck*, *Music for Strings, Percussion and Celeste*, and other masterpieces from the first half of the century, accepting the languages of these works as natural expressive vehicles rather than as radical novelties. They were anxious to move further ahead into the areas this music had made possible. And if these areas were in uncharted territory needing detailed elucidation, so be it.

The music that emerged in the late 1940s and continued to be written through much of the 1960s made this period one of the most exciting and fertile times in Western music history. Notwithstanding the encyclopedic explications, the rash of endless colloquia, and the impenetrable journal articles, the best of the music itself, unlike anything written before, created an unforgettable sense of exhilaration and vitality among all who participated in its genesis, whether as composers, performers, or listeners.

PART 3

The Postwar Period

CHAPTER SIXTEEN

Karlheinz Stockhausen and Pierre Boulez

World War II destroyed nearly an entire generation in Europe, and those who survived found cultural institutions that had endured for many generations in total disarray. In Vienna, Berlin, Paris, London, Warsaw, and elsewhere, people who had been disfranchised of any and all of life's potential amenities declared, surveying the material and psychological wreckage, that the year in which the war ended should not be called 1945 but, rather, the year zero. Everything had to begin again from the beginning.

If in the period between the world wars there had been a need on the part of certain composers to develop and codify new techniques of composition, the vast devastation and uprooting caused by World War II gave even greater impetus to the urge to put things in order. For some this became a fixation, a compulsion that may well have included a mixture of survivor's guilt and a craving for forgetfulness. Often this surfaced in statements of a strongly dogmatic, polemical nature, leaving no sympathy for persons who did not immediately perceive (or had not in past generations) the implications of certain basic discoveries and developments.

Among young composers of the early postwar period in Europe, the following verities were accepted: Debussy had emancipated sound, Stravinsky had freed rhythm, Schoenberg had released harmony from the bonds of tonality, and Webern had demonstrated how the arrangement of motivic cells, through rigorous application of row techniques, could be built into a complete musical edifice. Rejecting all else, these composers moved closer and closer to an all-inclusive serial system, eventually carrying it to its logical, if extreme, conclusion with the necessarily brief adventure into total serialism. Naturally any kind of tonal or neoclassic music was beneath consideration, at least among the composers meeting at the newly established Darmstadt International Summer Course for New Music in Germany.

Then, having reached an impasse, composers began spontaneously to assert a certain freedom, due at least in part to the infusion of the music and ideas of a certain smiling, dice-throwing, mushroom-loving man from the United States. Once this change had begun and the deterministic spell of the early postwar period was over, the proliferation of styles and manners had no bounds throughout a reviving Europe. Composers began moving in every conceivable direction, including west.

It became de rigueur, in fact, for European composers to visit America in order to pontificate at festivals featuring their music and to explain in detail their compositional rationales. Meanwhile, increasingly active American composers became restive, complaining quietly of being overlooked during the invasion of the "kleinemeisters," as some called the European visitors. They looked forward to the time, which they sensed was soon to come, when it would become apparent that the driving forces of new music were actually no longer in Europe but on the other side of the Atlantic.

One of the most brilliant members of the postwar generation has been Karlheinz Stockhausen (b. 1928). A man of tremendous intellect and industry ("I work from ten in the morning to half-past one in the afternoon, from half-past three to half-past seven in the evening, and from half-past eight to midnight"),[1] he epitomizes the composer as thinker and problem solver. A performer as well as a composer, he believes an essential part of the composer's task is to bring his own music to the public, not just in order to make a name for himself, but because this is the only way to test what he has done. "You have to organize yourself and do things on your own. You can't become a composer by avoiding the impact with reality. . . . The only road to take . . . is that of constant verification."[2]

Stockhausen was born near Cologne. During the early part of World War II he attended a teachers training college, where he studied the piano, violin, and oboe. In 1944 he left school to become a stretcher-bearer at a military hospital until the end of hostilities a year later.

When he was eighteen he entered both the Cologne Academy of Music and Cologne University as a student of composition, piano, musicology, philosophy, and linguistics. At the Academy he was able to study most of the works of the important early twentieth-century composers. Equally important, he made the acquaintance of Dr. Herbert Eimart of the West German Radio, who was instrumental in arranging broadcasts for Stockhausen. Eimart also recommended that he attend the International Summer School at Darmstadt. There he first heard, among many other things, Messiaen's "Mode de valeurs et d'intensité," a work that had a profound effect on him.

The following year he moved to Paris and attended Messiaen's classes. He was deeply impressed with Messiaen's keen musical insight as demonstrated in the analysis of twentieth-century works. Also, he met

Pierre Boulez and many other young French composers and performers in the circles around Messiaen and Pierre Schaeffer, director of the electronic music studio of the French radio.

Before moving back to Germany in 1953 he wrote, among other things, his first four piano pieces, *Klavierstücke I–IV*. Then, again thanks to Eimart, he became associated with the West German Radio's electronic music studio, which opened in May 1953. Since then, aside from travels in Europe and elsewhere to direct performances of his music, to lecture, and to teach, he has remained in Cologne, eventually succeeding Eimart as director of the electronic music studio in 1962.

Stockhausen has written a series of piano pieces that must be considered among the most important music for the instrument written during the present century. One notes that much of the piano music was written immediately after he had worked for some time on electronic compositions. Thus in discussing his piano music he has a tendency to contrast it with tape music.

> Composing electronic music involves describing sound in mechanical and electro-acoustic terms and thinking entirely in terms of machinery, apparatus, circuitry; reckoning with the single act of production and the unlimited repeatability of the composition thus produced.
> Writing instrumental music—after this—involves unleashing the performer's activities through optical signs and making a direct approach to the musician's living organism, and to his constantly varying and unpredictable capacities for response; bestowing the possibility of multiple acts of production from performance to performance, and that of unrepeatability.[3]

Characteristic of Stockhausen is that he would so aptly and succinctly point out the opposites involved in these two compositional activities: "single acts of production" and "unlimited repeatability" versus "multiple acts of production" and "unrepeatability." These distinctions are of enormous importance in Stockhausen's music, much of which describes and then mediates between opposites, as shall be seen in the discussion below. In so doing he has been able to create a new way of feeling time, something not altogether unrelated to the manipulation of psychological time discussed in the previous chapter, and for which his attendance at Messiaen's lectures may be at least partially responsible.

All of Stockhausen's work must be understood in light of his "zest for continually challenging the limits of perception."[4] This is as true in the vast sea of sound that composes *Kontakte* (1960), one of his greatest electronic works, as in the quiet intimacies of *Refrain* (1959) for three players (piano, celeste, vibraphone—each player doubling other smaller percussion instruments). Everything is investigated: notational possibilities, the physical motions of the performers, the rate of decay of a sound, and so on.

No composer in the postwar period has written more originally and, in a very real sense, more honestly for the piano. More than any other composer, Stockhausen has taken a fresh look at the instrument as if it had just been invented, saying something like the following to himself: "Here we have an instrument capable of producing eighty-eight sounds with twelve evenly spaced pitches in each of seven octaves plus a couple of extras at one end, and this instrument is playable from very soft to very loud, has three foot-pedals, each of which can do a variety of things, and has a set of levers (the keyboard) arranged in such-and-such a way so that the performer can get at things easily with both hands. It does not have a swell box nor any other way to keep a given sound, once begun, from decaying in a straight line until damped. What can I do with it?"

Klavierstücke I–IV (1953) are published together in one volume. The only piano pieces by Stockhausen to use traditional notation in every aspect, they demonstrate immediately a new approach to the instrument and to the performer (example 16.1). Rhythmic divisions of a measurable but nevertheless impracticable nature (who can really divide a $\frac{5}{4}$ measure into eleven parts and then, in addition, divide the final five of those eleven parts into seven?) indicate not that the composer is being obtuse but that he is attempting to impart "a new way of feeling time in music, in which the infinitely subtle 'irrational' shadings and impulses and fluctuations of a good performer often produce what one wants better than any centimeter gauge."[5]

EXAMPLE 16.1. Stockhausen, *Klavierstück I*, mm. 1–3. © Copyright 1954 by Universal Edition (London) Ltd., London. Copyright renewed. All Rights Reserved. Used by permission of European American Music Distributors Corporation, Sole U.S. and Canadian agent for Universal Edition, London.

Klavierstücke V–X (V–VIII, 1955; IX–X, 1961) are each published separately. The rhythmic nature of some of them, particularly the sixth and tenth, requires a new kind of temporal notation, which, when necessary, is explained in the score. Otherwise the notation is traditional except for the omission of barlines in all but the ninth piece. This omission does not mean that the rhythms of the pieces are free or "spatial," though Stockhausen is at pains to correlate tempo with space on the page as much as possible. Rather, what is indicated is simply that the traditional metric system, which organizes time into strong and weak beats, is no longer operative. Thus Stockhausen avoids the problem, discussed earlier, inherent in Webern's use of meter. In Stockhausen's music rhythm is organized (for the most part) according to a carefully gauged system of metronomic indications in some of the pieces and by graphic means in others.

Klavierstück VI is in the latter category. Above each system is a thirteen line "staff for tempi." As shown in example 16.2, a heavy line moves up and down inside this staff, indicating the precise tempo or change of tempo in every phrase or group of notes. The higher the line, the faster the tempo. The top line of the thirteen-line staff indicates $\downarrow = 180$, the bottom $\downarrow = 45$, with proportional gradations between.

Klavierstück VI is a rather long piece. The seventh and eighth pieces are very short, the latter lasting barely ninety seconds. *Klavierstück VII* is one of the most beautiful in the collection, making use of sympathetic vibrations created by holding certain keys down silently, then playing and releasing others, allowing harmonics from the held keys to ring. (This had been done for the first time by Schoenberg in a single passage in Op. 11, No. 1, half a century earlier.) *Klavierstück VII* requires considerable skill on the part of the performer, who must be able to depress the silent notes rapidly while playing other sounding notes at the same time, a technique requiring unusually delicate control.

Although the eighth piece is short, the compositional problems Stockhausen set for himself were so great that he despaired of solving them for a long time. These problems, having to do with serial parameters, do not affect the performance or perception of the work in its finished state, but it is of anecdotal interest to learn that Stockhausen, in considerable frustration, consulted his sometime friend Pierre Boulez concerning possible solutions in this matter of compositional craftsmanship, and they agonized over it together.[6]

The piece itself consists of five phrases, each involving quickly moving contrapuntal lines that lie primarily in the middle and upper ranges of the keyboard (example 16.3a). Each phrase is introduced and punctuated by grace-note "out-of-time" chord groups and ended with a single held note. It is a scintillating, sparkling piece, contrasting beautifully with its predecessor, the seventh piece, with which it may effectively be paired.

Many pianists are so intimidated by the look of Stockhausen's scores that they refuse even to consider working on his music. These pianists, who regularly learn and perform difficult Beethoven sonatas and Liszt études, seem to feel that not only is this music much more complex and

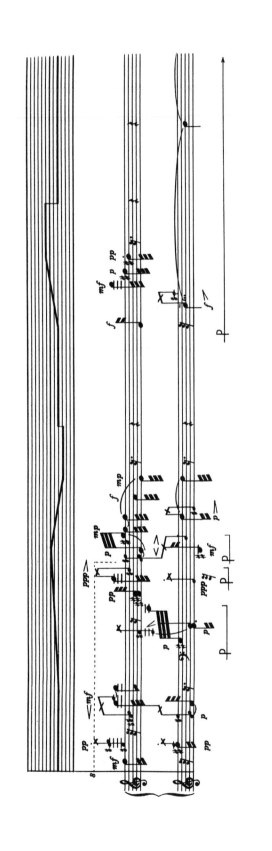

EXAMPLE 16.2. Stockhausen, *Klavierstück VI*, line 1. © Copyright 1965 by Universal Edition (London) Ltd., London. Copyright Renewed. All Rights Reserved. Used by permission of European American Music Distributors Corporation, Sole U.S. and Canadian agent for Universal Edition, London.

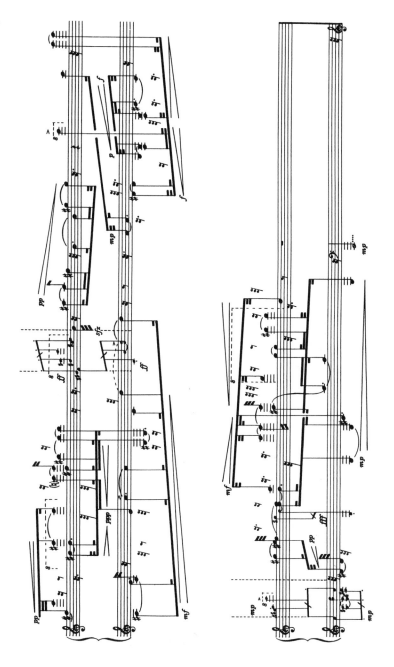

EXAMPLE 16.3a. Stockhausen, *Klavierstück VIII*, page 3, lines 1–2. © Copyright 1965 by Universal Edition (London) Ltd., London. Copyright Renewed. All Rights Reserved. Used by permission of European American Music Distributors Corporation, Sole U.S. and Canadian agent for Universal Edition, London.

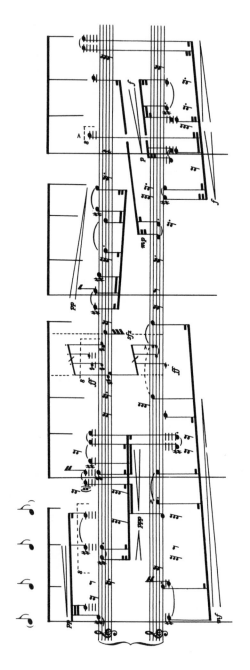

EXAMPLE 16.3b. First line of ex. 16.3a with meter lines superimposed.

technically demanding than the standard repertoire, but that special, mysterious learning and practice techniques must be invoked in order to begin at all.

I believe these misconceptions stem from the fact that, as opposed to the works of earlier composers, one cannot easily sight-read Stockhausen's piano music. This should not be such a formidable barrier, certainly not for a pianist who is willing to work through the intricacies of, let us say, Bach's *Goldberg Variations* or Ravel's *Gaspard de la nuit*.

Undeniably, preliminary study of the score is necessary before practice can begin. Let us examine the first of the two lines from *Klavierstück VIII*. First of all, I believe, one needs to find a way to organize the rhythm. Although individual lines in Stockhausen's carefully arranged counterpoint appear at first to be rhythmically irrational, it is possible to "line out" a regular meter, in this case $\frac{4}{8}$ (example 16.3b). To do this we must not include music written with small note-heads; these are to be played "as fast as possible," and therefore cannot fit into a metric scheme. Having done this, one can write out a "resultant rhythm" for the passage if it seems helpful to do so. This consists of a single series of rhythms including all attacks in all voices. The first half of example 16.3b is reproduced as example 16.3c.

EXAMPLE 16.3c. "Resultant rhythm" of beginning of ex. 16.3b.

This accomplished, we may now begin fitting these notes to the rhythms, working slowly on only a few beats at a time, jotting in fingerings (and even "handings") when necessary. From the first moment the counterpoint of dynamics must be carefully considered. Correct dynamics are just as important as correct notes; without the tonal variety and contrapuntal clarity they provide, the music becomes gray and uninteresting. Fortes, pianos, and the intervening crescendi and diminuendi must be strictly observed as one gradually internalizes the phrase under study, progressively bringing it up to tempo.

Fundamentally, this process is no different from that which pianists may use in learning a Bach fugue or Chopin étude. The learning process is, indeed, the same; one needs only to get past the initial fear that the music is somehow unreadable.

In the ninth and tenth pieces Stockhausen's endeavors to mediate between opposites is most clearly in evidence. In *Klavierstück IX* (which is the easiest of the piano pieces to play whereas the tenth is the most difficult) the opposites are two basic kinds of musical time, periodicity and aperiodicity. The composer describes the piece as transforming that which is "monotonous" into something else which he (amusingly) calls "polytonous."[7]

This is the only piece in the series to use meter signatures and, therefore, measure bars, but a glance at the first time signature, $\frac{142}{8}$, indicates that this is not exactly traditional. The work begins with a "monotonous" single chord played 227 times in two long diminuendos and ends with seemingly free, improvisatory cascades of "polytonous" notes in the treble. In between lies the mediation. Sometimes the two kinds of music oppose one another side by side, other times they mingle. All in all, the result is a charming and effective piece.

Klavierstück X is a perfect marriage between an extraordinarily bold concept of what the piano is capable of doing and a kind of notation that reflects exactly these startlingly original concepts. Among other things, the piece is "about" possible relationships between total activity and total inactivity. The latter become more and more a factor as the piece, which is at least thirty minutes long, moves toward its close. Total activity is exemplified in example 16.4, from the fourth page of the score. Of particular interest is the manner in which Stockhausen notates durations. Overall durations, corresponding roughly to the measure or phrase in more traditional music, are indicated by large notes written above the staves. The passages delimited by each of these is to have the duration of the time value given.

This arrangement allows for a kind of inner rhythmic fluctuation that traditional notation cannot so clearly indicate, a kind of written-in rubato. This is notated with beams between the top staves; some are horizontal, some rise, and some fall, indicating steady, accelerating, and retarding tempi, respectively. Since this use of beams automatically eliminates the possibility of traditional note values (eighth-notes also have single beams and thus cannot be used), durations are indicated in other ways, such as by the use of curved lines, which indicate that the notes affected are to be sustained.

The notation of cluster-glissandi, an extraordinary effect used extensively in *Klavierstück X*, should also be mentioned. At the same time, Stockhausen uses conventional signs whenever possible; dots are used for staccato notes, and dynamics are traditionally indicated.

For a relevant, clear description and explanation of every aspect of this work, Herbert Henck's study, *Karlheinz Stockhausen's Klavierstück X*,[8] is highly recommended. Performers will be particularly intrigued with the warmly written chapter entitled "Practice," a gratifyingly personal statement by one of the leading performers of contemporary piano music in the 1980s.

Klavierstück X, in a faithful and imaginative performance, has an extraordinary effect on the listener's perception of time. A single-movement work of considerable length, it contains passages of unbelievably intense, violent activity contrasting with long periods of virtually no activity or silence—Stockhausen's opposition of order and disorder. In so doing the piece seems to bend time—and here an analogy with the

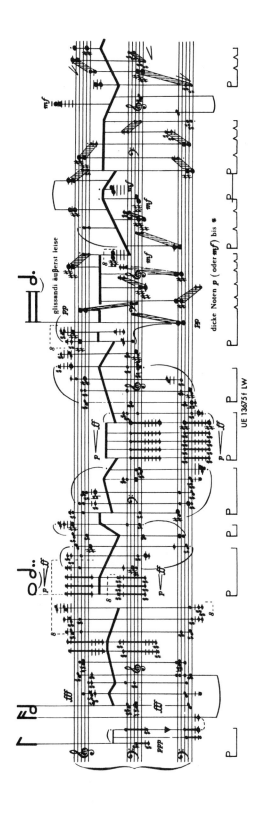

EXAMPLE 16.4. Stockhausen, *Klavierstück X*, page 4, line 2. © Copyright 1967 by Universal Edition (London) Ltd., London. Copyright Renewed. All Rights Reserved. Used by permission of European American Music Distributors Corporation, Sole U.S. and Canadian agent for Universal Edition, London.

curved space-time of Einstein's theory of relativity is more than appropriate—making the listener unaware of its passage. Henck, who agrees that the work has an undeniable effect on temporal perceptions, suggests that it may be due in large measure to the long periods of silence that are an integral part of the piece. "The rests give this piano piece its profile," he writes. The silences are

> experimental fields, test tubes, the laboratories of the piece, in which the material is subjected to various examinations. . . . Just why the silence . . . is so inescapable, and what it is that charges it with tension, would be worth a separate investigation, which would entail a reflection upon the total concert situation. . . . These stations of stillness . . . are moments in which the listener is thrown back into him-(her-)self and, thanks to the denial of sound, can become conscious of the role he(she) him-(her-)self plays.[9]

Lying behind such intuitive, subjective responses is a piece of music that in every respect is intellectually organized to a staggering degree. No composer in the postwar period felt more keenly the need to construct solid, rational compositional edifices. Even in his first and most famous brush with "chance" music, in *Klavierstück XI* (1956), the composer carefully thought through his organizational scheme in every detail. That the piece may not be as successful as some of his previous piano pieces is not directly due to any fault in construction but rather to more general problems inherent in music of "controlled" chance.

Klavierstück XI is printed on a large sheet, 21 inches by 36 inches, and consists of nineteen isolated musical fragments of varying lengths. To begin the piece the performer looks "at random at the sheet of music and begins with any group, the first that catches his eye. . . . At the end of the first group, he reads the tempo, dynamic and attack indications that follow, and looks at random to any other group, which he then plays in accordance with the latter indications."[10]

This means that after the first group, any one of the other eighteen groups may follow, depending solely on where the performer looks, and after that, using the same procedure, the performer chooses still another group, then another and another, without plan or route. In each case, however, the performer must follow the directions at the end of the previous group for tempo, dynamics, and attack—for each of which there are six possibilities, independent of one another, meaning that each group can, potentially, be played in one of 216 ways ($6 \times 6 \times 6 = 216$). Here lies the weakness of the piece, not because it is so difficult for the performer to make these adjustments, but because too many of these 216 possibilities lie in a gray area between extremes. In *Klavierstück IX* Stockhausen mediates between periodicity and aperiodicity, in *Klavierstück X* between order and disorder. Both pieces work well because the distinctions between opposites are made very clear. Stockhausen's music is at its best, in fact, when projecting these distinctions and then, in a kind of ruminative narration, negotiating between them, never allowing the listener to forget what the original extremes are. In the eleventh piece extremes of tempo and dynamics are necessarily in the minority—out of a possible six tempi, for example, there is only one "very fast" and one "very slow." In addition, it is difficult or impossible for the performer to "get close" to the piece, to internalize its emotional content, since so many of the interpretive decisions in a given phrase will change radically from one performance to the next through no choice or desire of the performer's own. David Tudor, who gave the first performances of *Klavierstück XI* in 1957, was very likely referring to this when he spoke of "how frantically I tried to get out of the four walls that the piece represented to me."[11]

Nothwithstanding its problems, *Klavierstück XI* is one of the first of a number of pieces written at the height of the serial vogue, which experiment with chance or "aleatoric" practices in one way or another. It is one of the important works, in fact, in the rather sudden swing away from tight compositional controls that occurred at the end of the 1950s.

The principal early architect of the movement toward total serialism was initially not Stockhausen but Pierre Boulez (b. 1925). A native of the small French town of Montbrison, the son of an engineer, Boulez as a boy was an exemplary student in all subjects, especially mathematics and science, and had to argue forcefully when he was seventeen to convince his father that he should continue his education as a musician.

A young man of quick tongue and unshakable opinions, he studied briefly with René Leibowitz, author of *Schoenberg et son école* (*Schoenberg and His School*, 1947)[12] and the first composer to write extensively about twelve-tone music after the war, and Messiaen. Through Leibowitz in 1945 Boulez became familiar with the music of Schoenberg and Webern, whose dodecaphonic scores appeared to him as revelations that would save the future of music; through Messiaen he not only became adept at musical analysis but was intrigued with the ideas discussed by Messiaen in his lectures, which eventually resulted in the "Mode de valeurs et d'intensité." Under the effects of these stimuli, Boulez wrote his first two sonatas for the piano, works of tremendous importance in the history of twentieth-century keyboard music.

The *First Sonata* (1946) was, according to Boulez, "influenced by the first pieces in Schoenberg's *Opus 23* as well as *Opus 11.* . . . The third piece of *Opus 11* introduced me to a style of piano writing that was different from anything I had known. There is a great density of texture and a violence of expression that conveys a kind of delirium."[13]

Given this statement, a comparison between the works of Schoenberg mentioned and the Boulez *First Sonata* is of particular interest. Both the *Five Piano Pieces*, Op. 23, and the two-movement *First Sonata* are primarily contrapuntal works, with great emphasis placed on the development of small cells. The cells in Boulez's first movement are more spread out over the keyboard than in Schoenberg's Op. 23, No. 1 (examples 16.5, 16.6). This difference aside, both composers use their principal motives throughout the respective movements in aurally comprehensible ways, thereby distinctly articulating formal structures. That Boulez alters his original cells through row manipulation does not make them less apparent since their essential shapes, rhythmically and intervallically, remains the same.

EXAMPLE 16.5. *Five Piano Pieces*, Op. 23, by Arnold Schoenberg. Used by permission of G. Schirmer, Inc. on behalf of Copyright Owner Editions Wilhelm Hansen Copenhagen.

EXAMPLE 16.6. Boulez, *First Sonata*, first movement, mm. 1–2. © 1916 Durand S.A. Used by Permission of the Publisher. Sole Representative U.S.A. Theodore Presser Company.

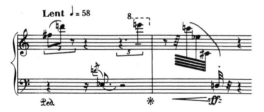

Both movements are, for the most part, lyrical. Rhythmically, however, the first movement of the Boulez *Sonata* has an underlying inquietude not found in the Schoenberg piece. This is due, partially, to the difference between Schoenberg's use of meter, which is traditional, and Boulez's use of barlines as little more than visual divisions between unequal amounts of time. Had Boulez used time signatures, the first ten measures of the first movement would have been designated as follows: $\frac{4}{4}, \frac{13}{16}, \frac{5}{8}, \frac{9}{16}, \frac{5}{8}, \frac{2}{4}, \frac{7}{8}, \frac{7}{8}, \frac{5}{8}, (\frac{3}{16} + \frac{2}{4} + \frac{1}{16})$. This would be meaningless, since the rhythmic implications of these changes (unlike the changing meters of Stravinsky, Bartók, and Copland mentioned in the previous chapter) are absent. Boulez's use of barlines is more akin to that of Messiaen, carried to a further extreme.

A more substantial difference between the Boulez and Schoenberg works lies in their approaches to form. Both develop small motivic ideas, but whereas Schoenberg's pieces in Op. 23 are each homogeneous expansions and elaborations of a single idea, Boulez juxtaposes dissimilar sections with mutually exclusive material in the same movement. In this he appears closer to the modular approach of Stravinsky and Messiaen than to Schoenberg.

In the first movement of the *First Sonata*, there are two principal sections, each with its own tempo. The first, *lent*, is followed by a much more brusque, nervous *beaucoup plus allant*. Three-quarters of the movement is taken up with the first presentations of these two contrasting ideas. The remainder consists of increasingly quick alternations between them, the interchange eventually taking place so quickly that it is barely perceptible.

The second movement alternates in similar fashion among three vastly differing tempo-motive sections: *assez large*, with widespread, declamatory single pitches; *rapide*, a fantastically fast contrapuntal toccata idea; and *modéré sans lenteur*, a lyric section with a fluctuating, undulating rhythm marked "excessivement souple" by the composer.

Boulez, stormy and belligerent at the age of twenty-one, was searching for a new kind of music and was shortly to call for an avoidance of "ce que l'on convient d'appeler les 'nuances expressives'" ("that which has come to be called 'expressive nuance' ").[14] Nevertheless, few works of the period under discussion exhibit fluid eloquence more than the *modéré sans lenteur* passages of this second movement, especially when they are contrasted with the vertiginous precipitation of the sections marked *rapide* (example 16.7a). The self-crossing, high-flowing contrapuntal cantilenas, rhythmically independent of one another and free of any sense of pulse other than the immediate agogics of the lines themselves, combine in a kind of lavish cantabile. The result is an astonishingly expressive, volatile piece of music, unprecedented in its approach to the piano, sounding like none of its antecedents (though coming closer to the spirit of Debussy than to Stravinsky, Schoenberg, or Messiaen).

Again, as suggested earlier in reference to Stockhausen's music, it may be helpful for the performer in the early learning stages to write out the resultant rhythms for passages such as this (example 16.7b). Here I would suggest keeping the rhythms for the two hands separate, the better to coordinate them. With the help of a pair of Messiaen-like added sixteenths the first three measures of example 16.7a can be written in $\frac{3}{4}$ time. Many pianists will find this procedure totally unnecessary, of course, but if it helps others to be more secure, why not try?

It is said that when René Leibowitz first saw the score of the *First Sonata*, he immediately began to criticize it. Boulez's reaction was to tear the manuscript from his hands, shouting imprecations, and parting company from his erstwhile teacher forever. While not every composer may feel the need to behave so strongly under criticism, one can empathize with this young man who knew that he had accomplished something genuinely new and had no need for it to be disparaged.

EXAMPLE 16.7a. Boulez, *First Sonata*, second movement, mm. 57–61.

EXAMPLE 16.7b. Resultant rhythm of example 16.7a.

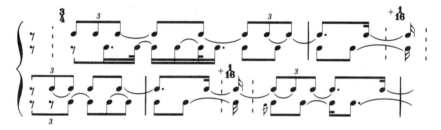

Then followed the *Second Sonata* (1948), a massive work in four movements that has inspired commentaries of the most conflicting nature. Even Boulez's own words on his treatment of motive and form in the piece are misleading. "What interested me was the manipulation of tones in a functional, not thematic way. This can be seen clearly in the first movement."[15] In fact, the first movement is in relatively clear sonata-allegro form with sharply defined themes, the first strong and contrapuntal (example 16.8) and the second ("Encore plus vif") homophonic. There is also a closing theme ("a Tempo: bien donner une impression de groupe"). After a short development there is a recognizable recapitulation, in which the closing theme in particular is considerably extended, and a short coda. It is, of course, completely atonal, and therefore traditional key relationships do not exist. However, the thematic use of motives is clearly evident. This is also true of the short third movement, a scherzo and trio that goes so far as to reuse the principal motive of the first movement at the outset (example 16.9). These are both strong, active movements, generally employing thicker textures than the *First So-*

EXAMPLE 16.8. Boulez, *Second Sonata*, first movement, mm. 1–2. Reproduced by kind permission of Heugel, owner and publisher for all countries.

EXAMPLE 16.9. Boulez, *Second Sonata*, third movement, mm. 1–2.

nata, but the actual large-scale structures are more traditional than in either movement of the earlier work.

The far more fascinating movements of the *Second Sonata* are the second and fourth. Here Boulez's comments concerning the "density of texture" and "kind of delirium" he felt in Schoenberg's Op. 11, No. 3, and the effect that kind of piano writing had on him, are much more understandable and seem to apply better than they do to the *First Sonata*, about which the comments were made. Both of these long, involved movements completely avoid reference to traditional formal procedures, just as in Schoenberg's Op. 11, No. 3. There is reference neither to the sonata-allegro procedures of the tonal period nor the modular forms of Stravinsky and Messiaen.

It is possible to make a case, in the recent history of instrumental music, for a progression from key-dominated forms (eighteenth century) through theme-dominated forms (nineteenth century) to forms that are structured on the relationships between psychological states (twentieth century). Schoenberg's Op. 11 crosses the line from the theme-dominated first movement to the relationship between psychological states that creates formal coherence in the last. Boulez, in his *Second Sonata*, moves back and forth, giving preference to the second type by employing it in the two largest movements, the second and fourth.

The slow movement (the second), which is as long as the entire *First Sonata*, is as beautiful as it is unpredictable. One listens moment by moment, moving from one constellation of sounds to the next. There is an occasional violent outburst, but with the exception of a somewhat extended pointillistic passage shortly before the end, the movement is one of cool contemplation of constantly expanding musical configurations.

The final movement, on the other hand, is alive with more immediate passions, building slowly and inexorably toward a huge, violent confrontation that is terrifying in its intensity. Near the end Boulez remonstrates, "pulvériser le son" ("pulverize the sound"). The climax achieved, there remains a brief, poignant epilogue, which brings the entire work to a moving, if not untroubled, close.

The *First* and *Second Sonatas* were written some years before the younger Stockhausen began to write his *Klavierstücke*, and they had an influence, just as they did on all who heard them. The relationship between Boulez and Stockhausen, who together quickly became the leading composers of the postwar period in Europe, is a complicated one. However, despite the existence of anecdotes now available from a number of sources, the only matter of importance in a study of their music is the fact that there has been a more or less regular interchange between them much of the time.

Perhaps as a result of this interchange, or because of ideas that were simply "in the air," when Stockhausen's *Klavierstück XI*, with its controlled chance parameters, was unveiled in 1957, Boulez was also working on a piano piece in which certain aspects of the structuring of the composition were left to the choice of the performer. In the *Third Sonata*, a far more elaborate conception than *Klavierstück XI*, the arrangement of movements (two were published in 1961—eventually there were to have been five), routes through fragmentary materials, the inclusion or omission of certain "free" passages, and other matters are ingeniously left "open." The large score of the "Constellation-Miroir" movement, with its structural groups printed in green or red and its intriguing many-shaped arrows serving as route markers, is one of the most fascinating-looking pieces of music ever published. In actual fact, however, as David Tudor suggested concerning *Klavierstück XI*, only much more so, the controls exercised by the composer are so strict that what is left to the performer's choice is little more than highly sophisticated game playing.

This, however, does not detract from the musical validity of the piece. The *Third Sonata*, written a decade after the second, is by a much-changed composer who, having plunged through total serialism in the first book of *Structures* (1952) for two pianos, a ghastly, aurally incomprehensible piece taking Messiaen's "Mode de valeurs et d'intensité" to its logical, forgettable conclusion, had turned to the ethereal beauties of *Le marteau sans maître* (1955), for mezzo-soprano and six instrumentalists, and found a style full of color and delicacy that he would pursue in all subsequent compositions.

Of particular interest among the many refinements of the *Third Sonata* is the use of harmonics, which are notated carefully not only as to the notes to be held down, but also the order in which they are to be released ("negative arpeggios"). As in Stockhausen's *Klavierstück VII*, considerable skill is required to keep the silent notes from sounding; it may be suggested that pianists depress these notes only as far as the after-touch—about halfway down the key dip—which raises the dampers sufficiently to allow the strings to vibrate and avoids, at least to some extent, the danger of going to the bottom of the key too swiftly.

The attractiveness of the two available movements, "Constellation-miroir" and "Trope," plus considerable published information as to the nature of the other three movements-to-be, has prompted much speculation as to the completion of the *Third Sonata*. In May 1969 I asked Boulez if he were still thinking of finishing the project. He was immediately forthcoming: yes, he would be getting at it soon, it was very important that he do so; the problem was only that he had committed himself to so many conducting engagements, allowing no time to compose, but these would soon be behind him and the *Third Sonata* would then be a top priority.

If memory serves, it was one or two weeks later that it was announced that Pierre Boulez had been appointed music director of the New York Philharmonic. I trust he was as surprised as I. In any case, the *Third Sonata* awaits conclusion as of this writing.

After 1961 Stockhausen, too, abandoned the piano as a solo instrument, returning to it only after 1980, when he made arrangements for piano of several portions of other pieces. *Klavierstück XII* (1983) is an arrangement of a scene from his opera *Thursday from Light*; *Klavierstück XIII* (1981) is also called "Lucifer's Dream" and is taken from a scene in *Saturday from Light*; and *Klavierstück XIV* (1984) is subtitled "Birthday Formula." The score of number twelve, elaborately packaged by the publisher, involves considerable vocal as well as pianistic activity, but appears less interesting than the extraordinary music of, especially, the *Klavierstücke V–X* portion of the entire cycle, which, with the Boulez sonatas and the music to be discussed in the next chapter, remain the most important contributions to the piano repertoire from Europe in the immediate postwar period.

CHAPTER SEVENTEEN

Luigi Dallapiccola and Luciano Berio

The first composer outside Germany and Austria to employ the twelve-tone technique effectively was the Italian Luigi Dallapiccola (1904–1975). He was, in fact, one of the few non-German composers to give much credence to Schoenberg's methods before World War II. Dallapiccola was a scholar, humanist, and linguist, and his wide-ranging interests are reflected in his music and his writings about music. His openness to early performances of Webern's music, for example, was in keeping with his lifelong eagerness to investigate new ideas of every sort, be they musical, literary, or theatrical.[1]

From a certain point of view there is considerable irony in this. When Dallapiccola was born in 1904, Istria, the province of his birth, was part of the Austrian empire. At the age of thirteen he was imprisoned for a considerable time with his family because of suspected pro-Italian sentiments. The eventual ceding of Istria to Italy after World War I could hardly have wiped out the trauma of this early brush with political reality, which was hardly conducive of sympathy to the music of his Austro-German contemporaries.

In fact, not all of Dallapiccola's music is dodecaphonic. Some of the early music shows neoclassic tendencies, and his first piano piece, the *Sonatina Canonica* (1943), a light, high-spirited piece in four short movements, is clearly tonal throughout and rhythmically rather square. However, it demonstrates a real lyric gift and strikes one immediately as the work of a talented composer with a penchant for interesting contrapuntal writing, especially of the canonic variety, but who had not yet found his style. That style was to blossom to the fullest in the postwar period as Dallapiccola returned to the techniques that had fascinated him earlier in the music of Schoenberg and especially Webern. He found that his love for canonic writing was well served by row techniques, and he developed an interest in rhythmic configurations (for example, four in the time of three followed by three in the time of four, i.e., |♪♪♪♪♪♪♪♪| that are simple but give the music a flavor not available in more conventional figures. Above all he applied his innate lyric gift to dodecaphonic writing,

working to equate row with theme in such a way that the series he chose
for a given piece was, perhaps more than with any other twelve-tone
composer, hearable.

Dallapiccola's masterpiece for the piano is the eleven-movement
Quaderno musicale di Annalibera (*Musical Notebook for Annalibera*), completed in 1952. The title has obvious reference to the *Musical Notebook for
Anna Magdalena Bach* by Johann Sebastian Bach, a composer Dallapiccola
revered ("Annalibera" is Dallapiccola's daughter, to whom he dedicated
this work on her eighth birthday). Various transpositions of the familiar
B-A-C-H (Bb-A-C-B♮) motive occur also, most evidently in the first
movement, "Simbolo" ("Symbol"). A far deeper link between the two
composers is found in the superior and elegant quality of the counterpoint that dominates most of the eleven pieces. Every sort of canonic
interplay is handled with apparent effortlessness.

Most of the eleven movements are short—eight are only a single
page long—and the total performance time is about fourteen minutes.
The order and relationship between movements are matters of great
importance to the composer. Indeed, Dallapiccola states on the title page
that the eleven movements must be performed as a complete unit; single
movements or selected groups may not be extracted. Furthermore, the
expressive continuity of the piece as a whole is a matter of such delicate
balance that the composer adds, "Fra un brano e l'altro le pause devono
essere piutosto significative" ("between one passage and another the
pauses must be rather significant"). Dallapiccola does not even use the
word for movement, referring rather to the eleven "passages" of the
work. His meaning is clear: every sound and every silence in the *Quaderno
musicale* adds up to a single, integral statement.

For the composer and performer both, this work is a marvelously
clear and musically exquisite demonstration of a unique and gifted composer's approach to the twelve-tone technique. The following remarks
on this subject were written two years before Dallapiccola completed the
Quaderno musicale and were published under the heading "Sulla strada
della dodecafonia" ("On the way to the twelve-tone system"):

> La tecnica seriale è soltanto un mezzo per aiutare il com-
> positore a realizzare *l'unità* del discorso musicale. Se qualcuno
> dice che la "serie" *garantisce* tale *unità*, sbaglia di grosso, in
> quanto in arte nessun artificio tecnico ha mai garantito nulla
> e *l'unità* dell'opera sarà, allo stesso modo che la melodia, il
> ritmo, l'armonia, un fatto interiore. Non sarà fuori luogo ram-
> mentare qui come la tecnica del Leit-Motiv wagneriano abbia
> avuto pure lo scopo de render possibile l'unità del discorso
> musical e che, se in *Tannhäuser*, se in *Lohengrin*, questa tecnica
> appare solo sporadicamente, è nel *Tristano* che raggiunge il
> suo completo sviluppo, nell'opera cioè in cui i rapporti

dominante-tonica (rapporti una volta destinati a realizzare l'unità del discorso) si sono indeboliti al massimo grado.[2]

[Serial technique is only a means to aid the composer in realizing *the unity* of the musical discourse. If anyone says that the "series" *guarantees* such unity, he is badly mistaken, in that in art no technical artifice has ever guaranteed anything and *the unity* of the work will be, in the same manner as the melody, the rhythm, the harmony, an interior fact. It is not beside the point to comment here how the Wagnerian Leitmotiv had the power to make the unity of the musical discourse possible and that, if in *Tannhäuser* and in *Lohengrin* this technique appears only sporadically, it is in *Tristan* that it arrives at its complete development, in a work, that is, in which the *dominant-tonic* relationships (relationships at one time employed to realize the unity of the discourse) are weakened to the highest degree.]

For simple elegance in the use of easily comprehensible row techniques nothing surpasses the final movement of the *Quaderno musicale*, "Quartina" ("Quatrain"). Each of the four versions (original, inversion, retrograde, retrograde-inversion) of the row sings expressively for one of the four lines of the piece, each time accompanied by one of the other versions of the row arranged as a succession of chords. Example 17.1 shows the third line of the final piece. In the top staff (right hand) is the retrograde-inversion of the row, to be played "with the maximum expression." The bottom two staves (left hand) accompany the melody with a chordal version of the original row beginning on A-natural.

EXAMPLE 17.1. Dallapiccola, *Quaderno musicale*, No. 11, mm. 11, mm. 10–13. Used by permission of Edizioni Suvini Zerboni, Milan.

For contrapuntal mastery the seventh piece, "Andantino amoroso," should be examined (example 17.2). It is a crab canon, written on two staves. The first time through this is played just as it is; the second time ("2ª. *volta*") one hand plays in normal left-to-right fashion while the other begins at the end, meets the first in the middle, and finishes at the beginning. The result is breathtakingly beautiful. (Incidentally, Dallapiccola supplies a "realization" in the score.)

EXAMPLE 17.2. Dallapiccola, *Quaderno musicale*, No. 7 (complete short version).

Although Dallapiccola was a professor at the Cherubini Conservatory in Florence from 1934 until 1967, he was never allowed to teach composition there, serving as a teacher of secondary pianists (!) for more than thirty years. If he was neglected in his own country, he was welcomed as a master composer, teacher, and man of cultivation, wit, and kindness elsewhere. He had the sophisticated Italian love of literary allusion combined with an internationalist's pride in exceptional linguistic ability. In addition, he was incapable of forgetting a name, even after a brief acquaintanceship had allowed many years to go by without contact (the author can attest to this personally).

Luigi Dallapiccola left not only the legacy of his own music but the music of others he inspired them to write. The list of piano music dedicated to him stretches at least from George Rochberg's *Twelve Bagatelles* (1952) to Roger Sessions's *Five Pieces for Piano* (1975) and includes a particularly beautiful early composition, *Cinque variazioni* (1953), by Dallapiccola's compatriot, Luciano Berio.

Berio was born in Oneglia in 1925 and first met Dallapiccola, oddly enough, at Tanglewood in 1951 when they were both in the United States for the first time—Dallapiccola to preside over composition seminars, and Berio, with his new wife, the singer Cathy Berberian, to investigate musical life in the United States. Berio quickly developed an interest not only in serial music, which was on everyone's mind in 1951, but in the possibilities of electronic music, still in a rather primitive state at that time. Taking these interests with him to Darmstadt in 1954, he met Stockhausen and the Belgian Henri Pousseur, among others, whose music stimulated him still further.

Taking over the directorship of the newly founded Studio di Fonologia in Milan in 1955, he remained in Italy until 1961, by which time he was clearly the most active Italian composer on the international level. The strength and novelty of his musical imagination have kept him at the forefront of the musical scene for several decades. *Circles* (1960), for soprano, harp, and two percussionists, was the principal work giving impetus to the entire "action-music" movement of the 1960s. The electronically produced *Visage* (1961), based on the voice of Cathy Berberian, displayed a fresh, improvisatory approach to the possibilities of dramatic tape music. And *Sinfonia* (1968) opened the doors to a return to tonality.

His first piano piece, already mentioned, is the *Cinque variazioni* (1953). The dedication to Dallapiccola is embedded in the fifth and last variation, which begins with a quotation from Dallapiccola's *Canti di Prigonia* (1941), as shown in example 17.3. The first four variations unfold gradually, beginning extremely quietly—*appena percettibile e vago* (scarcely perceptible and vague)—reminding one somewhat of the spirit, if not the sound, of Debussy's "La cathédrale engloutie," which emerges from its quiet opening, "peu à peu sortant de la brume" ("little by little emerging from the fog"). Berio's first variation also emerges slowly, cautiously picking up speed in what can best be described as an impressionist atmosphere, measureless, but with occasional staccato interruptions, premonitions of what is to come.

EXAMPLE 17.3. Berio, *Cinque variazioni*, variation 5, mm. 1–6, original version. Used by permission of Edizioni Suvini Zerboni, Milan.

The second variation, considerably more active, continues to pick up speed and energy, leading to the scurrying, frantic pointillism of the third variation, with staccato notes bursting like firecrackers all over the keyboard. This in turn leads quickly to the climactic fourth variation, in which fast-flying scales combine with dissonant *martellato* gestures, ending with the hands flying in both directions to the ends of the keyboard, "precipitando molto." There is a long pause, and the simple, beautiful, final variation, with its quotation from Dallapiccola, begins, leading eventually back to the same vague, impressionist sounds with which the piece began.

Thus far the discussion has centered on the original version of the *Cinque variazioni*, originally published in 1954 in a facsimile of the composer's manuscript, but now no longer available. Some years later, when Berio had arrived at a different place in his career, he became uncomfortable with the knowledge that this early piece was still in circulation. He was especially concerned with the final variation, which he found embarrassingly artless in its lyric simplicity. In 1966, with the complexities of *Sequenza IV* (see below) incubating in his mind, he determined to rewrite portions of the *Cinque variazioni*. Then (as now) rather fond of the original version, I had occasion to argue that youthful works should be left alone, not overlaid with encrustations from more mature styles. Berio, following his conscience, listened politely but paid no attention, eventually rewriting and extending several passages in the piece, with particular attention devoted to the final variation. The revised version, engraved, is now the only one available. The first four variations are, for the most part, the same. A comparison of the opening measures of the two versions of the last variation, however, tells one a great deal about Berio's compositional thoughts in the mid-1960s (examples 17.3 and 17.4).

EXAMPLE 17.4. Berio, *Cinque variazioni*, variation 5, mm. 1–4, revised version.

The new version is, indeed, beautiful, but in a different way from the original. Ornamental filigree, the kind of all-enveloping embellishment that had become an essential part of his later style, now surrounds almost every melodic note, and simple simultaneities (compare the bass lines) have been displaced by more improvisatory, less straightforward relationships.

Later in the same year (1966), when I visited with Berio in his house in Cambridge—he was lecturing at Harvard University—he spoke with great excitement of Karlheinz Stockhausen's *Klavierstück X*, which he had just heard for the first time. This "new way of playing the piano" had inspired him, he said, to write a big piece for the instrument that would also use clusters, but in a different way than Stockhausen had used them. It would also require the employment of the middle (sostenuto) pedal "most of the time," he continued. "The pianist will not be able to play wrong notes," he added with a smile, alluding to the fact that inadvertently striking a note held by the sostenuto pedal would immediately be heard as an error because the note would be unduly prolonged.

The work, which was quickly completed, is the fourth in Berio's *Sequenza* series, which has now extended to ten pieces—the other works in the series are for other instruments or, in one case, solo voice. *Sequenza IV* (1966) is one of the most ingenious, colorful piano pieces of the postwar period. Berio's piano writing—with its entrancing superimpositions of staccato and legato chords made possible by the middle pedal, and its shimmering, dissolving filigree passages—is as original in its way as Stockhausen's *Klavierstücke* and Boulez's three sonatas.

For the pianist, there are many learning problems in *Sequenza IV*. The tempo, given in metronomic units, changes constantly. For example, there are eleven tempo changes in the first twenty-three measures, and these should be observed with great care. A relatively easy way to learn these changes correctly is to make a "click track" on tape with the help of an electric metronome. One then practices while listening to the tape through earphones. By no means should the piece be learned in a single tempo with the idea that adjustments will be made later. This will give one a skewed initial conception of the music, comparable to learning a Mozart sonata movement with a tempo change every two bars!

The most difficult problem is to learn how to play clusters sensitively; sometimes they are rolled upwards, sometimes down, and often they are to be played with the most delicate touch possible at high speeds, as in example 17.5—which the composer insists is reminiscent of Chopin's *Étude in A-flat Major*, Op. 25, No. 1.

Many listeners have commented on the "rightness" of the ebb and flow of the piece. There is, in fact, a kind of sequence, as the title implies, a collection of chords that Berio uses as a point of departure. Although these chords are adjusted and altered almost from the start, especially when the filigree breaks them down into the smallest particles, recognizable shapes return at cadence points[3] to remind the listener of what has happened before, after which the filigree again departs into another swirling, sparkling exploration of sound.

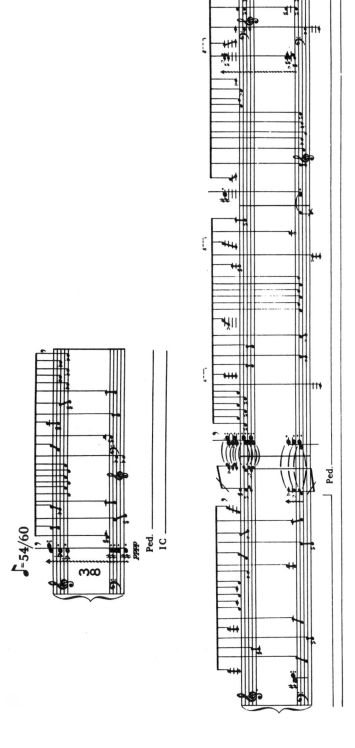

EXAMPLE 17.5. Berio, *Sequenza IV*, mm. 153–56. © Copyright 1967 by Universal Edition (London) Ltd., London. Copyright renewed. All Rights Reserved. Used by permission of European American Music Distributors Corporation, Sole U.S. and Canadian agent for Universal Edition, London.

CHAPTER EIGHTEEN

Other Composers in Europe

As the music of Boulez, Stockhausen, and Berio was disseminated and hotly discussed at meetings of the International Society for Contemporary Music (ISCM), at the Darmstadt summer courses, and at the Donaueschingen festivals, composers throughout Europe were attracted to the excitement of the new avant-garde movement. Some went off in their own directions while others built on the ideas promulgated by the three composers mentioned above. Meanwhile, older composers remained less affected by the new ideas, continuing to write in already established ways.

Iannis Xenakis

Iannis Xenakis (b. 1922) was born in Romania of Greek parents. During World War II, as a member of the Greek resistance movement, he was badly injured in the face, losing an eye. Later he was captured and narrowly escaped death.

Two years after the war he became a French citizen. In France he met the architect Le Corbusier, who was so impressed with his mathematical and designing skills that he accepted him as a collaborator. Xenakis also met Messiaen and discussed with him his ideas concerning the application of mathematical concepts to both architecture and the composition of music. Messiaen was so impressed with these ideas, coming as they did from a man with almost no formal musical training, that he suggested that Xenakis pursue them on his own without risking the diluting effects of academic musical study.

Xenakis's music finds its basis in abstract mathematical structures. It is music of many notes, "clouds" of notes, as he says. He has called his handling of these sound masses "stochatic" music. The word, of Greek origin, is a statistical term used to define observations of randomness. In music it implies a large number of small, "molecular" events—single notes, chords—packed so closely together in a "cloud" that the consequence of no single one of them can be determined, yet the overall effect is predictable.

166

Xenakis's solo piano pieces—*Herma* (1961), *Evryali* (1973), and *Mists* (1980)—were created using stochastic principles, with note choice determined through algebraic applications of set theory. The results, fascinating in both conception and realization, present formidable problems to the performer, who must move almost constantly with the utmost speed over the entire keyboard. Example 18.1, from *Herma*, is the first half of a typical "nuage" ("cloud") near the middle of the piece. At the tempo requested by the composer, ♩=180, each measure should last exactly two seconds, no more.

EXAMPLE 18.1. Xenakis, *Herma*, mm. 99–102. © Copyright 1967 by Boosey & Hawkes, Inc. Reprinted by permission.

The problem in these pieces lies neither in the unique conception nor even in the pianistic difficulties they present. Rather, the constant intensity of the action, always covering the entire keyboard, seems eventually to result in a lack of differentiation. This is hardly a problem unknown in the music of other composers, of course, but the very fierceness of the activity exacerbates the dilemma. In short, the "clouds" are too much the same.

Xenakis designed the soaring Philips Pavilion for the 1950 Brussels World's Fair. He writes of it as being the result of "an intimate connection" between music and architecture, with similar processes being applicable to both.[1] The beauty of the architectural result in the Pavilion is instantly apparent. The application of Xenakis's ideas to music may, indeed, be just as valid, esthetically, but for the moment, at least with regard to his piano pieces, the success of the realization is not immediately evident.

Kazimierz Serocki

The Polish composer Kazimierz Serocki (b. 1922) graduated from the Łódź Conservatory of Music immediately after the war and spent the next five years traveling as a concert pianist and attending Nadia Boulanger's classes in composition in Paris. Giving up his performing career in 1951 in order to concentrate all his energies on composition, he remained a relatively conservative composer, not necessarily by choice, until the loosening of political and artistic controls took place throughout Poland later in the decade. At that time he became a central figure in the organization of the famous Warsaw Autumn Festivals, which were for many years the principal point of interchange between musicians of the Eastern and Western bloc countries.

Serocki's true compositional colors are indicated in the vast difference in style between the conservative *Piano Sonata* (1955) and the post-reform *A Piacere* (1963). The title of the latter piece, meaning "as you wish" or "at your pleasure," is an apt one; *A Piacere* is among the best of the many offspring of Stockhausen's *Klavierstück XI* in that it consists of many separate "structures" that are to be arranged in an order chosen by the performer. As in the Stockhausen piece, all of the fragments are printed on a single sheet, in this case divided into three panels. Each panel contains ten structures, each of which is enclosed in a box and given a suggested duration in seconds. Either through previous decision or in an impromptu manner at the moment of performance, the pianist decides in what order to play the three panels and in what arrangement to perform the ten structures within each panel. All structures must be played, none repeated. Most are short, consisting of one or two musical gestures. Unlike the Stockhausen model, Serocki's piece, though it always consists of the same material, can be arranged to have a considerably different musical effect from one performance to the next, and therefore the performer has a genuine sense of having made compositional decisions of a substantive nature.

Henri Pousseur

The Belgian composer Henri Pousseur (b. 1929) first met Pierre Boulez in 1951 while he was still a student at the Liège Conservatory, observed Stockhausen's work in the Cologne electronic music studio in 1954, and collaborated with Berio at the Studio di Fonologia in Milan in 1957. Since then he has attempted to emulate something of each of these men. The founder of the Studio de Musique Électronique in Brussels in 1958, he is the composer of some of the better tape music of the postwar period, including the dramatic *Trois visages de Liège* (1961) which, though it owes something to Stockhausen's *Gesang der Jünglinge* (1956), has a sheen and pathos all its own.

Pousseur has always been intrigued with the development of his own compositional theories and notational systems. He has been at the forefront in adapting variable, mobile forms (of which Serocki's *A Piacere* is a relatively simple example) to large works, most notably in an extended composition for theater that dominated his thinking for an entire decade, *Votre Faust* (1960–67, first performance 1969). He was one of the first composers to reintroduce tonality, proscribed by serial techniques, by using quotations from music of earlier centuries embedded in the building blocks of his mobile structures.

All of this is seen in his several works for solo piano, some of which, in fact, are extracted from *Votre Faust*. His first piano composition, *Exercises pour piano* (1956), shows the composer straining at the bonds of conventional notation, particularly with regard to minute subtleties of rhythm and tempo. In this case, however, the subtleties are lost in the too-uniform textures created by the constant thickness of the material.

Caractères I (1961) is Pousseur's most interesting, exploratory piece. It consists of two movements, 1a and 1b, each of which is a mobile that may be played in a number of ways. Movement 1a has six sections; choices for their succession and/or repetition are provided (example 18.2). Within each, as in the Stockhausen-Boulez prototypes, there are rules for the ordering of segments.

In addition, the composer has done away with accidentals. Filled-in notes (black notes) are naturals, open notes (white) are flatted. (That this makes black notes white keys and white notes black keys takes a bit of getting used to for the performer.) This, of course, necessitates a new kind of rhythmic notation, since stemmed white and black notes can no longer be used as half- and quarter-notes. Whether or not the notation devised by Pousseur in this case emerges from the inherent needs of the music he is writing is a moot question.

Movement 1b adds another dimension to mobile-chance procedures. Several single sheets of music, each with "windows" cut in several places, are arranged in any sequence and inserted in a cover or "envelope." One plays the music in conventional fashion, including whatever shows through the randomly arranged windows. The idea is amusing and clever. Unfortunately, however, in both parts of *Caractères I*, Pousseur seems more interested in his newly discovered procedures rather than the sound of the instrument for which he is writing. Unlike Stockhausen, Boulez, and Berio, whose piano music always seems to emerge from properties inherent in the instrument, requiring notational adjustments only when it is impossible to accommodate the musical conception, Pousseur seems to treat the piano as incidental to his pursuit of new ways of scoring.

Pousseur's later piano music includes the relatively easy *Apostrophe et six réflexions* (1966), seven short pieces, traditionally notated, which could be useful as an introduction to avant-garde piano music. Move-

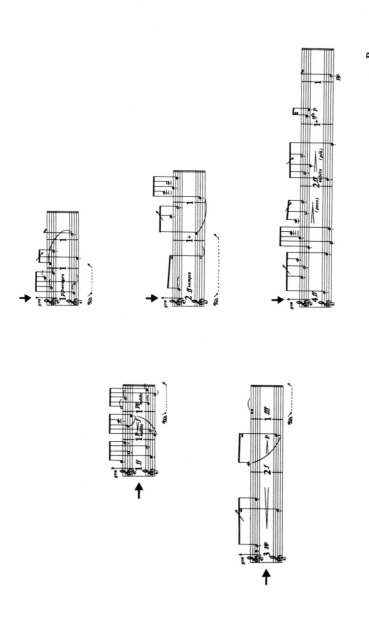

EXAMPLE 18.2. Pousseur, *Caractères I*, 1a, Section A. © Copyright 1962 by Universal Edition (London) Ltd., London. Copyright renewed. All Rights Reserved. Used by permission of European American Music Distributors Corporation, Sole U.S. and Canadian agent for Universal Edition, London.

ments are entitled "About Dynamics," "About Touch," "About Sonorities," and so forth.

The three movements of *Miroir de votre Faust (Caractères II,* 1965) are a fascinating compendium of the composer's stylistic and notational experiments. The second piece, "La chevauchée fantastique" ("The fantastic ride"), takes the listener on a gallop from Haydn and Mozart to Wagner and Schoenberg through a series of stylistic modulations. The other two movements are elaborate extensions of all the modular techniques that first appeared in *Caractères I.*

Sylvano Bussotti

Sylvano Bussotti (b. 1931) grew up in Florence, where he studied piano with Dallapiccola. His family included a number of avant-garde artists, and his subsequent career was as much influenced by them as by the musicians he knew.

However, the imprint of Dallapiccola is clearly seen in his first published piano composition, *Musica per amici* (1957), a charming short piece, more nervous than the music of the *Quaderno musicale,* but obviously related to the kinds of sounds favored by Dallapiccola.

Bussotti's meeting with John Cage and David Tudor in 1958 had a tremendous impact. His compositional aims changed radically, and though much of his energy was subsequently poured into the creation and direction of musico-theatrical works of the most bizarre nature, two compositions are documents of some significance in the chronology of new piano music.

The *Five Pieces for David Tudor* (1959) may be viewed as a set of musical compositions incorporating elements of design, or as visual creations incorporating elements of musical notation (example 18.3). Obviously taking his point of departure from Cage and other American composers who had already published graphic scores, the *Five Pieces* are particularly intriguing not because they are so far from standard notation but because the very use of familiar signs in unfamiliar circumstances leaves the performer wondering if such-and-such a mark is meant to be taken literally, as an abstraction, as an enigma, or as none of the above. The composer replies to such dilemmas by writing in the brief notes that the manner in which sounds are generated by the designs "resta nelle mani del pianista" ("remains in the hands of the pianist").

Pour clavier (1961) is a massive work, the notation of which is not quite as abstruse as in the *Five Pieces for David Tudor,* but which requires imagination and initiative nevertheless. There are twenty-three pages, some more easily interpreted than others. The actual beauty of the layout, combined with the sheer audacity of the various, changeable pianistic conceptions, makes the work both fascinating and challenging.

EXAMPLE 18.3. Bussotti, *Five Pieces for David Tudor*, No. 1. © Copyright 1959 by Universal Edition; Copyright Renewed. Copyright assigned to G. Ricordi & C. SpA, Milan. Reprinted by permission of Hendon Music, Inc. Sole Agents.

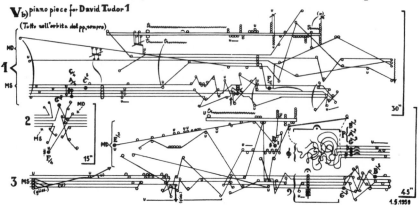

Per Nørgård

Much less intimidating is a calm, quiet piece by the Danish composer Per Nørgård (b. 1932) called *Grooving* (1968). Nørgård's early music, including several large works for the piano, reflects his affection for the music of Sibelius as well as a kind of Nordic modality. However, attendance at a meeting of the ISCM in 1959 opened his mind to more international trends, and his music thereafter is of a considerably different nature.

Grooving reflects Nørgård's attraction to a minimalist movement, which (if one does not count Cage's early prepared piano pieces, though they exhibit the mesmerizing, repetitive qualities associated with the genre) had blossomed earlier in the 1960s in the United States with such works as Terry Riley's *In C* (1964). Nørgård's piece, which is extremely slow for most of its quarter-hour duration, is through-composed, not using the constant repetitions that are a trademark of minimalism. One might say it is a kind of developmental minimalism in which figurations are constantly being adjusted, however slightly, while new pitches are added and others phased out.

However, the last section of the piece, emerging suddenly in this otherwise motionless atmosphere, is very different from the first part, and it is what makes one remember *Grooving*. In these last few moments Nørgård "grooves" on a series of high repeated notes that go in and out of phase with one another (much as in Steve Reich's *Piano Phase* for two pianos written the year before), finally leaving a single high C repeating over and over, softer and softer, until it eventually disappears.

Zsolt Durkó

Zsolt Durkó (b. 1934) is the best known Hungarian composer of his generation. A 1960 graduate of the Budapest Academy of Music, he subsequently studied in Rome until 1963. His early works, including his best-known composition for the piano, *Psicogramma* (1964), consist of collections of short pieces or fragments built on identical note-cells.

Psicogramma has nine such sections, some as long as two pages but others considerably shorter. The effect, however, due to the fact that one part leads directly into the next, is that of a single movement. It is a work of color and drama. The opening movement, "Prologo," begins with strong, intense chords, then proceeds to a single-note tremolo surrounded by jumping, flashing figurations. The fourth movement, "Psicogramma II," is a somewhat Bartókian "night music," with murmuring double trills inflected by grace-note figurations. The fifth movement, "Canone alla Prima: Logicogramma," is a fascinating chordal canon at the unison (an "echo" canon), disappointing only in that it is so short. The next movements, "Anti-evidenze" and "Un enfant terrible," make dramatic use of long repeated figures, played in one hand out of synchrony with what is being played on the other. There is brief use of glissandi, played directly on the treble strings, and a few plucked notes in the bass; neither effect is integral to the piece, which would not suffer from their absence. However, taken as a whole, it is a kaleidoscopic piece of an almost theatrical nature, making beautiful, varied use of the instrument.

Cornelius Cardew

The English composer Cornelius Cardew (b. 1936), whose early piano sonatas, written while he was a student at the Royal Academy of Music, are Webernesque in nature, became an assistant to Stockhausen at the Cologne electronic music studio soon after his graduation in 1957. A meeting with John Cage and David Tudor at that time caused him to redirect his thoughts completely, and by the time he returned to England a few years later he had become the leading figure in the field of experimental, indeterminate music in his country, a position he held throughout the 1960s.

Of Cardew's numerous piano pieces involving indeterminate procedures, the best known is actually a double publication, *February Pieces for Piano* (1961) and *Octet '61 for Jasper Johns* (the latter not necessarily for piano, though it may be if desired). These pieces, printed together in a facsimile of the composer's manuscript, reflect not only the influence of Cage's music but, interestingly enough, his calligraphy as well.

February Pieces for Piano consists of three short works plus the skeleton of a fourth; each work has thirteen sections, each printed in parallel (the first sections of all four pieces are on the first page, one above the other, all the second sections are on the next page, and so on). Cardew gives several options for the structuring of the work, which may be played as four separate pieces or with sections mixed together any way one wishes. "It is not necessary to follow a scheme . . . when combining the pieces," he writes in the score. The music is written more or less traditionally, though the rhythm is notated spatially rather than metrically.

Octet '61 for Jasper Johns is another matter. It consists of a single page with sixty small figures or signs on it (example 18.4). These signs look like single notes or chords on a music staff, but closer examination reveals that all have something unusual about them. Cardew writes:

> The signs should be allowed to suggest something concrete; a sound, a technique. The traditional connotations of signs or parts of signs should provide sufficient context for a concrete interpretation of at least one sign by almost any musician. This done, his utterance of the one sign should provide sufficient context for the comprehension of neighboring signs. And so on.[2]

EXAMPLE 18.4. Cardew, *Octet '61 for Jasper Johns*. © 1962 by Hinrichsen Editions, Ltd. Used by permission of C. F. Peters Corporation, sole selling agents.

He then suggests specific ways in which these figures may be interpreted and calls the piece "an opportunity for an interpreter," suggesting later that "the stimulation of the interpreter is a facet of composition that has been disastrously neglected."

Of particular interest here is the almost complete lack of intentionality in Cardew's work. As we shall see in the following chapter, the sublimation of the ego was one of John Cage's chief compositional aims during a major portion of his career. So it is with much of Cardew. In the

Klavierstück XI and *Third Sonata*, Stockhausen and Boulez circumscribe the performer's possibilities with strict rules of procedure. Holding out the possibility of the performer's participation in the compositional process, they offer options only on their terms. This is echoed directly in Pousseur's *Caractères* and, to a lesser extent, in Serocki's *A Piacere*. In these two pieces, however, Cardew offers his work as a friendly challenge to the performer to use "that modicum of creativity that is available to all," allowing the pianist complete freedom in his decisions concerning the manner in which his suggestions may be interpreted.

This attitude continues in later works for the piano such as the amusing *Memories of You* (published in 1967) which is played on and around a grand piano, though almost never on the keys. Other pieces such as *Three Winter Potatoes* (1965) return to a more through-composed style. Cardew's piano music, like that of Cage, runs the gamut between complete determinism and total freedom, with numerous in-between stages as well.

Bo Nilsson

Bo Nilsson (b. 1937) produced a few astonishing avant-garde pieces despite little training or contact with the musical world outside his native Sweden. All are from his twenties, including the short, powerful *Quantitäten* (1958) for piano, a work of great originality and singular beauty. It is a great misfortune that later works, such as *Rendezvous* (1968), do not measure up to his earlier efforts.

Frank Martin

Among the older composers in Europe who contributed to the piano repertoire in the period following World War II, mention should first be made of the Swiss composer Frank Martin (1890–1974), whose *Eight Preludes* (1948) are the most popular of his several works for solo piano. Lasting about twenty minutes, the preludes are traditional in every aspect, never straying far from what he termed "extended tonality." He was particularly fond of employing extended ostinato figures as a means of binding long sections together; these are found in virtually every one of the preludes. The music is strong and expressive, given the nature of the style. The final prelude in particular, with its heavily accented, fanfare-like themes, is extremely effective.

André Jolivet

André Jolivet (1905–1974) was unusual for his time in that he disliked all theoretical systems. He was much influenced in his early works by his study with Varèse, but he eventually developed a style more reminiscent of Debussy and Bartók. His two sonatas, from 1945 and 1957, are remarkably pianistic, considering the fact that he professed to understand little concerning the instrument and played it hardly at all.

Elizabeth Lutyens

Elizabeth Lutyens (1906–1983) introduced twelve-tone writing to England before World War II began and was ostracized for her efforts. A formidable personality, she persevered, finally receiving a measure of recognition in the 1960s when it became more acceptable in England to emulate continental musical trends. Her *Piano e forte* (1955) and *Five Bagatelles* (1962) for piano, both serial works, give a measure of her indomitability.

Grazyna Bacewicz.

Grazyna Bacewicz (1909–1969) was one of the leading and most prolific composers in Poland. A fine violinist—the composer of eight violin concerti, seven string quartets, and many other works for strings—she was also a talented pianist, as her dozens of keyboard works clearly demonstrate. Her major contribution to the pianist's concert repertoire is the *Second Sonata* (1953), a strong, important work. Interestingly enough, a complete list of her keyboard compositions, now available,[3] includes unpublished piano sonatas from 1930, 1935, 1938, 1942, and 1949, of which the last is identified as the *First Sonata*. Given the strength of her compositional voice, one would hope to be able eventually to examine her earlier attempts in the form.

Isang Yun

One of the most interesting older composers in Europe today is the Korean-born Isang Yun (b. 1917). Before the war, Yun studied composition in Japan at the Osaka Conservatory and in Tokyo, then immediately set about writing works of unprecedented (for Korea) scope and dimension. Receiving the Seoul City Award in 1955, two years after the end of the Korean War, he was able to travel for the first time to Europe, living first in Paris, then in Berlin.

Greatly attracted to German cultural life, Yun decided to settle there. His colorful, dramatic works for large orchestra and for theater brought him immediate attention. His fundamental aim became to develop Korean themes through the means of Western music.

Basically apolitical, Yun was sometimes indiscreet in his casual comments. Returning from a summer at the 1967 Aspen Institute in the United States, he was detained in Berlin by members of the South Korean secret police and returned to Korea, charged with being a communist. He would have remained in jail longer than the two years he spent there were it not for the international outcry from those who recognized his talent and the injustice of the allegations against him. Released and returned to Berlin in 1969, he became a West German citizen two years later.

Yun's *Fünf Stücke für Klavier* were composed in 1958, during his early residency in Germany. Brief, expressionistic pieces of a Schoenbergian-Bergian cast, they demonstrate a compositional talent of a high order. Unfortunately for pianists, Yun, with his predilection for symphonic and operatic works, has not written more for the piano. That his skills in keyboard writing have become still more sophisticated is already in evidence in an extraordinary composition for clarinet and piano entitled *Riul* (1968), written while he was a prisoner, in which both instruments are led to transcendental heights, both musically and technically, by a composer capable of extraordinary emotional projection.

CHAPTER NINETEEN

John Cage

Stockhausen can dispel one of the many misunderstandings that arise in assessments of the supposed influence of Cage on European music. Time and again one reads that the incorporation of controlled chance in the work of Stockhausen, and subsequently of Boulez and Pousseur, was induced by the work of Cage. Stockhausen reports that the development of the forms he calls 'statistical,' 'variable' and 'polyvalent' was germinated as early as 1953 by his researches with Meyer-Eppler into phonetics and information theory, and has made its mark on his thinking independently of Cage.[1]

Pierre Boulez has recently been quoted as saying of John Cage, "he was refreshing but not very bright. His freshness came from an absence of knowledge."[2]

The two leaders of the postwar European avant-garde have not, it seems, been kind in their assessment of the influence on themselves and other European composers of the American composer John Cage (b. 1912). What remains unclear is whether this reflects a lack of generosity or a deep-seated fear that an American *could* in fact threaten the dominance of European musical culture.

The facts suggest that Cage's relatively brief appearances in Europe after 1949 had profound effects on any number of composers there. Arguably, this influence was due more to his ideas, his compositional concepts, and his persona than to the music he brought with him, as is often charged.[3] This would hardly be unprecedented in a time in which discussions of method and philosophical stands pertaining to compositional concepts were as much a part of the new music scene as actual performances of the music illustrating these methods and concepts. That Cage's thought-provoking esthetic position made a long-lasting impression can hardly minimize the importance of his creative work.

John Cage was born in Los Angeles and attended Los Angeles High School, from which he graduated class valedictorian in 1928. After two years at Pomona College he spent some time in Paris where his attraction to the arts—particularly poetry, painting, architecture, and music—was greatly enhanced. Encouraged by several musicians in California, among them Henry Cowell, to study composition seriously, he worked briefly with Arnold Schoenberg, who had recently arrived in the United States after fleeing from the Nazi regime.

Always attracted to the piano, Cage wrote many of his early pieces for that instrument and continued to employ it in many ways throughout his career. From the first it was important to him to experiment with ideas that were untraditional, either in the manner in which pitches were chosen or in the way the sound of the piano was modified. These modifications began with simple kinds of muting, but eventually Cage learned to change the timbre of pitches either slightly or to the point of unrecognizability by inserting various kinds of materials between the strings. Pieces of felt, rubber, and metal were used in what quickly became known as the "prepared" piano. The first piece written for the prepared piano, *Bacchanale*, was composed in 1938 and given its first performance in 1940. As with many of Cage's works, it was written for a small dance company; Cage earned a meagre living playing the piano for dance classes at the time and has always been closely associated with dancers in subsequent years.

Cage has always enjoyed doing things that are not "supposed" to be done. In *The Wonderful Widow of Eighteen Springs* (1942) for voice and piano, the fallboard is closed and the pianist knocks on various parts of the instrument with his knuckles. In 1948 he wrote an extended, serious *Suite for Toy Piano*. However, the majority of Cage's scores from 1942 until 1951 are for prepared piano, the amount and character of the preparation varying with the musical demands of the individual pieces. Among the more extended works in the genre are *Amores* (1943) and the *Sonatas and Interludes* (1948), but there are also more than a dozen shorter works with such remarkable titles as *Our Spring Will Come* (1943), *Tossed as It is Untroubled* (1943), *Root of an Unfocus* (1944), *A Valentine Out of Season* (1944), *Daughters of the Lonesome Isle* (1945), and *Music for Marcel Duchamp* (1947).

Music for Marcel Duchamp is about five minutes long (example 19.1). It is written on a single staff with a C clef in an unchanging $\frac{5}{4}$ meter. There are only eight pitches in the entire piece, and all are prepared. The preparation, carefully described in the score, is quite simple. Seven of the notes are prepared with weather stripping; their original pitches remain intact but their timbre becomes something like a series of small, muted cowbells. The eighth pitch is stopped with a piece of rubber and a small bolt, the latter placed between the second and third of the three strings; when played, this note sounds like an unpitched wood block.

The music itself is very simple, making considerable use of repetition of figures as short as two beats and as long as four measures. There is much use of measured silence, but no sense of buildup, development, or climax. There is no counterpoint nor change of tempo. The music

EXAMPLE 19.1. Cage, *Music for Marcel Duchamp*, mm. 97–111. © 1961 by Henmar Press Inc. Used by permission of C. F. Peters Corporation.

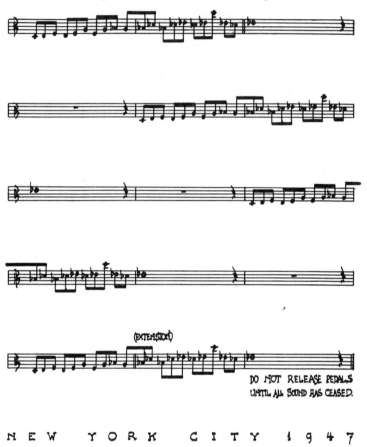

NEW   YORK   CITY   1947

exists, nothing more—its simple repeating figures interspersed by periods of silence.

Sonatas and Interludes, in contrast, is an hour and ten minutes long. More than half of the piano's eighty-eight pitches are prepared with a variety of screws, bolts, nuts, pieces of rubber, and plastic. Unlike *Music for Marcel Duchamp*, one cannot tell from the score how the music will sound because of the radical changes in pitch, timbre, and sonority the preparation creates. The textures are more complex, and the rhythmic and metric schemes are much more variable.

Nevertheless, the *Sonatas and Interludes* resemble the music of the earlier pieces in many ways. In fact, they may be said to sum up the kinds of things Cage was working toward in the smaller works for piano and prepared piano before 1948. First of all, everything is carefully notated. No chance procedures are involved. There is a conscious effort to integrate pitch and non-pitch elements through the use of varying kinds of timbre modifications. Cage's concern for rhythmic proportion extends to the relationships between groups of sounds and the durations of silences.

The success of the *Sonatas and Interludes* in the first performances by Maro Ajemian in Carnegie Recital Hall in early 1949 brought Cage to the attention of an influential audience. His distressing financial situation was much improved by a grant from the Guggenheim Foundation and from the American Academy and National Institute of Arts and Letters. With this money he was able to return to Europe in 1949.

In France he met the young, outspoken composer Pierre Boulez, and the two became close friends almost immediately, finding they had much to discuss. Some of the discussion was extremely profitable for Boulez. Cage, thirteen years older and with more connections, was able to convince two Paris publishers to bring out several of Boulez's works, including the *First Sonata* and *Second Sonata*. He was also able eventually to assist Boulez's entrée into the United States. Remarkably, the two men carried on a correspondence for the better part of three years in which Boulez described in great detail much of what he was striving for as a composer. That the two were basically different kinds of people, personally and musically, surfaced only rather slowly. Three productive years passed before the inevitable breakup occurred.

Meanwhile Cage, already deeply involved in Oriental studies, had been introduced to the *I Ching*, a collection of commentaries that may be consulted using chance methods, such as the tossing of coins.[4] Following certain procedures, he utilized the *I Ching* to make compositional choices in writing the *Music of Changes* (1951) for "unprepared" piano. The results are much different from the earlier keyboard writing. A totally new period opened up in his work, involving the use of chance and, later, indeterminate procedures.

Music of Changes, in four volumes, lasts about forty-five minutes. While by no means allowing the performer any chance operations—the notation is specific throughout—the score demonstrates Cage's new interest in chance as a compositional tool. That he chose to use procedures resulting in much more complex rhythmic detail than ever before is quite clear from a glance at the score (example 19.2).

EXAMPLE 19.2. Cage, *Music of Changes*, Book I, mm. 39–40. © 1961 by Henmar Press Inc. Used by permission of C. F. Peters Corporation.

Almost inevitably, this new interest eventually led to giving the performer more "open" opportunities. The first step for Cage, however, was to refine his compositional practices with regard to chance operations. One of his principal aims became that of removing himself from the act of composition by bypassing personal choice. He wished to find methods by which his own ego and taste could be prevented from being applied.

In the subsequent works called *Music for Piano* (1953), notes are determined by the locations of imperfections in the paper on which he was writing. In *31'57.9864" for a Pianist* (1954) for prepared piano, the materials and placement of preparations are, to a considerable extent, left up to the pianist, dynamics and kinds of attack are indicated by enigmatic graphic means, and the spatial rhythmic notation leaves considerable leeway to the performer. *Winter Music* (1957) goes much further (example 19.3). It may be performed by from one to twenty pianists. There are twenty pages, which may be played in any order or omitted. Tempo is completely free, the choice of clefs is variable within certain limits, and some notes are played as harmonics or prepared ahead of time if they cannot otherwise be reached.

EXAMPLE 19.3. Cage, *Winter Music*, page 10. © 1960 by Henmar Press Inc. Used by permission of C. F. Peters Corporation.

-10-

For some ten years after *Winter Music* was published a large group of Cage's scores consisted only of drawings—lines, circles, points—from which performances can be extracted. Though these pieces, such as the series of *Variations* (1958–1966), may be played by pianists, they are not so specified, being offered to "any number of players, any sound-

producing means." This period, then, carries Cage's denial of compositional intentionality to its furthest extreme.

In the late 1960s Cage suddenly returned to a more conventional
kind of writing. The principal work for piano to emerge from this new
period is the set of twenty-four *Études australes* (1975) (example 19.4).
These pieces, each two large pages long, are notated on conventional
treble and bass clefs, though the fact that each hand has its own pair of
treble and bass clefs gives an indication that Cage has not discontinued
his search for innovation. The title is derived from the fact that note
choice was determined by charts of the stars in the southern sky.

EXAMPLE 19.4. Cage, *Études australes*, No. 6, Systems 1 and 2. © 1975 by Henmar
Press Inc. Used by permission of C. F. Peters Corporation.

From the performer's point of view, some of Cage's keyboard music
is quite easy, but most is not. In many cases, to learn all the notes and
correct rhythms is taxing. In addition, piano preparation requires pa-
tience, skill, care, and a considerable amount of time.[5] The complete
Sonatas and Interludes, for example, require preparation of an instrument
hours before and after a performance. Also, once a piano has been prepared for a particular piece, no other music can be played on that instrument until all the materials have been removed (and even then the
piano may require retuning). Thus the pianist wishing to incorporate a
group of prepared piano pieces into a recital program must arrange for
(at least) two instruments. In addition, one is well advised to solicit the
approval and help of the resident piano tuner-technician before beginning preparations.

It is a commonplace that those who influence us the most often disturb us the most. The more we are affected, the more we resent those affecting us. Boulez, for example, found Cage fascinating at first and discussed with and wrote to him about matters that were of the utmost concern. Finding he was being influenced by Cage and actually doing some of the same things Cage had already done, he found it necessary to reject him vehemently, saying he was "not very bright." Stockhausen was instrumental in bringing Cage to Darmstadt in 1954 and was, by all contemporary reports, greatly intrigued by what he heard him say in his lectures there. His eventual denial that Cage could have influenced him or any other European composer may be viewed with a certain scepticism today.

Today's music would be different had John Cage not made his unique contribution. People will, of course, make up their own minds as to the worth of individual pieces, remembering that Cage himself has commented, "if my work is accepted, I must move on to the point where it isn't."[6] Some of his piano music is entrancing, some is dull. There is a bewitching naiveté about some of the work for prepared piano, while elsewhere the meditative qualities become so intense that one is reminded of Messiaen, albeit a secular Messiaen. Finally, a certain Zen calmness pervades the exterior of other pieces, with only the silences being loud.

CHAPTER TWENTY

Aaron Copland, Roger Sessions, and the Mid-Century Piano Sonata

A thirty-minute single-movement composition for a solo instrument is a daring idea; such works are rare. Large sets of variations (the Bach *Goldberg*, Beethoven *Diabelli*, Rzewski's *The People United*) should not be considered in this category because they have a built-in structural capability, variation being added to variation as long as the imagination allows. Only a handful of pieces of such size exist in the repertoire for piano, including Donald Martino's *Pianississimo* (1970), which is fascinating for awhile but just too long, Stockhausen's *Klavierstück X*, surely one of the best in this genre, and the Liszt *Sonata in B Minor*, an all-time masterpiece which, however, is really a multi-movement work skillfully molded into a single unit.

Aaron Copland's *Piano Fantasy* (1957) most closely resembles the Liszt model in many respects (examples 20.1 and 20.2). Elements of a four-movement conception are clearly evident. However, Copland set out to write an improvisatory piece—a fantasy—and he achieved the desired sense of spontaneity by blurring the outlines between sections and by centering the listener's attention on a series of motives, each of which is worked out in leisurely fashion.

In the *Piano Variations*, completed in 1930, concentration and economy of means had been essential to Copland, nor was he, at that time, concerned with anything more than the pursuit of his craft and the expression of his feelings. The *Sonata*, coming a decade later after considerable success with more popular, accessible styles, returned to this private, introspective world. But though the economical use of motive and theme remained compositionally essential, Copland was now confident enough to relax in the lightness and humor of some parts of the music (second movement) and in the unhurried expansiveness elsewhere (third movement).

EXAMPLE 20.1. Copland, *Piano Fantasy*, mm. 1–15. © Copyright 1957 by Aaron Copland, Copyright Owner. Copyright Renewed. Reprinted by Permission of Boosey & Hawkes, Inc., Sole Agent.

EXAMPLE 20.2. Copland, *Piano Fantasy*, mm. 66–69.

The *Piano Fantasy* signals another return to these inner musical thoughts, something Copland could rarely do except when writing for the instrument with which he felt the greatest intimacy. As in the earlier piano works, one again hears the emphasis on single notes and characteristic open sonorities.

The form is greatly expanded, the moods are savored longer and change more slowly, and transitions are carefully rounded, taking longer to arrive at their goals. Though there is a long scherzando section in the middle of the piece, an overall sense of contemplation pervades most of the work.

Copland was, of course, well aware of the activities of the postwar avant-garde in Europe and America, and he has always been keenly interested in and supportive of new music activities. But by 1957 his musical language was firmly established, and though he found certain serial procedures worth pursuing—the *Fantasy* employs a ten-note row at the outset, and Copland suggests, not unreasonably, that the 1930 *Variations* may also be said to use serial procedures—these procedures did nothing to alter the grammar and syntax of his clear, articulate, and highly individual musical speech.

Roger Sessions (1896–1985) distinguished himself as a composer, theorist, essayist, and teacher. A musical prodigy, he entered Harvard University at the age of fourteen and received his first faculty appointment when he was only twenty. During the period between the two world wars he lived primarily in Europe, after which his life alternated between Princeton and Berkeley, where his pupils numbered among the most important American composers for two generations.

Sessions was always thoughtful and articulate concerning the state of music, and his lectures and essays[1] demonstrate his willingness to tackle larger cultural issues facing musicians in the twentieth century. He felt strongly that music should reflect the emotional life of the society in which it was written:

> The central problem of contemporary art . . . is that of developing an artistic vocabulary in terms of which the sensations, feelings, impulses and attitudes of contemporary human beings can be given articulate organization.[2]

He was concerned that so much of Western musical heritage had been neglected in this century:

> Our time . . . has seen that tradition called into question and challenged in a way that can only mean one of two things — either a major cultural catastrophe or a major turning point.[3]

Those who studied with Sessions have been unanimous in their gratitude not only for his concern with the development of their compositional craft, of whatever style, but also for inculcating appreciation and understanding of their heritage. These concerns manifest themselves not just in his lectures and essays but in his music as well.

Sessions's music ranks with the best of the century. It is fully emotional but without extramusical implications — no mystical titles, no idiosyncratic notation, no references to or quotations from music of other composers. Uncompromising, it stands on its own merits and inner logic, each work justifying the relationships between motive, development, and form. At the same time the solid crafting and perfect equilibrium between form and content link it to the music of the past in a manner rarely equaled by any of his contemporaries. All of this is beautifully exemplified in his three finest works for solo piano, the *Second Sonata*, the *Third Sonata*, and the *Five Pieces for Piano*.

The short (thirteen-minute) *Second Sonata* (1946) is in three movements, arranged in a conventional fast-slow-fast order and played without pause. The first movement, in sonata-allegro form, seems barely able to contain the driving energy that virtually never lets up from beginning to end (example 20.3). The opening right-hand figure, a pair of six-

EXAMPLE 20.3. Sessions, *Second Sonata*, first movement, mm. 1–2. © 1948 Edward
B. Marks Music Company. International Copyright Secured. Made in U.S.A. All
Rights Reserved. Used by permission of Hal Leonard Publishing Corporation.

teenths leading up to an accented two-note slur, dominates the movement, appearing in many configurations but always reaching upwards. It
is initially accompanied by vigorous adaptation of an Alberti bass figure,
the intensity of which is magnified by irregular meters such as the $\frac{11}{16}$ in
the second measure of example 20.3. The constantly driving rhythm
propels the movement forward, and even the appearance of the more
lyric second theme is underlined with a stream of rhythmic sixteenths
that quickly lead to the heavily accented, syncopated closing idea (example 20.4). In two places the energy is allowed, for structural reasons,
to subside momentarily: in the bridge to the development section—that
juncture is clear—and in the parallel passage that ends the movement
and makes way for the second.

EXAMPLE 20.4. Sessions, *Second Sonata*, first movement, mm. 63–65.

Sessions, master of the long line, spins out a beautiful slow movement, the melody never stopping, the accompaniment now chordal, now
quietly contrapuntal. Particularly attractive is the middle section in
which, over an undulating left-hand figure, the line reaches higher and
higher in lyrical, expressive melismas (example 20.5).

If some aspects of Sessions's earlier music seemed to emulate
Stravinsky, with this movement his conversion to Schoenbergian romanticism is confirmed. If anything, Sessions's almost uncanny feeling for
musical form, something not always so apparent with Schoenberg, makes
his music even more convincing than that of the older composer.

The final movement of the *Second Sonata* opens with a Bartókian
idea that, with its many repeated notes, leads into some overly percussive

EXAMPLE 20.5. Sessions, *Second Sonata*, second movement, mm. 191–95.

writing at points of climax. The movement is well shaped and logical, but the pianist must guard against jarring sonorities in a number of passages.

The *Third Sonata* (1965) is Sessions's masterpiece for the instrument. Like the *Second*, it is in three movements, but the playing time is much longer, about twenty-five minutes. This is in part because the outside movements are slow, leaving only the middle movement with a fast tempo. Far more important is the magnitude of Sessions's message in this deeply felt work. Here, as in certain pieces by Schoenberg, one has the sense that the composer has started a movement with the simplest possible motive (see example 20.6), then quietly begins to explore the emotional ramifications of that sound (see example 20.7), until, after awhile, it takes on more affecting significance, not through constant repetition and development as employed by Schoenberg, but because of a certain presence that is hard to define. When, at the close of the long first movement, the opening chords unroll themselves in reverse order, ending with the original sound from the first measure of the piece, one feels that the process has almost totally transformed a simple, innocent sonority into something full of grief and pathos (see example 20.8).

EXAMPLE 20.6. Sessions, *Third Sonata*, first movement, m. 1. © 1969 Edward B. Marks Music Company. International Copyright Secured. Made in U.S.A. All Rights Reserved. Used by permission of Hal Leonard Publishing Corporation.

EXAMPLE 20.7. Sessions, *Third Sonata*, first movement, mm. 1–5.

EXAMPLE 20.8. Sessions, *Third Sonata*, first movement, mm. 93–96.

To say that this exquisite movement is built on a single sound does it a gross injustice, of course. Other ideas emerge in the first measures of the piece, presenting themselves in a seemingly artless way with no presentiments as to how they will develop. For example, the triplet figure first heard in measure 9 (see example 20.9) is later, at the most climactic moment of the movement, revealed in the fashion shown in example 20.10.

EXAMPLE 20.9. Sessions, *Third Sonata*, first movement, m. 9.

The second movement, a giant, soaring rondo, is Sessions's biggest and most difficult work for solo piano. Its more-than-two-octave martellato theme remains unmistakable, even with the myriad permutations it goes through in its remarkable journey. The final movement, headed with the inscription "In memoriam: Nov. 22, 1963," is only four pages long, but it conveys and embodies better than any other single statement

EXAMPLE 20.10. Sessions, *Third Sonata*, first movement, mm. 72–73.

the feelings of millions of people who, with Sessions, cried in anguish that day and grieved profoundly in the days thereafter.[4]

The fourth of the *Five Pieces for Piano* (1975), completed when Sessions was approaching his eightieth birthday, is another memorial, this one for Luigi Dallapiccola, who died in February 1975. Quite unlike the tragic final movement of the *Third Sonata*, this is a vigorous, galvanic tribute to his Italian friend and colleague, marked "Molto agitato" and rarely departing from that mode. It is fascinating to speculate why this piece was chosen to commemorate the day of Dallapiccola's death when, in fact, the entire set is dedicated to his memory. That Dallapiccola's enquiring mind, robust energy, and interest in practically everything required a statement of confirmation, even in death, is a salute from another positive man.

Beyond such speculation, one marvels at the colors that Sessions, almost half a century after the *First Sonata*, could still elicit from the piano in this remarkable set of pieces.

Copland, Sessions, and Cage (the rebellious outsider) made the principal contributions to American literature for the piano in the generation after Charles Ives. Unlike Cage, both Copland and Sessions wrote personal, emotional, and basically traditional music. The piano was a greater outlet for Copland's inner musical life, and yet one can say that his music conveys more of a sense of distance, of scope, and of landscape than a feeling for the human condition. Still a New Yorker who had lived in Paris when he wrote his tightly knit *Piano Variations*, he seemed to move, spiritually speaking, into the Great Plains and Rocky Mountains with the final movement of the *Piano Sonata* and in much of the spacious *Piano Fantasy*. Sessions, on the other hand, beginning with a certain impersonal quality in the *First Sonata*, grew closer to people with *From My Diary* and the *Second Sonata* and became, in the last works, a composer who, possessed of craft and human empathy no longer needing rationalization or intellectualization, wrote about feelings and humanity.

Such generalities may do these two composers a certain injustice, but they are made only by way of comparison and, much more importantly, with appreciation for the transcendent accomplishments of both.

The final harvest of the neoclassic movement occurs with the rush of symphonies and sonatas, most of them by American composers, dated in close proximity to the mid-century mark. Excluding the first two sonatas by Boulez (1946, 1948), which in any case have no kinship with neoclassicism, and the sonatas of Copland and Sessions already discussed, there remains a sizable group of works for the piano from the immediate postwar years that employ many aspects of the traditional multi-movement sonata.

Elliott Carter

Elliott Carter (b. 1908) completed his single *Piano Sonata* in 1946. The work is in two movements and may be termed a transitional piece in his output, lying between the colorful, sprightly works of his early, neoclassic period (he, too, had been a student of Boulanger) and the diabolically complex works of his later years. The sonata owes much to Copland in its sonorities, though Carter's exploration of harmonics with those same sonorities is highly original for the time.

What is specifically Carteresque in this work is the alternation between two tempi and pianistic styles, one slow and homophonic, the other quick and contrapuntal. The latter passages, marked "scorrevole," scampering up and down the keyboard in what might be called random diatonicism with irregular rhythms and constant cross accents, become one of the trademarks of the composer's later music.

Ross Lee Finney

Ross Lee Finney (b. 1906) wrote the most popular of his five sonatas, the *Piano Sonata No. 4 in E Major*, in 1945. Finney, who for many years was a member of the composition faculty of the University of Michigan, studied with Boulanger, Alban Berg (his *Variations on a Theme by Alban Berg* for solo piano, written in 1952, is an interesting if not altogether successful experiment), and Sessions. The *Fourth Sonata* is strongly tonal, exhibiting more than a hint of American folk idiom. There are five moments, "Hymn," "Invention," "Nocturne," "Toccata," and "Hymn," which, though there are double bars between them, are played without pause.

The work epitomizes the best of conservative American neoclassicism in its final surge immediately following World War II. Though Finney's later music became markedly more chromatic, he was never able to assimilate more advanced idioms in the same assured manner with which he handled diatonic tonality in this pleasant work.

Leon Kirchner

Of the several important sonatas by American composers written in the late 1940s, the one that comes closest to the high emotional level of

Roger Sessions's last two sonatas is the *Piano Sonata* (1948) by Leon Kirchner (b. 1919). Kirchner is a much more intuitive composer than Sessions, and this score is both powerful and enigmatic. The power lies in the nature of the thematic material and in the convincing manner in which Kirchner leads the listener from one emotional state to another. Kirchner's skill with transitions and his flexible approach to form, resembling Ives to some extent, make his work compelling and original.

Despite the three-movement format, this work goes considerably beyond the limited horizons of neoclassicism. Ironically, this very flexibility is also part of what makes the work enigmatic; the performer must take an active role in shaping the composition and must also come to terms with some minor notational ambiguities. Overall, however, the energy and conviction of the sonata make it one of the most impressive works for piano of this time.

Particular mention should be made of the slow movement, which owes more than a little to the "Musiques nocturnes" of Bartók's *Out of Doors* suite. Giving the impression of a quiet extemporization, it is in perfect contrast to the strong, malleable first movement and the hard-charging finale.

Ernst Krenek

The venerable Ernst Krenek (b. 1900) has spent a long life in constant creative activity, never allowing himself to settle into one specific style but always investigating the latest trends and trying his hand at them. Possessed of a brilliant and incisive mind, he has written countless articles on the subject of new music. *Music Here and Now*,[5] a book first published in German when he was in his thirties, demonstrates that Krenek was not only deeply involved in his own prolific compositional career, but that he could, at a relatively early age, make wise and objective appraisals of the musical questions of the day.

Born in Austria and coming into international prominence with the phenomenal success of his jazz opera, *Jonny spielt auf* (1926), he moved to the United States in 1938. After stints as a teacher (Vassar College) and administrator (Hamline University) he settled in southern California, where he continues to produce operas, symphonies, and vocal, chamber, tape, and piano works in quantities now numbering in the hundreds.

Of Krenek's six piano sonatas, the most important are the *Third Sonata* (1943) and, especially, the *Fourth Sonata* (1948). The latter, in four movements, is an atonal work of great power and effect. The first movement may be one of the most unusual examples of sonata-allegro form ever devised. In a conversation with the author many years ago, Krenek explained that before writing the *Fourth Sonata* he had noticed that in the first movements of some of the late Beethoven sonatas the recapitulation was actually a second development section, and the coda a third development section. So why not have a movement that was structured Exposition-Development-Development-Development?

One may question Krenek's view of the first movements of Beethoven's Op. 109 or Op. 110, but his unusual analysis makes for a strikingly effective opening movement of the dodecaphonic *Fourth Sonata*. To make the progression from section to section clear, Krenek changes the tempo at the beginning of each. The slow exposition, "Sostenuto," moves to "'Poco più mosso, deciso," then to "Allegro ma non troppo," and finally to an energetic "Allegro assai." In each section certain kernels of ideas are heard, their articulations changing as the pace increases. This is one of the most ambitious movements in all of Krenek's piano sonatas; it makes an impressive effect as it accelerates to a fiery conclusion.

This is followed by a slow, emotional movement in three-part song form. The composer employs a hexachordal technique rich in minor-triad associations, which give the work a sonority that is unusual for this style. The principal feature of the movement, however, is the expressive melodic line, which rivals Schoenberg for pathos and *Angst*.

The third movement is a flying rondo, contrapuntal at first, full of trills and tremolos later, and ending with a bit of jazzy syncopation, a hair-raising scale to the top of the piano, and a plunge to three *sforzando* chords deep in the bass. The final movement, in contrast, is a beautifully written set of variations on a quiet minuet theme, which, before it closes, reminisces briefly on the opening theme of the first movement, then quietly dances away to the end.

Samuel Barber

By far the most popular of the sonatas written at mid-century is that of Samuel Barber (1910–1981). Introduced in sensational fashion by Vladimir Horowitz in 1949, the four-movement work by one of this country's most successful romantic composers challenges performers and pleases audiences with its mixture of driving energy, scintillating pianism, and broad, Chopinesque lyricism.

That Barber was a very gifted composer was evident from the start. His *First Symphony*, Op. 9, written when he was only twenty-six, is a marvel, and many of his songs and works for strings are exquisitely beautiful. That the *Sonata for Piano* is basically a decorative piece, not matching the substance of any of its models (Chopin sonatas, Liszt études), demonstrates the difficulty of writing an extended work for the piano. It makes one appreciate all the more the accomplishments of Ives, Bartók, Copland, Sessions, Krenek, and Kirchner in this form, which, by 1950, was quickly becoming an anachronism.

Alberto Ginastera

Alberto Ginastera (1916–1983) from Argentina is considered by many to be the leading South American composer of the century. Much involved in the music of his own country, he produced charming, delightful collections for piano such as the *Danzas argentinas* (1937) and *Suite de danzas criollas* (1952), much as Bartók and Falla had absorbed and then redefined the folk music of their own countries.

The *First Sonata* (1952) is in four movements, of which the most unusual is the second, "Presto misterioso," which begins with a lithe, pianissimo theme played in both hands three octaves apart. The third movement, sounding rather like an extemporized guitar solo, is haunting and melancholy.

The outer movements are difficult to control, tonally, due to a profusion of quickly repeated chords, interlocking figures, and excessive use by the composer of *ff*, *fff*, and *sfff* markings, plus such directions as "violento" and "feroce." There is no denying, however, the potential effectiveness of these movements in a performance that maintains rhythmic control and tonal restraint.

The *Second Sonata* (1981) and *Third Sonata* (1982), written at the end of the composer's life, do his memory no service. Both are severely overwritten and, musically speaking, rely almost totally on barren formulas. Neither has any of the charming, imaginative qualities of the 1952 sonata, but both exaggerate its faults.

The list of mid-century American sonatas hardly ends there. A host of lesser figures attempted the genre, with results ranging from the suffocating pretension of David Diamond's lengthy *Sonata* (1947) to Norman Dello Joio's blithe, frivolous *Third Sonata*, written the same year. Vincent Persichetti's *Fourth Sonata* (1949) is probably the most consistently strong of his huge and variable output for the piano, and the Canadian Jean Coulthard's *Sonata* (1948) has its impressive moments. Ingolf Dahl's *Sonata Seria* (1953) is, indeed, serious and well crafted but limited, and George Walker's short *Second Sonata* (1956) has many fine points despite certain formal imbalances.

Sometime in the middle of the 1950s the need to write a piano sonata suddenly evaporated. Composers in America, jarred by the resonances of strange sounds and echoes of new procedures coming from overseas and even from rebels in their own midst, set off in new directions.

CHAPTER TWENTY-ONE

The American Avant-Garde

An awakening of interest in the twelve-tone technique took place among young composers in the United States soon after the end of World War II, just as it had with Stockhausen, Boulez, Berio, and others in Europe. Some Americans, having embraced the potential of dodecaphonic writing, never abandoned its principles; many of these composers were soon involved in the development of set theories and other expansions of serial thought. On the other hand, a number of composers became disenchanted with the esthetic of twelve-tone music and found the challenges of compositional indeterminacy compelling. Soon there was an unprecedented variegation of compositional styles throughout the United States as composers looked in all directions for new pathways to explore.

The influence of John Cage in Europe has already been detailed. His extraordinary effect on serial composers there was repeated often in this country, as contact with his ideas and music steered such composers as Morton Feldman and Earle Brown away from twelve-tone writing and toward indeterminate compositional modes, which were then adopted and developed still further by younger composers.

The brilliant composer-theorist Milton Babbitt represented a different point of view. Babbitt's precision and rationality have done much to keep a number of extremely talented composers, such as Charles Wuorinen and Donald Martino, close to the twelve-tone camp. Babbitt has also been at the forefront in electronic music, thus maintaining leadership in two of the three principal branches of compositional activity (interdeterminacy being the third) in the postwar era.

Composers not only continued to push out the boundaries of composition but redoubled investigations of the possibilities of the instruments themselves, experimenting with new ways of playing the piano (Crumb), tuning it (Eaton, Johnston), and combining it with tape (Davidovsky) and live electronics (Austin). Inevitably, new techniques and freedoms occasionally resulted in anarchy; in the 1960s, burning a piano could also be considered a legitimate piece of music (see illustration 21.1). In a decade including drugs, assassinations, Vietnam, Elvis, the

Illustration 21.1. Reproduction of a photograph of a performance of Anna Lockwood's *Piano Burning* from the cover of *Source: Music of the Avant-Garde*, 5, (1971). Courtesy of Larry Austin, University of North Texas.

Great Society, Woodstock, the Kent State massacre, and the Beatles, responses of a nihilistic or revolutionary nature were common.

Composers were finding the gap between performers and themselves growing wider. Pianists, singers, and most other instrumentalists busied themselves almost exclusively with the repertoire of the past. In this situation, composers again became increasingly involved in the performance and dissemination of their own music. The ONCE group was formed in Michigan in 1961; the Group for Contemporary Music at Columbia University gave its first concerts in 1962. From California, *Source* magazine lavishly promulgated the most avant-garde music, and the American Society of University Composers (ASUC)—its title suggesting a composer's almost unavoidable destiny—had its first quarrelsome meeting in 1966.

Throughout America in the affluent 1960s, an unprecedented explosion of activity took place in the contemporary music scene. The piano continued to have its role, though one could sense that its function as a solo instrument was beginning to wane. This was in part because training to become a pianist meant, more and more exclusively, the study of traditional repertoire. Nevertheless, major figures in the field of composition continued to contribute to the repertoire as a few performers remained willing to devote their time to the cause of new music.

Milton Babbitt

Milton Babbitt (b. 1916) grew up in Jackson, Mississippi, where his expertise as a jazz clarinetist and saxophonist was recognized at an early age. The son of a mathematician, his interest in music was parallel to a fascination with numbers, and his extraordinary intelligence was able quickly to grasp and synthesize the most complex aspects of both fields.

As a student at New York University he discovered the music of the Second Viennese School and became absorbed in their compositional processes long before the twelve-tone technique was considered respectable in the United States. When, after World War II, he became Conant Professor of Music at Princeton and Director of the Columbia-Princeton Electronic Music Center, he had already adapted Schoenberg's hypotheses to his own stimulating theories and had applied them to the composition of both instrumental and electronic music.

Babbitt's music is discussed more often than it is played, a situation he has always found annoying. His numerous piano pieces, which form an integral part of his oeuvre, demonstrate his preoccupation with the integration of row techniques with rhythmic structure, registral shifts, and other parameters. It is "important" music—daring in what it sets out to do and demanding on the performer. It is influential music, but as an example of an extreme stance.

Unfortunately, for most listeners the music is hermetic and lacks emotional content; it is the product of intellectual tabulations rather than the expression of human feelings. Aficionados of Babbitt's music will disagree, of course, and rightly so if they have found the key to the emotive secrets of his work. Most serious listeners have not.

The *Three Compositions for Piano*, written in 1947–1948, do indeed anticipate some of the serial developments that took place in Europe shortly thereafter, as is habitually reported (example 21.1). The pieces are often described as Schoenbergian, but this is true only insofar as compositional techniques are concerned. The rather dry layout of Babbitt's linear structures contrasts with Schoenberg's expressive phrases and romantic climaxes.

Partitions (1957) and *Post-Partitions* (1966) exemplify Babbitt's further explorations of linkages between sets, rhythms, attacks, range, and dynamics (example 21.2). Each note in these complex, concentrated, difficult studies has its own dynamic level on a scale from *ppppp* to *fffff*. The sequence of attacks is so dense that four staves are needed for each system.

EXAMPLE 21.1. Babbitt, *Three Compositions for Piano*, No. 1, mm. 1–6. © Copyright 1957 by Boelke-Bomart, Inc., copyright assigned 1977 to Mobart Music Publications, Inc. Used by permission.

EXAMPLE 21.2. Babbitt, *Post-Partitions*, mm. 1–2. © 1975 by C. F. Peters Corporation. Used by Permission.

The problem with this music, similar to that with the piano works of Xenakis, is the lack of differentiation. Rhythms are infinitely more complex in Babbitt than in Xenakis's "clouds," but their complexity and density keep them from being interesting. The organization may be elegant, but the attacks arrive so quickly that they begin to sound random. Also, the range of the piano is employed more or less in its totality throughout entire pieces; again, there is no differentiation, nothing is "saved." One begins to think of these pieces as calculation in sound rather than as music.

Later works—*Reflections* (1974), for piano and tape, *Canonical Form* (1983), and *Lagniappe* (1985)—continue Babbitt's compositional investigations along lines similar to the pieces mentioned above.

Charles Wuorinen

One of this country's chief spokesmen for the cause of contemporary music has been composer-pianist Charles Wuorinen (b. 1938). As a graduate student at Columbia University in 1962 he was, with Harvey Sollberger, a co-founder of the Group for Contemporary Music, the first such organization to be formed in this country in the postwar period.[1] In 1964 he joined the Columbia faculty and soon was instrumental in forming the ASUC, which, in spite of early squabbles that did not leave Wuorinen unscarred, did an enormous amount to bring composers together from all over the country for colloquia and concerts of their music.

Wuorinen has remained his own person, willing to speak his mind on issues of major concern. More than just a gadfly, he has been an ardent supporter of a rational approach to composition, very much in the tradition of his friend and associate, Milton Babbitt, with whom he shares more than a few points of view.

Wuorinen's first and most successful composition for piano is the *Piano Variations* (1963), a splendid, ringing piece of virtuoso writing. As with Babbitt, serial procedures are employed at all times, but, unlike the older composer, Wuorinen's sense of drama, both in the overall shape of the piece and in the inner workings of local events, makes the piece colorful and convincing. The two *Sonatas* (1969 and 1976) are considerably longer than the *Variations*. As one would expect from the composer, both are highly organized. In fact, the two works seem to overemphasize intellectual concerns, eventually stifling the confrontation with human feelings, which the earlier work so vigorously projects.

Ben Weber

Initially a medical student, Ben Weber (1916–1979) quickly turned to music and was attracted to the twelve-tone technique as early as 1938. Never truly an experimentalist, he wrote works that attempt to fuse serial techniques to more traditional melodic, rhythmic, and figurative contexts.

Most successful among these works is the beautiful *Fantasia (Variations)* for piano, completed in 1946. The piece, lasting about nine minutes, is in three sections. Opening with a set of free variations, it moves to a slow "Passacaglia," which leads in turn to a final, rhapsodic "Fantasia." Weber has said that in this work he specifically wished to combine Lisztian pianistic style with dodecaphonic procedures. He has succeeded admirably in this expressive, deeply felt work.

George Rochberg

The intensely serious George Rochberg (b. 1918) is one of this country's most interesting, articulate composers. In his thoughtful, forceful, sometimes outspoken way, he has pursued the destiny of music in this century, commenting on its many foibles and shifts in words and in his music as well.

At the conclusion of World War II Rochberg became a student at the Curtis Institute, where he studied with Menotti. His music at that time was strongly influenced by Stravinsky and Bartók. However, upon meeting Dallapiccola in Rome in 1950, he developed a passion for serial music. His *Twelve Bagatelles* (1952), written soon after this meeting, employ a strict application of "classical" twelve-tone procedures and are, appropriately, dedicated to Dallapiccola.

Becoming Director of Publications at Theodore Presser Company in 1951, a position he held until 1960, he continued to develop serial procedures in his writing, culminating in the *Sonata-Fantasia* (1958), a very large work for solo piano in which, for the first time, brief quotations from the music of others—in this case a few bars from Schoenberg's Op. 23, No. 1—are employed.

In a conversation with the author in the late 1950s, Rochberg expressed his concern as a publisher and composer that his music and the music of other contemporary composers "sat on the shelf gathering dust." It was evident at that time that he was looking for a way to communicate with performers and listeners in a way his present style was not doing.

This change took place in the 1960s through, first, a greater use of quotation from earlier twentieth-century composers and then, quite soon, from composers before the twentieth century. Such works as *Nach Bach* (1966) resulted, mixing snippets of Bach's keyboard music with original figurations. Eventually, determining that it was no longer necessary to quote in order to employ tonality, he "reacquired" tonal procedures, using them freely in such works as the *Carnival Music* (1971) and *Partita Variations* (1976), which juxtapose styles in a manner that has become familiar in his other works for chamber ensembles and orchestra.

The early *Bagatelles* remains his best work for solo piano. Honest, expressive music, the set covers a wide range of emotional nuance from lyric melancholy (numbers five and seven), through humor and sarcasm (numbers two, six, and twelve), to intense drama (numbers one, three, nine, and eleven). The longer *Sonata-Fantasia* is worth investigating, though its unremitting seriousness and lack of variety in its materials require a great deal of empathy from the performer. The later works have good moments, but Rochberg's attempt to reach out to his listeners leads to some less than persuasive writing, spoiling what otherwise might have been a successful blend of styles.

Salvatore Martirano

Salvatore Martirano (b. 1927) was born in Yonkers, New York. He spent much of the 1950s in Italy, studying with Dallapiccola in Florence from 1952 to 1954 and living in Rome as a Fellow of the American Academy from 1956 until 1959. Soon after he was invited to join the faculty of the University of Illinois, a position he still holds.

As with so many others, Martirano began as a twelve-tone composer, encouraged by Dallapiccola. In a fascinating composition for piano, *Cocktail Music* (1962), he links durations with pitches and tempi, then begins to shift one or the other to achieve different combinations of parameters. Informed also by his interest in assimilating pop music into his concert works, the piece remains tightly controlled yet bubbles effervescently in a spontaneous, impromptu fashion, leading finally to an improbably long tremolo-crescendo. Composers in the early 1960s found the work entrancing, and it may well have been the most often imitated work of the time.

After this work Martirano, too, felt the need to put twelve-tone writing behind him. Subsequent works, in fact, avoid any reference to traditional notation—as in the cataclysmic *L's. G. A.* (1968) for actor, tape, and multiple projections—and the endless splicing together of various electronic systems, such as the "Sal-Mar Construction," has occupied much of his subsequent compositional energies.

Earle Brown, Morton Feldman, and Christian Wolff

Earle Brown (b. 1926), Morton Feldman (1926–1987), and Christian Wolff (b. 1934) were, with John Cage as the senior member, known in the 1950s as the "New York Group." Feldman had studied with Wallingford Riegger and Stefan Wolpe earlier, writing dodecaphonic scores under their tutelage, but a meeting with Cage in 1950 transformed his thinking about music. Brown, too, had begun as a twelve-tone composer, but under the influence of the sculptor Alexander Calder as well as Cage, he moved into the exploration of graphic notation and open forms.

Wolff, youngest of the group, became a professor of classics at Harvard and Dartmouth and was active as a composer. As a high school student he had studied the *I Ching* and it was he, in his teens, who introduced the book to Cage in the early 1950s.

Feldman's first Cage-inspired music consists of graphic scores, but as his need for more control increased, he developed notation in which note heads are written on traditional staves but without any rhythmic indications, other than the suggestion that a piece or a section should be fast or slow. His *Last Pieces* (1959) are scored in this way (example 21.3). They also illustrate his characteristic request that *all* notes be very soft.

EXAMPLE 21.3. Feldman, *Last Pieces*, first line. © 1963 by C. F. Peters Corporation. Used by Permission.

MORTON FELDMAN (1959)

Much later music, such as *Triadic memories* (1981), a lengthy piece in which everything is *ppp* from beginning to end, embraces aspects of minimalism.

Earle Brown's *Twenty-five Pages for one to twenty-five Pianos* (1953) is his first open-form composition (example 21.4). The twenty-five pages may be played in any order, with either end of each page up, and with any clef applied to any staff. Notes and durations are written legibly whichever way the page is turned. The composer suggests, in addition, that each two-line system take somewhere between five and fifteen seconds, but even this can be adjusted. Given that as many as twenty-five pianists on twenty-five pianos may perform the work at a given time, this composition would seem to have carried indeterminacy close to its limits, verging on pure improvisation.

Wolff's works in the early 1950s, such as the *Suite I* (1952) for prepared piano, are fully notated and have a Webernesque austerity about them. Later, Wolff became more interested in giving more initiative to the performer and systematically explored the possibilities of total indeterminacy.

George Crumb, John Eaton, and Ben Johnston

If new ways of playing the piano had been considered experimental in the 1920s, and if dividing the octave into something other than twelve

EXAMPLE 21.4. Brown, *Twenty-five pages for One to Twenty-five Pianos*, page 1. ©
1959 Universal Edition (London), Ltd., London. © Renewed. All Rights Reserved. Used by Permission of European American Music. Distributors Corporation, sole U.S. and Canadian agent for Universal Edition London.

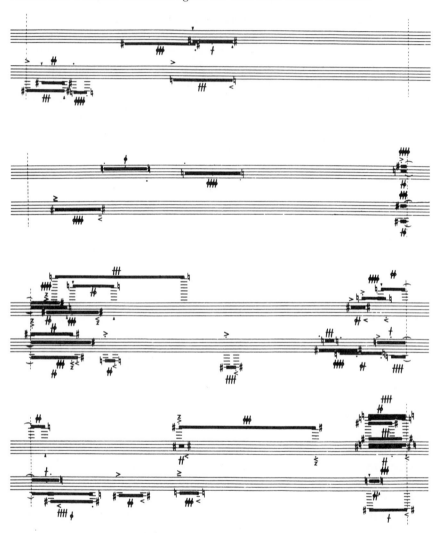

equal parts had been tentative before World War II, a number of composers in the 1960s found such matters so natural that no trace of self-consciousness remains in their music.

The piano music of George Crumb (b. 1929) will be treated more fully in the next chapter. The *Five Pieces for Piano* (1962), his first mature composition, masterfully integrates the sounds of plucked and strummed piano strings with those made on the keys. The composition is notable for the elegance of its form—an arch—and for the ingenuity of its microserial approach to pitch choice.

John Eaton's *Microtonal Fantasy* (1964) is for one pianist at two pi- anos tuned a quarter step apart. The beauty of this composition's sinuous lines can only make one wonder why it was not done before. The special problems encountered by the pianist—playing two pianos with key- boards at right angles and simultaneously operating two damper pedals—are well worth solving. In an ideal performance one hears what sounds like a single piano with 176 keys.

Eaton (b. 1935), a student of Babbitt and Sessions, teaches at In- diana University.

The *Sonata for Microtonal Piano* (1965) by Ben Johnston (b. 1926) is one of several works the composer has written using tunings other than the well-tempered variety. This is the only one for solo piano, however.

Johnston, for many years on the faculty of the University of Illinois, explains that the piano is tuned through an interlocking system of just- intonation triads. The A below middle C is tuned to its normal frequency, 220 cycles per second. By moving out from this note with just-tuned triads, every note on the piano eventually becomes part of such a triad. The result, however, is that there are no octaves. In Johnston's scheme, for example, if A = 220 is in tune, the A that would be tuned 440 is 62 cents sharp (up ca. two-thirds of a step), A = 880 is 24 cents sharp (up one quarter step), A = 1760 is 31 cents flat (down ca. one-third of a step), and so forth.

Johnston has admitted in conversation that although he conceived the music with the just-tuned intervals and triads in mind, he was shocked when he first heard the piece. The absence of octaves in the tuning had an unforeseen side effect, which was to take away much of the resonance of the instrument, the strong sympathetic vibrations provided by octaves now being unavailable. Once he became used to the differ- ence, however, he found the purity of the just thirds and fifths to be very pleasing, exactly as he had hoped. Indeed, it takes some time for the listener to get used to the tuning so that it does not simply sound "out of tune."

The rhythm is difficult, a great deal of metric modulation making the initial learning process extremely challenging. Beyond that the tech- nical difficulties are not excessive. And the performer may find the four movements, of vastly differing emotional content, to be worth the effort.

Larry Austin

The ultimate emblem of the American avant-garde, and perhaps also the signal of its forthcoming dissolution in the late 1960s, is *Source: Music of the Avant Garde*, a publication initiated at the University of Cal- ifornia at Davis by composer Larry Austin (b. 1930) (see illustration 21- 1). A luxuriously mounted periodical that seemed to know no financial restraints, it was the antithesis of the staid, professional, Ivy League *Per- spectives of New Music*, with its dignified format and sometimes impenetrable prose. Both represented strong views on contemporary music and presented musicians with extreme poles against which to make esthetic decisions.

The plausible endgame of indeterminacy would be, logically, a piece of silent music in which only mistakes would be heard. This is what Larry Austin provided with his live-electronic piece, *Accidents* (1967), described in the July 1968 issue of *Source*. In *Accidents* the piano has wind-chime shells strewn over its strings and a large number of contact microphones lying on the shells. The slightest vibration activates the microphones, sending a signal, possibly including feedback, through an amplification system with a ring modulator. Six speakers picking up these signals surround the audience.

The music, in which notes are "correct" only if keys are depressed silently, is to be played as fast as possible. A sound will occur only when a hammer accidentally strikes a string. "With successive performances it is possible that the player may develop techniques to avoid *accidents*," writes the composer; "this happening, the performer should counter such gradually acquired technique by playing faster and with more abandon."[2] The piece is in ten sections, called "gestures." Each gesture must be performed "successfully," that is, silently, for the piece to be concluded.

A subsequent issue of *Source* included a composition entitled *Piano Burning* by Anna Lockwood.[3] Photographs of a performance were featured on the front and back covers (illustration 21.1). The composer suggests an upright piano with the strings overtuned as high as possible, thereby achieving the most sound when the heat snaps them. She also explains how to amplify the sounds electronically with asbestos-covered microphones and suggests, for a night performance, the inclusion of firecrackers and rockets. A little kerosene in one corner helps get things underway, she concludes.

Was this act, relatively tame compared to the rock stars who burned their electric guitars onstage in a 140-decibel orgy, an artistic counterpart to the anger that swept through the inner cities of America in the 1960s; to the loss of innocence brought on by live television coverage of the body counts, napalm, and corruption of the Vietnam War? Perhaps one could say that Anna Lockwood was more honest in her reaction to the world than other composers dared to be.

Whatever one's interpretation, the 1960s—affluent, carefree, imaginative, tragic—ended. Money became tight, people who would "never trust anyone over thirty" became thirty, drugs and other social problems did not go away, and the slide toward fundamentalism and conservatism began.

Composers, having gone all out with musico-theatrical productions, total serialism, total indeterminacy, and group improvisation, also stepped back a bit and pondered where their audiences had gone. Like George Rochberg, they felt a sudden nostalgia for tonality, and the appearance of Berio's *Sinfonia* (1968), with its lengthy quotations from Mahler (Berio called it his biggest "experiment"), provided the loophole. Brought up in the firm belief that writing tonally was anathema, the aging postwar composers could receive remission for their sins if they quoted from the works of earlier composers. Once again the old-fashioned key signatures of F-sharp major and B-flat minor appeared sporadically. And, interestingly enough, the composer's performing directions and other esthetic excuses were shorter than they had been in twenty years.

Suddenly what had seemed so new and exciting in the 1950s and 1960s became restrictive. The cogitations of Stockhausen or Babbitt no longer seemed so awe-inspiring; the indeterminacy of Cage and the aleatoric processes of Boulez no longer had fresh impact. New directions needed to be taken and *could* be taken. All compositional systems could be embraced. Even the quotation marks surrounding earlier composers' music could be thrown off. Somehow, permission was given for composers to be themselves.

Piano music in America in the 1950s and 1960s is not plentiful. Between Cage's *Music of Changes* in 1951 and Anna Lockwood's *Piano Burning* twenty years later, there are just a few pieces—the Copland *Fantasy*, the Sessions *Third Sonata*—of large scope. Other works of lasting worth are short: pieces by Rochberg, Crumb, Martirano, Wuorinen, and a few others. As 1970 approached, pianists interested in new music had cause for discouragement. They could not have guessed that the 1970s and 1980s would see the creation of a substantial group of major works of great expressive beauty for their instrument, nor that the coming years would form a period as prolific as any in music history.

PART 4

The 1970s and 1980s

CHAPTER TWENTY-TWO

George Crumb

George Crumb (b. 1929) was born and grew up in Charleston, West Virginia. The Crumbs were a close-knit family that blended West Virginian conservative traditions with devoted loyalty to one another; they all loved music, played instruments, and enjoyed performing together. The father, an accomplished clarinettist, had a large collection of classical scores, and as a boy George Crumb would study these by the hour, trying to figure out how all the parts sounded together. He developed a passion for reading and, with it, a lifelong fascination for the mysteries of life, the deeper aspects of humanity's relationship with nature, some of which could not, and *should* not, he thought, be explained, only expressed. (Much later, having written *Night of the Four Moons* as the Apollo 11 spacecraft took astronauts to the moon for the first time, he expressed a certain sorrow that human beings had set foot there; the moon would not be the same anymore, he said, for some of its mystery was gone.)

Quiet and self-effacing, he demonstrated unusual talent as a teen-age pianist and composer, writing dozens of pieces of various kinds. At the University of Illinois and later at the University of Michigan, where he studied with Ross Lee Finney, he continued to absorb music in great quantities, remembering everything he examined, piecing together, little by little, the musical ideas, sounds, and gestures that would, in a few years, emerge suddenly as his own unique and unprecedented style.

Crumb found particular reference to life's mysteries in the sounds of Debussy's music, the autobiographical confessions of the songs and symphonies of Mahler, as well as the poems of Rilke. He also found them in the magically evocative images of García Lorca, a Spanish poet whose language he did not speak but whose incisive linguistic concepts and sonorities were in tune with his own inner visions. Equally important, he learned about musical form from the classical masters and Bartók, admired the transparent lyricism of Dallapiccola, and was profoundly affected by the ecstasies of carefully prepared, hyperromantic climaxes in the music of Alban Berg.

As a member of the faculty (like Dallapiccola in Florence, he taught secondary piano) of the University of Colorado from 1959 until 1964, he, like many others at that time, became fascinated with the precision and craft of Webern's music. After the years of absorbing and digesting the music of so many others, the study of this carefully wrought, deeply expressive music seemed to provide Crumb with the final, cathartic impulse necessary to throw off past influences and begin writing in his own new style. Music began to flow out of him, not quickly, but steadily: *Five Pieces for Piano* (1962), *Night Music I*, for soprano, piano (celeste), and two percussionists (1963), *Four Nocturnes* for violin and piano (1964), the first two books of *Madrigals* (1965), *Eleven Echoes of Autumn*, for flute, clarinet, violin, and piano (1966). After that the progression was rapid and secure; Crumb moved in a very short time from being an unknown piano teacher to becoming the best-known American composer of his generation, winning every major prize and honor, receiving more commissions than he could accept in a lifetime, and being appointed to a prestigious position as a member of the composition faculty at the University of Pennsylvania, a position he still holds today. For a certain period in the 1970s he became a cult figure, an incongruous and uncomfortable position for a person of such shy demeanor, but one with which he had to contend despite himself. Such works as *Ancient Voices of Children*, for soprano, boy soprano, and seven instrumentalists, including pianist (1970), *Black Angels*, for string quartet (1970), and *Voice of the Whale*, for flute, cello, and piano (1971) captured the imagination of audiences as no other composer of the time could do. Crumb provided his listeners with something of the sensation of awe, wonder, and enigmatic beauty that he himself felt concerning the "mysteries." He named movements after geological eras, referred to images as coming from "the Dark Land," invented visual symbols for his scores, and concocted numerological schemes. For many listeners these extramusical trappings provided an avenue into the music itself, allowing them to listen to it openly and with interest rather than with resistance and scepticism.

The music itself is carefully wrought, hypnotic, ecstatic, no mere accompaniment to extramusical flights. It tends to be uncomplicated, often all foreground with little background and with a minimum of counterpoint. Crumb's masterful use of the most disparate, far-ranging sounds has tended to overshadow his harmonic consistency, just as his dramatic effects tend to obscure the care with which he plans sonority and range, which make these effects possible. Much of his music is tonal, sometimes traditionally so, as when he writes "in the style of" or quotes from an earlier composer's work.

There are six works for solo piano, of which four are of primary interest here: *Five Pieces for Piano* (1962), the first two books of the *Makrokosmos* cycle (1972, 1973), and *Gnomic Variations* (1981). The other two piano pieces are *A Little Suite for Christmas, A.D. 1979* (1980) and *Processional* (1983).

As the first work written in Crumb's mature style, *Five Pieces for Piano* is an excellent starting point for the study of his music. In these pieces the composer's meticulous attention to matters of compositional craft are clearly evident, uncolored by extramusical materials.

The five movements are arranged in an arch similar to that used by Bartók in a number of his ensemble works. The arrangement is best shown in a diagram (figure 22.1).

Figure 22.1.

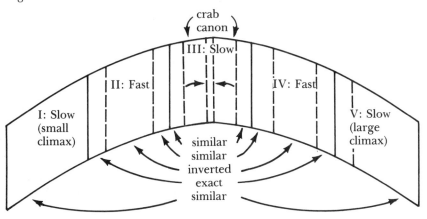

The first and last pieces employ sounds made both inside the instrument (pizzicato, tremolos, harmonics) and on the keys; the pitch-cell groups that open the first piece are used to round off the fifth. The second and fourth pieces are almost entirely played on the keys; the main portion of the fourth piece is a free inversion of the second, the rhythms remaining exactly the same; also, the short introduction of the second piece is almost exactly repeated as the epilogue to the fourth, and the introduction to the fourth is similar to the epilogue of the second.

The third piece is the center of the arch. Played "sempre pizzicato" (one can close the fallboard during this piece since no keys are employed), its main section is a crab canon, the second half repeating the first exactly, but in reverse order and as an "echo" in quadruple piano. Example 22.1 shows the middle three measures of the piece, the single high E in the center measure being the mid-point of the canon, the movement, and the entire composition.

In order to give this symmetrical work dramatic impact near the end, Crumb makes the outer movements the freest in their relationship to one another. While the first movement, improvisatory in nature, has a relatively quick, fleeting climax, the parallel fifth movement involves a rather long contrapuntal buildup (the longest real contrapuntal passage in any of Crumb's piano works) to a very large, sustained climax marked "molto drammatico, fuocoso!", with heavy chords played on the keys and thunderous tremolos directly on the strings.

EXAMPLE 22.1. Crumb, *Five Pieces for Piano*, third movement, mm. 8–10. © 1973 by C. F. Peters Corporation. Used by permission.

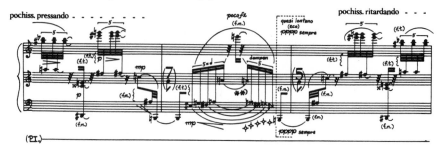

EXAMPLE 22.2. Three-note row used to construct Crumb's *Five Pieces for Piano*.

As a counterpart to this formal organization, Crumb is extraordinarily economical in his choice of notes throughout the *Five Pieces*. A three-note row and its transpositions are used to construct every sound in the piece (example 22.2). Obviously, had he used four of these three-note cells, Crumb could have written a strictly twelve-tone piece; in fact, the opening line of the first piece alludes to the possibility (example 22.3). However, this is not the case; rather, the three-note cell, transposed and combined freely, is the building block of the entire set, thereby giving it extraordinary harmonic consistency.

None of this would be of great importance if the music itself were not so compelling. Combining sounds made traditionally and untraditionally, thereby expanding the coloristic possibilities of the instrument, Crumb does so without allowing the inside-the-piano sounds to give the impression of being special effects or gimmicks. *Five Pieces for Piano* is an integrated blend of expanded piano sounds. The sounds and the gestures formed with them create an aura from the first note, suspended in time, floating in the air. Tremolos in the bass, buzzing tones, and flashing triplets give a sense of menacing thoughts and fleeting drama, and the final climax, the whole piano vibrating like a giant cimbalom, is masterfully conceived.

Before we proceed to Crumb's later piano music, a few words concerning playing inside the piano are in order. What the pianist needs to do in order to be able to play inside the instrument in the music of George Crumb is not "preparation" in the Cageian sense. Crumb writes for the piano, not for the prepared piano. Immediately before or after a work by Crumb, other traditional piano music may be played on the

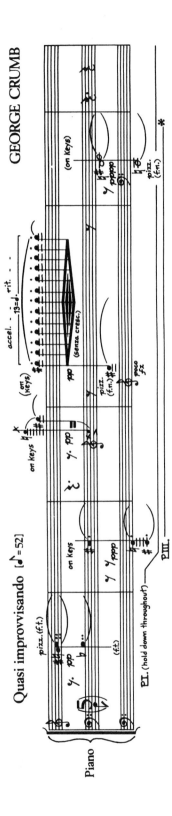

EXAMPLE 22.3. Crumb, *Five Pieces for Piano*, first movement, mm. 1–6.

same instrument with no time necessary to add or remove anything. However, the pianist does need to develop a scheme whereby he can find exact pitches quickly inside the instrument. One glance at the harp of a grand piano is enough for one to see that individual notes are quite anonymous. Just finding the first three-note chord of the *Five Pieces* can take several seconds unless the performer adopts a clear system, harmless to the instrument, for indicating pitches.

"The piano was not made to be played on the inside!" This is the most frequent reaction of tuners and technicians to this music. It is most important for pianists to understand that, in fact, the statement is correct. Whether preparing an instrument for music by John Cage or marking the inside for the music of Crumb, one must understand the potential dangers and proceed with caution at all times.

The best procedure known to the author for identifying strings is the following: First, prepare tiny pieces of masking tape, not larger than one-half inch by one-quarter inch. Second, with the damper pedal depressed so the damper felts are off the strings, *lightly* apply these pieces to the tops of the dampers that correspond to the black keys in the mid-range of the piano, being very careful not to press or twist the dampers in any way. When this has been done, the pianist has a rank of $2+3+2+3+2+3$ and so on, directly in the front of the instrument. There is no need to write any further identification on the pieces of masking tape, since the pattern on the dampers corresponds exactly to the keyboard. With proper practice, notes can be found just as quickly inside as out.

In the bass rank it is best simply to memorize where the notes are: on a Steinway "D," for example, from the lowest A up to E are single strings, F to A are double strings, and B-flat to E are triple. Other pianos have somewhat different arrangements, but one can quickly learn to find any bass string with a little study and adaptability. Therefore, the dampers of the bass rank need no markers; in any case, the line of sight would make them more confusing than helpful.

All markers should be removed immediately after a performance, again with the damper pedal held down so as not to press the damper felts into the strings.

Harmonics in the mid-range are marked very simply. First, the pianist finds the exact node necessary for the required harmonic and makes a single chalk mark on the strings *of the next higher note*, thereby avoiding the possibility of erasing it while playing. Fifth-partial harmonics on the bass strings need no marking—in any case, one should *never* rub chalk or anything else into wound strings! Nodes for fifth partials (Crumb's "bell"-harmonics) are close enough to the dampers that one can estimate their position easily and accurately with practice, being careful, as always, not to touch the dampers themselves while playing.

Crumb suggests (or requires, in some cases) that his piano music be amplified in order to give more presence to the delicate sounds inside the piano. This suggestion should be followed, of course. The amount of amplification needed is rather slight. At no time should the tone of the instrument shatter or be otherwise distorted. With or without amplification, pianists will need to learn to match the sounds made inside the instrument with those played on the keys, which almost always means increasing the apparent dynamics of plucked or strummed notes.

Finally, it is strongly recommended that the pianist stay seated at all times. It is rarely, if ever, really necessary to stand. Shorter persons may need to use a somewhat higher bench than usual, but the distracting sight of the performer alternately standing and sitting should be avoided at all costs.

Ten years after *Five Pieces for Piano*, Crumb completed the two solo volumes of *Makrokosmos*. Each volume is subtitled *Twelve Fantasy-Pieces after the Zodiac for Amplified Piano*. Each takes approximately thirty minutes to perform, much longer than the nine-minute duration of the *Five Pieces*.

In the ten years between solo piano works, Crumb further developed special techniques for inside the piano (many of the ensemble pieces written in the interim employ the instrument), and his confidence as a composer had grown, allowing his imagination to follow more daring pursuits. Nevertheless, though the writing in the two *Makrokosmos* volumes may seem to be freer than in the *Five Pieces*, his attention to matters of compositional craft—harmonic consistency, sense of inner formal logic, careful use of sonorous contrasts, and sense of cumulative drama— is, if anything, stronger than before.

Crumb has stated that he used the two books of *Preludes* by Debussy, each of which has twelve pieces, each with a fanciful title, as a model for the two-volume solo *Makrokosmos*. In some of the titles of individual movements Crumb lets his fertile imagination run wild: "Pastorale (from the Kingdom of Atlantis, ca. 10,000 B.C.)," "Ghost-Nocturne: for the Druids of Stonehenge," "Tora! Tora! Tora! (Cadenza Apocalittica)." In others he links the title with a special "symbolic" manner of notating the movement, as in the "Crucifixus," notated as a cross, "The Magic Circle of Infinity," a circle, "Spiral Galaxy," a spiral, and so on.

In addition to the titles, each of the twenty-four pieces is labeled with a sign of the zodiac and with the initials of someone born under that sign—a friend, colleague, family member, or respected composer.

In both volumes the pianist is required not only to play in and out of the piano, but almost must whistle, sing, shout, and whisper in various specified ways. Singing is always notated in the bass clef only because the pianist-dedicatees of each volume are men; women may transpose pitches up an octave. Whistling is notated at exact pitch; in both volumes the whistling requirements are demanding and will need (for most) practice over an extended period of time to develop range, breath control, and precise intonation in order to achieve an accurate and effective performance.

The two volumes of *Makrokosmos* are not difficult once the routines of playing inside the instrument are worked out and the vocal effects coordinated. Because of Crumb's harmonic consistency, and because in these volumes he uses relatively simple, small forms of individual pieces, the music is easily memorized, a necessity if only because the pianist needs to look at what he is doing.

The effect of either volume on an audience can be spellbinding, but the spell must not be broken from start to finish. Though each set has twelve separate pieces, the attention of the listener must not be allowed to waver, either because of the actions of the pianist (who *must* stay seated and minimize all gestures inside the piano) or because of failure to move rapidly from the end of one movement to the next. Crumb's music is full of fermatas; these rarely, if ever, mean silence. Some reverberation should be heard at all times in order that the momentum, the thread of the total conception, not be lost.

All of Crumb's scores are published in a facsimile of his beautiful, clear calligraphy. Any pianist can learn to play the music from the score without additional help. The notation is explicit in every detail as to how each sound is to be made.[1] Example 22.4 from "The Phantom Gondolier" in volume 1 is Crumb's solution to one of the most difficult passages to notate in all of his music. In just a few seconds of music there are various kinds of pizzicati, harmonics, singing, shouting, glissandi on the strings, and so on. He notates the passage perfectly in the simplest manner possible.

In all of his music, but particularly in the two sets of *Makrokosmos*, a certain dramatic abandon is necessary. The vocal effects must be done with conviction and strength, the various climaxes should be well approached and powerful, and all sound combinations must be fully understood and executed with complete assurance.

The *Gnomic Variations*, completed almost ten years after the solo *Makrokosmos* sets, is in a way a return to the "pure" music of *Five Pieces for Piano*. Although still making extensive use of inside-the-piano techniques, there are no extramusical connotations or vocal sounds. The title uses the word *gnomic* in a somewhat obscure sense: an aphoristic expression of a terse, pithy idea. The short, seven-measure theme consists, "gnomically," of a single two-note idea (a tritone) repeated a number of times on various pitches without rhythmic alteration.

The theme is followed by eighteen variations. Initially they follow the same structural plan as the theme, then become more extended as the piece continues. Each, however, refers specifically to some aspect of the

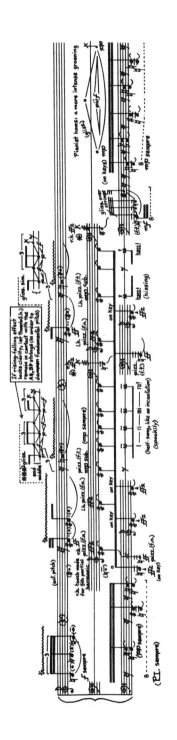

EXAMPLE 22.4. Crumb, *Makrokosmos*, Volume 1, "Phantom Gondolier," line 2. © 1974 by C. F. Peters Corporation. Used by permission.

theme, particularly with regard to the initial tritone and its harmonic ramifications. The final variations lead to a typically sonorous climax (Var. 17) and final peroration (Var. 18), the latter being a restatement of the theme with only the timbres of the original version changed.

In a number of ways this is Crumb's most difficult solo piano piece. Some of his most challenging sonic effects are employed, requiring agility on the keyboard and inside the piano, and exacting pedaling. Variations succeed one another without pause, and the pianist must constantly think ahead to the next maneuver with a rapidity not required in the more spacious *Makrokosmos* or the separate movements of the *Five Pieces for Piano*.

Crumb's teaching and music have had enormous influence on composers. His style is specific, however, and composers attracted to it find that their music quickly "sounds like Crumb" if they are not careful. His legacy, in addition to his now universally known music, is not so much this specific style but the care with which Crumb approaches the craft of composition, the fantasy of his conceptions, the beauty and clarity of his calligraphy, and the imagination with which he combines sounds of the most disparate nature into an integrated, unified whole.

CHAPTER TWENTY-THREE

Donald Martino

In every musical age one can find the composer whose style changes, sometimes radically, sometimes more than once, during his lifetime. On the other hand there is always the composer who, once his musical grammar and syntax have been found, speaks with the same voice from youth to age with little modulation. The changes in Beethoven's style from Opus 1 to Opus 135 are dramatic, those from Wagner's *Lohengrin* to *Tristan* arguably more so, and the similarities between Stravinsky's *Rite of Spring* and *Agon* are difficult enough to perceive to require the aid of a specialist to discern them. Early and late Mozart, if not identical, are recognizable as being by the same person, and the Chopin who appeared in Paris at the age of twenty wrote in a manner that was not substantially altered, even if it was refined in the next two decades.

Of the four composers treated in some detail in chapters 22–24, both George Crumb and Donald Martino belong to the Mozart-Chopin category, whereas William Albright and Frederic Rzewski have both moved away from entrenched stylistic positions to a stance much different from where they started. This is not a case of steadfastness versus instability (if it were, Beethoven would come up short and Stravinsky would be positively untrustworthy). Rather, it is a matter of temperamental necessity, on the one side to hold fast to a developed congenial language through the elaboration of which a composer may express all things, and on the other to switch to another mode in order to say those things that have been blocked by achieved systems of rhetoric.

For all its thoroughgoing craftsmanship, George Crumb's music is about sound and color. Crumb paints sonic pictures of strange and bizarre places; he focuses on inchoate mysteries and unmoving states of being. In his music one rarely hears the raw emotion itself, but rather a somewhat disembodied depiction of the emotion, as seen from a distant (spiral?) galaxy. His gondolier is a phantom, his voices come from the "Corona Borealis," and if he asks the performer to sing words, they are usually from an unknown language.

Donald Martino (b. 1931) writes about human feelings and how they change from moment to moment. His musical style, as personal as Crumb's is to him, is tuned not to unchanging states of being but to the transitions that are always taking place in real life. Martino's "mysteries" are the fluctuating emotions of living, feeling souls.

Martino was a student of both Babbitt and Sessions at Princeton and, in the mid-1950s, lived in Florence and worked with Dallapiccola. His career has taken him from one prestigious academic post to another: Princeton (1957–59), Yale (1959–1969), the New England Conservatory (1969–1981), Brandeis (1980–1983) and, since 1983, Harvard.

A strikingly successful early piece for piano is the *Piano Fantasy* (1958), completed shortly after Martino returned to the United States from Florence (example 23.1). A short work of five minutes's duration, it demonstrates that the composer's style was well developed when he was in his twenties. Watchwords of that style are "expressive nuance." Martino, writing in a dodecaphonic idiom, exerts great care through every available notational means to convey to the performer the exact nuance of feeling from one phrase to the next. Note that even the extent of a *ritardando* is indicated ("fin'a ♪ = 84") as the music changes from "espressivo, drammatico" to "espressivo, dolce."

EXAMPLE 23.1. Martino, *Piano Fantasy*, mm. 33–37. Copyright 1970 by Ione Press (E. C. Schirmer), Boston. Reprinted by permission.

Pianississimo: A Sonata for Piano (1970) is a formidable work, one of the most imposing and intimidating scores of recent decades (example 23.2). Lasting almost half an hour, it is in a single movement. That it is not completely successful does not, in the case of a composer of Martino's sensibilities, mean that it should be disregarded. Such a heroic attempt must be given its due, whatever the outcome.

Stockhausen begins his *Klavierstück X* (see chapter 16), a somewhat longer single-movement work, with a tremendous outburst of activity of nearly superhuman proportions. This outburst continues for several

EXAMPLE 23.2. Martino, *Pianississimo: A Sonata for Piano*, mm. 136–55. Copyright 1970 by Ione Press (E. C. Schirmer), Boston. Reprinted by permission.

minutes, but then the violent commotion is balanced by long periods of silence or, more often, fading resonances. Beginning with flagrant disorder, he subsequently mediates the near hysteria with the calming timelessness of near silence.

Martino, in *Pianississimo*, investigates the landscape of the piano as few have done. Clusters, pizzicati, muted notes, pedal effects of all kinds, and rapid changes of tempo appear in detailed and unremitting agitation. The activity at the outset is not quite as frantic as in *Klavierstück X*, but it is much longer. In fact, it continues with little letup for more than half the piece. No remonstrance on the part of the composer that this note is "timido," that one "dolce," the next three notes "nervoso" and the next "austero" can keep the overall effect from fatiguing the listener. There is simply too much activity too much of the time and for too long. This is not to suggest that Martino should have written another *Klavierstück X*. But certain styles suggest (or even dictate) certain temporal possibilities, just as in theater certain kinds of dramatic situations cannot be sustained beyond a certain length of time. In the first twenty-five pages of *Pianississimo* (there is a total of forty-three), Martino exceeds the promise of the chosen metier to such an extent that the felicities of the remainder are lost.

The details of *Pianississimo* make it one of the great unsuccessful pieces for piano of our time. The concept of a "counterpoint of sentiments" expressed on page 6 of the score could only come from a composer who senses the exact feeling of every note he writes. The assigning of specific, named emotions to dynamic levels is almost naive. (*Mezzopiano* is "expressive" while *mezzoforte* is "elegant"? Even for a few measures? How wonderful if it could be so!) But the attempted fusion, far from being an abstraction, is something other composers can envy. That the composition of this incredible work would help the composer to come even a little bit closer to his dream of notating human emotion in his music is justification enough for its existence.

A decade after *Pianississimo*, Martino produced his masterpiece for solo piano, *Fantasies and Impromptus* (1981). Like the earlier work it has a playing time of about thirty minutes. Unlike *Pianississimo*, however, it is divided into three large sections, and two of these sections are subdivided still further. As a result, given the composer's ongoing narrative style, there are closed segments of aurally satisfying dimensions within a clear beginning-middle-end structure. The balance between style, form, and content is nearly perfect, thus allowing the detailed emotive ideas each to be savored by having been placed in an appropriate context.

There are three relatively long "Fantasies" and six short "Impromptus." In his notes, printed in the score, Martino suggests the following program listing; this listing provides a clear idea of the overall structure, including the placement of pauses, and this can be quite helpful to someone who is hearing the work for the first time.

Fantasies and Impromptus for Solo Piano
Fantasy
    Maestoso—Andante cantabile; Sempre ansioso;
    Maestoso giubilante—Cadenza and Coda
Impromptu
    Sospeso; Tempo rubato
Impromptu
    Giocoso
Impromptu (Omaggio)
    Andante flessibile

—pause—

Fantasy
    Meditativo—Adagietto cantabile—Meditativo

—pause—

Impromptu
    Tempo rubato, sempre ansioso

Impromptu (Omaggio)
Vivace; Animato

Impromptu
Tempo di cadenza

Fantasy
Drammatico; Allegro molto—Allegretto—Allegrettino—
Andantino sentimentale—Allegro molto—Allegretto—
Andante sostenuto; Veloce—Ipnoticamente—Maestoso

As in all his music, the composer is at great pains to inform the performer as to the precise manner of playing and feeling each passage in the work. In the first Fantasy, for example, after an opening bravura passage, a simple melodic phrase moves from "smiling" to "caressing" to "capricious," all of which are related but different, and then changes at the beginning of the next phrase to "anxious" (example 23.3). These admonitions are stimulating, challenging, and helpful to the performer.

EXAMPLE 23.3. Martino, *Fantasies and Impromptus*, Fantasy 1, mm. 6–15. Copyright by Donald Martino. Used by permission of Dantalian, Inc., 11 Pembroke St., Newton, MA 02158.

In Martino's music there is always a line. Sometimes the counterpoint or accompaniment is complex enough that the line is difficult to discern, but the skillful, sensitive performer will always make the projection and shaping of this line a top priority. Naturally, the line reflects the prevailing mood of the moment. It can be agitatedly anxious, as in the crescendo from pianissimo to triple forte near the end of the first Fantasy, or it can be contemplative, as in the third Fantasy with its Mahleresque cantabile (examples 23.4 and 23.5).

The two groups of Impromptus provide colorful, quickly changing styles, thereby making a nice contrast with the longer Fantasies. Each

EXAMPLE 23.4. Martino, *Fantasies and Impromptus*, Fantasy 1, mm. 118–21.

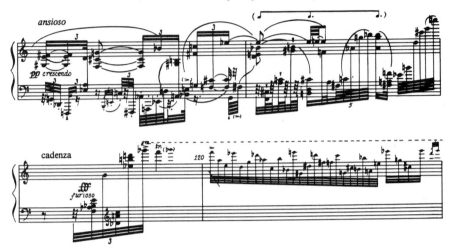

EXAMPLE 23.5. Martino, *Fantasies and Impromptus*, Fantasy 3, mm. 115–26.

group is played without pause, one Impromptu proceeding directly to the next. Particularly beautiful moments of reminiscence are found in the two Impromptus parenthetically entitled "Omaggio." These two movements are not really quotations from earlier composers, nor do they abandon dodecaphonic techniques. In their Brahmsian ardor, they seem nevertheless to reflect the composer's feelings about the highly charged music of late romanticism.

In fact, the writing throughout is basically romantic, as befits the directly emotive intentions of the composer. The writing is technically difficult, but never excessively so. Although the emotional range of the *Fantasies and Impromptus* is enormous, Martino avoids theatricality and showiness, preferring to convince his listener of the genuineness of his music's message through the subtle and refined presentation.

Martino has written two other works for the piano. *Impromptu for Roger* (1977) is an expressively pointillistic hommage to Roger Sessions on his eightieth birthday. It is two pages long. The *Suite in Old Form* (1982) is just what it says it is. Using what he calls "twelve-*tonal*" procedures, the composer writes an Allemande, Courante, Sarabande, and so forth, in a work for students that is rhythmically baroque and melodically and harmonically somewhere between now and then. It is fun to play. Note especially the "Gavotte," which changes key signatures sometimes as often as every two or three beats, just long enough for the composer to move his tongue from one cheek to the other.

Earlier it was suggested that Martino, like Crumb, has not changed his style through his long career. Yet each of his major piano pieces—the *Fantasy, Pianississimo, Fantasies and Impromptus*—is quite different. In fact, the basic langauge of these pieces, written over a quarter of a century, is the same. Martino has never forsaken the constructive qualities of twelve-tone composition (even when writing a little "baroque" work for fun) nor the need to express deep concerns. The expressive differences between works may be extreme, but this is not a matter of style. That the style's emotive possibilities are better expressed in one framework rather than another is a matter that depends largely on the original intent and how well that intent and how well that intent is in synchrony with the final realization. In *Fantasies and Impromptus*, Martino's finest inspiration has been realized, providing pianists and listeners with a musical and emotional experience of rare substance and significance.

CHAPTER TWENTY-FOUR

Frederic Rzewski and William Albright

Two younger American composers, Frederic Rzewski (b. 1938) and William Albright (b. 1944), have composed major works for solo piano, and these works are of a different nature from those of Crumb and Martino. Both Rzewski and Albright were initially influenced by the serial music of the postwar period before they broke away in the 1960s into a kind of music Rzewski describes as "human realism," an eclectic fusion of Western art music, American folk idioms, jazz, and (with Albright) ragtime. Both are splendid pianists (Albright is also a well-known concert organist) and both have virtually unlimited capabilities as improvisers in all styles, an attribute clearly detectable in the spontaneity of their compositions.

Frederic Rzewski was born in Massachusetts and studied at Harvard and Princeton. Like Martino and many others, he worked with Babbitt and Sessions in this country and, on a Fulbright grant, with Dallapiccola in Florence from 1960 to 1961. Remaining in Europe, he became increasingly active as a pianist and teacher, creating something of a sensation as the first performer of Stockhausen's *Klavierstück X*. Interested in live electronic music and improvisation, he co-founded Musica Elettronica Viva in Rome in 1966. Accepting a post as professor of composition at the Royal Conservatory in Liège in 1976, he now divides his time between Belgium and Italy and continues to tour as a pianist.

Rzewski's first important work for solo piano is the astonishing set of variations, *The People United Will Never Be Defeated!* (1975). An hour long, this composition is already recognized as one of the masterworks in the history of variation form.

The theme is perhaps the best-known protest song of the Chilean resistance, "¡El Pueblo Unido Jamás Será Vencido!" (example 24.1). Rzewski's association with political movements in several parts of the world has been close and long-lasting and is reflected in many of his compositions; it is, therefore, no surprise to find such an emotion-charged melody used as the theme for this, his lengthiest work for solo piano. The twelve-bar tune has a number of melodic and harmonic felicities that make it particularly appropriate as the basis for an extended set of vari-

EXAMPLE 24.1. Rzewski, *The People United Will Never Be Defeated!* Theme, mm. 5–16, simplified. © Copyright 1979 by Zen-On Music Co., Ltd. All Rights Reserved. Used by permission of European American Music Distributors Corporation, sole U.S. agent for Zen-On Music Company.

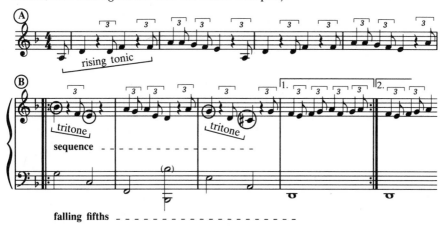

ations: the rising tonic arpeggiation at the beginning, the subsequent melodic sequence with its prominent tritones over an implied cycle of falling fifths, and the easily recognizable, four-square phrase structure— A-B-B, each part four bars long.

Rzewski's setting of the theme, with introductory material and repetitions, is thirty-six measures long. Following the theme are the thirty-six variations, arranged into six groups of six variations each. In the first four of these groups, certain procedures are followed precisely. All of these variations (except Var. 24) are twenty-four measures long; the twelve-bar A-B-B structure is heard twice in each variation, the second setting usually a more complex setting of the first. As an example of this, the simple pointillism of the first four measures of Variation 1, when the tune is repeated to start the second half of the same variation, is filled in with sixteenth notes (examples 24.2 and 24.3).

EXAMPLE 24.2. Rzewski, *The People Untied Will Never Be Defeated!* Variation 1, mm. 1–4.

The first five variations in each group follow this pattern; each has its specific, characteristic figurations. In the sixth variation of each group, however, a summation of the previous five variations is heard. For ex-

EXAMPLE 24.3. Rzewski, *The People United Will Never Be Defeated!* Variation 1, mm. 13–15.

ample, in Variation 6, four measures using figurations from Variation 1 are followed by four measures derived from Variation 2, and so on. By the conclusion of measures 17–20 of Variation 6, all of the previous variations in the group have been sampled. This leaves four final measures (mm. 21–24) in which to make a transition to the next group, where the entire process begins again: Variations 7–11 are followed, in Variation 12, by their summation and a transition to the next group.

Rzewski interrupts this pattern with a sudden rapid tremolo, fifteen to twenty seconds long, appearing, at the end of Variation 24, with its summation of the fourth group. This tremolo seems to signal that the next group will be much freer, as it is indeed is. None of the variations from Variation 25 through Variation 30 is twenty-four measures long, meter signatures change or are omitted, and there is a general feeling of the throwing off of formal constraints. Variation 30, in summing up this freer group, is, appropriately, the longest variation in the entire set.

Variation 31 begins the final group by returning to the twenty-four measure format, but now each variation is retrospective. Variation 31 devotes four bars each to recollections of the first variation of each previous group (i. e., Variations 1, 7, 13, 19, and 25) before moving on through four final measures to Variation 32, reminiscent of the second variation of each group (Variations 2, 8, 14, 20, and 26). Following this procedure, which continues in Variations 33, 34, and 35, the final variation, Variation 36, becomes a summary of *all* previous variations. This is succeeded by an optional improvisation of "anywhere up to five minutes or so" before the theme is restated in a final, extended version.

Such a gigantic structural plan could be a recipe for boredom, with three dozen lengthy variations, most of which are of a predictable formal shape. That the composer captures the listener's interest throughout is a tribute to the fertility of his imagination and ability to work with the most diverse musical materials. The melody is completely tonal, some variations are functionally tonal and diatonic, some are chromatic and less tonally stable, and there are atonal pointillistic variations, pop-style melody-and-accompaniment variations, avant-garde disjunct variations, minimalist-repetition variations, and so on. One cannot predict what will happen from variation to variation, except that the basic form of the |:ABB:| theme will always underlie whatever is going on. Even the summing-up variations, hopping as they often must from style to style, do so convincingly.

It is a matter of interest to investigate how Rzewski makes this melange persuasive. Most pieces, traditional or avant-garde, establish a style at the outset and, no matter how varied the emotional content may be, maintain that musical language to the conclusion. One could say that the initial establishment of a style is a kind of a promise, giving the listener a sense not necessarily of what is going to happen in the piece but of the idiom to be employed. In *The People United*, Rzewski establishes eclecticism as his style. One hears as soon as the theme is completed and the first group of variations begins that the style of the work is, literally, any style. Thereafter he delivers what he has promised, legitimizing stylistic change as a facet of variation technique. To maintain stability he makes sure that each variation remains stylistically homogeneous, never losing sight of the harmonic underpinnings of the fertile Chilean tune, and regularly includes the summing-up variations to reinforce eclecticism as a unifying stylistic device. Taken as a whole, the work is a fantastic musical, emotional, and pianistic experience for performer and listener.

Rzewski's other important works for solo piano include *Four Pieces* (1977), *Squares* (1978), and *North American Ballads* (1979).

The *Four Piano Pieces*, lasting slightly over half an hour, are the composer's least "specific" piano music insofar as extramusical connotations are concerned. No folk tunes or other songs are quoted in any of the movements. The music is charged with emotion, nevertheless. The first piece, starting with what might be described as a folk tune waiting to be born (example 24.4), quickly turns to subterranean tremolos and

EXAMPLE 24.4. Rzewski, *Four Piano Pieces*, first movement, m. 1. © Copyright 1981 by Zen-On Music Co., Ltd. All Rights Reserved. Used by permission of European American Distributors Corporation, sole U.S. agent for Zen-On Music Company.

violent, agitated gestures requiring virtuoso control of the entire keyboard (example 24.5). When the opening tune reappears it is no longer so innocent, with its tremulous, menacing accompaniment.

The second movement, by way of contrast, is labeled "Light + Bouncy." The opening idea, reminiscent of many a jazz lick, sets the tone for this scherzo-like piece (example 24.6). The third piece is slow and brings together an astonishing melange of thoughtful recitative, cimbalom-like broken chord figurations, and passionate, widespread, quasi-"three-handed" counterpoint. As in the Chilean variations, Rzewski proves himself a master at bringing together the most unlikely musical styles in one piece.

EXAMPLE 24.5. Rzewski, *Four Piano Pieces*, first movement, mm. 10–11.

EXAMPLE 24.6. Rzewski, *Four Piano Pieces*, second movement, mm. 1–4.

The fourth movement is a piece about repeated notes and pianistic sonority. To call it a "toccata" is to do it a disservice, but that may be the best conventional term to use. At a measured, steady pace the pianist "opens up" the resonances of the piano, starting at the top and moving rather slowly to the bottom, the constantly repeating notes and chords becoming a subliminally perceived frequency rather than any kind of bravura technical device.

Throughout *The People United* and the *Four Piano Pieces*, Rzewski's ideas surprise and fascinate the listener. With his music, one feels one is dealing with a composer who has come to terms with a century of musical, philosophical, and esthetic decisions by several generations of composers, each affected by individual personalities, national prejudices, and musical heritage. Rzewski has had to make his decisions, too, and has tested them in public as a composer and improviser. Basic to his music seems to be a tremendous need to communicate ideas and feelings by using whatever musical system is appropriate, always adhering to the idea that no matter how free the musical concept, there must be formal coherence for it to be convincing. Neoclassicism, serialism, chance music, jazz, rock, and folk music are all ingredients in his art, as was the ideological breakthrough, unique to the 1970s, that declared that no specific procedure need be adhered to exclusively; that, in fact, there are no mutually exclusive musical territories.

Crumb began to reach tentatively for this conclusion in his quotations (Chopin's *Fantasy-Impromptu*, Beethoven's *Hammerklavier Sonata*, *Dies Irae*, Berlioz's *Damnation of Faust*, and so forth) in the first two volumes of *Makrokosmos*, and goes a step further with the quasi-Spanish song in *Night of the Four Moons* and the long peroration in B major in *Voice of the Whale*. Martino makes wondrous reference to unspecified tonal music in the "Omaggio" sections of *Fantasies and Impromptus*, and, as we shall see, Albright mixes tonal and atonal styles deftly in *Five Chromatic Dances*. Rzewski's music seems to suggest that there is no need to be self-conscious about such things. There are, he is saying, various kinds of music in the world, each with its own set of social and personal connotations. Why not take the endowment we have received from Debussy, Stravinsky, Schoenberg, Ives, Bartók, Stockhausen, Berio, and Cage and, combining it with folk and other popular idioms, apply it freely to the expression of that which was so often concerned the real composer, the personal, political, and social issues of the day?

Thus, in *North American Ballads*, Rzewski can set the grand old tune, "Down by the Riverside," in both a straightforward D major over a down-home bass figure, and then launch into an atonal-contrapuntal discussion of the same tune in a stylistic leap that would have been unthinkable in the flamboyant but restrictive 1960s (examples 24.7 and 24.8).

EXAMPLE 24.7. Rzewski, *North American Ballads*, third movement, mm. 1–6. © Copyright 1982 by Zen-On Music Co., Ltd. All Rights Reserved. Used by permission of European American Distributors Corporation, sole U.S. agent for Zen-On Music Company.

In a setting of an old political tune, "Which Side Are You On?", in the same collection, Rzewski is able to mix complex, many-keyed settings with minimalist techniques and then suggest that the pianist improvise in the same manner(s) "at least as long as the preceding written music."

EXAMPLE 24.8. Rzewski, *North American Ballads*, third movement, mm. 19–20.

Rzewski's music is bold and confrontational, just like his political thinking. As with the music of Crumb and Martino, it has something unique to say that is not heard elsewhere.

William Albright became a student at the University of Michigan at the age of nineteen and a faculty member there at twenty-six. A prodigious talent, he maintains a career in performing, composing, and teaching. As a concert organist he has commissioned and recorded many of the best new works for the instrument, and as a composer he has contributed to the organ repertoire as significantly as anyone after Messiaen. As a performer of piano rags he is largely responsible for the reawakening of interest in Joplin and other early ragtime composers, and he has written several sets of rags and extended piano pieces such as *Grand Sonata in Rag* (1968) in the ragtime idiom.

Pianoàgogo (1966), Albright's earliest published composition for the piano, shows the composer attempting to construct a bridge from the styles of the postwar avant-garde to popular idioms, as Martirano had done a few years before in *Cocktail Music*. Passages of a skittish, atonal nature, written in spatial notation, are interspersed with quiet, dissonant chords that develop a jazz flavor as the piece moves on. Tension accumulates until finally, after a furious, loud trill, the music breaks into a "faster-than-possible" jazz riff with "standard," cliché jazz chords jabbing nervously in the left hand. This breaks off into additional atonal pointillism before the brief work concludes.

During the next ten years Albright found ragtime to be an avenue through which he could completely escape the postwar styles that still haunted him in such works as *Pianoàgogo*. As already mentioned, he not only wrote short rags using traditional formal procedures, he also composed extended pieces in the style. His ear for colorful harmonies and his sense of humor—characteristics shared in abundance with Rzewski— enabled him to endow a somewhat limited idiom with extraordinary variety and vitality.

This is particularly true of *The Dream Rags* (1970), three of his most delightful compositions. The first movement, "Sleepwalker's Shuffle," is a slow, chromatic rag in F-sharp Minor, the trio of which is a boisterous, amusingly scruffy section entitled " 'Chicken Scratch' . . . Harlem Style." The next, "Nightmare Fantasy Rag," subtitled "A Night on Rag Moun-

tain," is undoubtedly one of the longest and most varied rags ever written. After a brief flourish and cadenza at the beginning, the principal
theme, "hard and driving," enters over a boogie bass, (example 24.9).

EXAMPLE 24.9. Albright, *The Dream Rags*, second movement, mm. 19–26. © 1980
Piedmont Music Company. International Copyright Secured. Made in U.S.A. All
Rights Reserved. Used by permission of Hal Leonard Publishing Corporation.

This leads into the first of many digressions, one of Albright's clev-
erest rhythmic ideas (example 24.10). Although scored as simply as
possible—three bars of $\frac{2}{4}$ plus one of $\frac{3}{8}$—the right hand is actually in
groups of five and the left in three, so that they do not coincide until after
fifteen eighth-notes. This somewhat tipsy effect is very amusing. There
is a long, swinging foxtrot for a trio before the opening section returns,
and then, after a cadenza, the coda, in "cruel rock tempo," brings the
work to what can only be described as a rousing conclusion.

EXAMPLE 24.10. Albright, *The Dream Rags*, second movement, mm. 35–38.

The final movement, a "slow drag," is called "Morning Reveries."
The most conventional of the three, it brings the set to a warm and
serene conclusion.

Albright's masterpiece for the piano, *Five Chromatic Dances* (1976),
is full of various dance rhythms (ragtime is not one of them). In this
thirty-minute work the composer takes full advantage of the eclecticism
of the 1970s to reminisce in a personal way about the music of the past.
Specifically, he chooses moments of great emotional intensity in keyboard works of earlier composers and synthesizes them into his own

many-faceted style. This work clarifies the fact that the brief adventure with musical quotation as a subterfuge in order to write tonally, an adventure indulged in by Berio, Rochberg, Crumb, and others, was, by 1976, no longer necessary. Having used ragtime as an avenue to tonality for ten years, just as Rzewski had utilized folk and protest songs, Albright was now able to change harmonic hats confidently without fear of losing the focus of his individual style.

Not all five movements of the *Chromatic Dances* are actually dances. The opening and closing pieces, in fact, have nothing dance-like about them. The second movement, "Masquerade," is indeed a dance, a humorous, lighthearted Debussyan trifle that constantly interrupts itself with little atonal explosions. The "Fantasy-Mazurka" is considerably longer. Improvisatory in nature, its outer sections seem bent on capturing the style, melancholy, harmonic progressions, and melodic figures of the highly chromatic Mazurka in A Minor, Op. 17, No. 4, by Chopin, and almost quote it directly before breaking it off. The middle section, by contrast, is starkly rhythmic, with quiet staccato chords moving steadily over a half-pedaled resonance. The fourth movement, a wildly fiddling "Hoedown" of tremendous, driving energy, has a quieter middle section, habanera-like in character.

To return to the outer, non-dance movements: the first, in two distinct sections, is called "Procession and Rounds." These two contrasting kinds of music may be said to define the expressive and mechanical limits of the piano. The "Procession," slow and steady, is almost entirely in the bass register. "Rounds," fast and unsteady, is in the treble throughout. Both sections are atonal, in contrast to much of the music in the following movements.

The final movement, "The Farewell," is also concerned with the limits of the keyboard. The opening idea is a quiet, simple tune played seven octaves apart at the extremities of the keyboard. Eventually, however, a tremolo-reverberation is established in the center of the instrument and builds to a giant roar, the entire piano vibrating, before the movement dies away, ushering back the return of the simple tune.

The emotional effect of this final movement, the longest of the five, is extraordinarily poignant. The expressive chromatic diversity of the previous four movements is welded together, the sense of "Farewell" being aptly portrayed by the anguished reverberations and lonely, widespread melody. It is a stunning conception, beautifully realized.

In *Sphaera* (1985), for piano and four-channel computer-generated tape, Albright attempts the near impossible: to construct a piece in which there is constant coordination between instrument and tape, yet providing performers with the illusion they are not constricted by the inflexibility of the tape's chronometry. The result is an extended, impressive work in several sections.

Crumb, Rzewski, and Albright all regard the piano as the most important instrument in their musical lives. Like Mozart, Liszt, Debussy, and Bartók before them, they are performer-composers who have found the piano congenial to their most personal musical thoughts on the one hand and most daring compositional experiments on the other. All three, plus non-pianist Martino, completed a substantial list of solo pieces and ensemble works including the piano before they were fifty years old.

Unfortunately this is true of only a few other composers in the 1970s and 1980s. Takemitsu in Japan, Tippett in England, Perle and Helps in this country, as well as Babbitt, Cage, and Rochberg, have each written several works for the instrument in recent years, but the majority of today's composers, many of whom are clearly interested in writing for the piano, have at best produced only a single work. As previously suggested, this has been caused to a great extent by the attitudes prevalent today in almost all institutions devoted to the training and promotion of pianists. These institutions, if they are aware that there is a problem at all, blame the composer and the public, forgetting that the performer has always been the necessary link between creation and dissemination in music. The almost total abdication of responsibility on the part of pianists, their teachers, and their managers for several generations has, ironically, left pianists stranded on a shrinking island as their chosen repertoire washes away and, in turn, leaves composers little choice but to look elsewhere.

That the music for solo piano of the four composers discussed in these three chapters is as expressive, profound, and beautiful as any ever written for the instrument is a value judgment testable under the fingers of any good pianist. The performance of it has a relevance to today's world, just as Beethoven's music had meaning to his day. Performing it, or any of the music mentioned in the following chapters, helps to sustain a vital art—the venerable art of playing the piano.

CHAPTER TWENTY-FIVE

Composers in the Far East and Europe

The explosion of interest in Western music among the peoples of Asian countries in recent years is well documented. Pianists and other instrumentalists, hard-working, highly disciplined, began arriving in this country from Japan and Korea in the 1960s. Taiwan was already sending its best young performers to the United States and Europe for additional study by the time the People's Republic of China began to give its students permission to leave its borders following the disasters of the Cultural Revolution. Malaysians, Thais, and eventually Vietnamese soon were added to the stream of expert young keyboardists who appeared in ever-growing numbers at the doorsteps of Western conservatories and music schools. The influx became so great that special programs had to be established for talented people with minimal skills in English, and activities in the major cities of the Orient were transformed to such an extent that more than one wag suggested that the geographical center of Western musical culture was being transplanted to a spot lying somewhere between Tokyo and Seoul.

That this eruption of interest did not at first include contemporary concert music is hardly surprising. In our own society its place remains somewhat peripheral, a fact hardly lost on bright Oriental visitors. Therefore, interest in advanced Western composing styles did not, at first, grow as quickly as interest in performance areas. However, as a number of composers from the Far East began to win international reputations, a host of younger composers hastened to follow in their footsteps. Entire programs of Japanese, Korean, and Chinese piano music are still rare, but they are possible. The overall Oriental impact on both pianism and the composition of music for the piano will be fascinating to observe in the next generation.

Isang Yun, from Korea, has already been mentioned (chapter 18). Piano music by at least two other older composers from the Far East, both Japanese, should be briefly discussed.

Toru Takemitsu

Toru Takemitsu (b. 1930) is from Tokyo. He is essentially a self-taught composer, which is surely one reason that his ideas are so refreshing. In contrast to Isang Yun's desire to write Korean music on Western instruments, Takemitsu has often written Western-style music featuring Japanese instruments.

Takemitsu's primary compositional interests have to do with texture, timbre, and silence. Even his early piano pieces, such as *Piano Distance* (1961), a slow, four-page work, involve long, quiet resonances and extended, silent fermatas. There is little if any sense of climax or progression from one musical place to another; rather, a scene is set, remains unmoving, and disappears.

For Away (1973) is Takemitsu's most extended work for piano, lasting five or six minutes (example 25.1). The sound of the piece may remind one of a fine piece of jewelry, shining and glowing quietly with brief flashes of surging energy and power.

EXAMPLE 25.1. Takemitsu, *For Away*, lines 1 and 2. Used by permission of G. Schirmer, Inc. on behalf of copyright owner Editions Salabert.

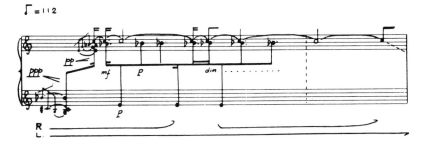

Though there are no bar lines, the composer employs conventional note values and assigns a metronomic value to the eighth-note.

One is tempted to suggest that there is an Oriental aura of contemplation in *For Away* and in a later work by Takemitsu, *Les yeux clos* (1979). Indeed, the music easily conjures up visions of Japanese silkscreen wall hangings with their exotic, unreal perspectives and other-worldly mountains, waterfalls, and misty clouds.

Akira Miyoshi

Akira Miyoshi (b. 1933) was also born in Tokyo. He studied composition in Japan and France and also has advanced degrees in French literature. Presently he is chairman of the Toho Gakuen School of Music, Tokyo's finest music school.

An early *Piano Sonata* (1958), skillfully written for the instrument, is not as interesting as the composer's later work, though its extraordinary difficulty has given it a certain notoriety in Japan as a "test piece" in which pianists may exhibit their technical prowess.

Miyoshi's mature compositional style, first coming to the fore in his wonderful *Concerto for Orchestra* (1964), reflects not only the effect of his work with French composers but also a preoccupation with Buddhist concepts of time, space, life, and death. This is most evident in what may be his most successful composition for piano solo, *Chaînes* (1973). In this work Miyoshi creates a notation that attempts to link music to the unconscious rhythms of breathing, rhythms that change speed and intensity in accordance with different moods, emotions, and states of being.

Chaînes is in five sections. The first, third, and last sections are extended, usually beginning softly and slowly and leading to exciting, violent climaxes. The shorter second and fourth sections serve as quiet interludes.

The notation is purposely ambiguous much of the time, leaving considerable room for interpretive nuance. The opening, for example, is spatially notated (as is much of the work) and includes such devices as arrows delineating sound decay, time spans marked in seconds, short-lived metronomic indications, and unusual grace-note figures. There is also the initial indication, "respiration longue" ("long breath"), which shortly becomes "respiration pressée" ("short breath") (example 25.2).

EXAMPLE 25.2. Miyoshi, *Chaînes*, section 1, line 1. © Copyright 1976 by Zen-On Ltd., Tokyo, Japan. International Copyright Secured. All Rights Reserved. Used by permission of European American Distributors Corporation, sole U.S. agent for Zen-On Ltd.

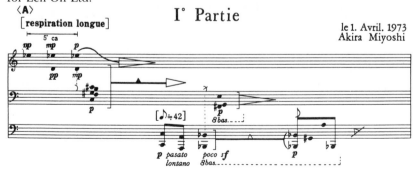

Other unusual kinds of notation include passages such as the one shown in example 25.3 in which the music in "balloons" is to be inserted *ad libitum*, and the nature of the performer's (and the music's) breathing changes more rapidly than before—slow, fast, calm, slow, fast (example 25.3). Also, notes with and without stems intermingle freely and ambiguously.

EXAMPLE 25.3. Miyoshi, *Chaînes*, section 3, mm. 1–4.

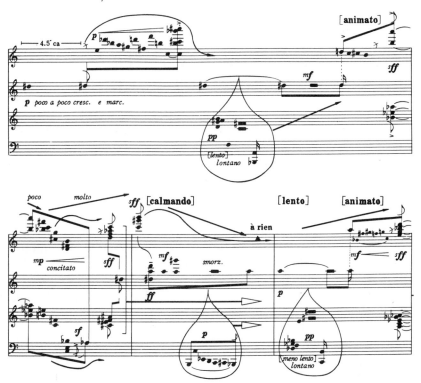

Harmonically the work is fascinating and beautiful. Miyoshi's musical language is somewhat reminiscent of Messiaen, with the latter's use of "color chords" clearly an influence. His use of different portions of the keyboard for diverse harmonic effects is sumptuous and dramatic. The writing can be virtuosic, moving rapidly around the instrument as climaxes start to develop (example 25.4).

Above all, however, the emotional impact of the work, its involvement not just with breathing (life) but, at the end, the cessation of breathing (beyond life), makes *Chaînes* a unique work. A thoughtful, beautiful piece, it is the most substantial recent work for solo piano from the Orient.

Example 25.4. Miyoshi, *Chaînes*, section 5, mm. 60–68.

Sir Michael Tippett

The distinguished English composer Sir Michael Tippett (b. 1905) has written two piano sonatas in recent years. The *Third Sonata* dates from 1973 and the *Fourth Sonata*, which was premiered in this country, from 1984. Both are large works, especially the latter, which is more than thirty-five minutes long.

Both sonatas utilize neoclassic forms and gestures, but although Tippett is an imaginative, forceful composer, the piano perhaps no longer responds well to these styles. There is in this music a surprising amount of repetition that is difficult to justify, especially given the composer's limited concepts of pianistic sonority. These large works are difficult to bring off and should be approached with caution.

Other European Composers

More successful is a set of pieces by the Scottish composer Iain Hamilton (b. 1922) called *Palinodes* (1972). Written in an assured, individualistic manner, the work is subtitled "Seven Studies after Lines of Rimbaud," and each of the seven movements has the appropriate line printed in French at the top of the page. The style is pleasantly evocative, leaning toward impressionism in an exploration of the sensuous, coloristic potentialities of the piano. Hamilton is also the composer of three sonatas for the piano (1973, 1976, and 1978) of varying strengths and attractiveness.

One of the very best short pieces from Europe in recent times is the exciting *Improvvisazioni* (1972) by the Hungarian composer Miklós Kocsár (b. 1933), professor of composition at the Budapest Conservatory. The work makes an extremely strong musical statement with clearly presented, well-developed ideas and a dramatic exploitation of pianistic color.

Improvvisazioni employs a mixture of spatial notation and traditional rhythmic durations, a notation that may pose a few queries in the mind of the pianist in the initial learning stages. The performer can be assured that these minor inconsistencies become insignificant as one becomes familiar with the style and procedures of the piece.

The principal ideas are strong, simple, and eminently recognizable. Kocsár makes excellent use of immediately varied repetition to reinforce the importance of motivic ideas when they are first presented. For example, the opening figure is partially repeated as an echo (*quasi eco*) and then played again in full in an altered tempo and dynamic. This convincingly establishes the importance of the motive (example 25.5). A second prominent idea is even simpler than the first: a rhythmic, two-note "call," which returns in countless configurations (example 25.6).

EXAMPLE 25.5. Kocsár, *Improvvisazioni*, lines 1 and 2. © Copyright 1974. Reprinted by permission of Boosey & Hawkes, Inc., U.S. Agent.

The title refers to the many passages in which figurations, usually moving in an upward direction, are partially written out by the composer and then, with the appearance of wavy lines, improvised by the pianist (example 25.7).

There are also passages in which one hand repeats a figure over and over while the other plays rhythmically unrelated chords or phrases. These improvisatory devices are well integrated into the style of the piece; the listener is never aware of seams between written and improvised music.

Improvvisazioni contains three parts, the middle section being slower and quieter than the outer parts. The sections are well balanced, and transitions between them are completely convincing. The final climax, in which single repeated notes in the center of the instrument are punc-

EXAMPLE 25.6. Kocsár, *Improvvisazioni*, page 4, lines 3 and 4.

EXAMPLE 25.7. Kocsár, *Improvvisazioni*, page 7, lines 4 and 5.

tuated by accented versions of the second motive, now at the extremities of the keyboard, is unique and extremely impressive.

A Hungarian composer whose name is more familiar to most musicians is György Ligeti (b. 1923). His first important work for the solo piano, *Études pour piano—premier livre*, was completed in 1985. These six pieces are as much studies in composition as pianistic études. Each explores a certain compositional process; for example, the barlines are gradually displaced, figures are systematically and continuously transposed, or irrational rhythmic complexities are methodically introduced. Each study begins with a certain characteristic figuration, usually quite simple at the outset, then subjected to a logical and continuous series of operations.

All of these operations bear directly on the increasing pianistic difficulties they bring about, of course. This is particularly noteworthy in the third étude, "Touches bloquées" ("Blocked Keys"), in which one hand silently holds down a small but changing cluster of notes while the other plays quick chromatic figures involving keys of which some are held and some are not. Obviously, the keys that are blocked do not sound, but striking them is, nevertheless, essential to the rhythmic configuration of the music. The results are ingenious if not compelling.

Klavierstück n. 5 (tombeau) (1975) by Wolfgang Rihm (b. 1952) and *Lemma-Icon-Epigram* (1981) by Brian Ferneyhough (b. 1943) epitomize the piano music now coming out of Germany (Ferneyhough is English, a native of Coventry, but he is strongly influenced by Stockhausen and has held important academic posts in German universities). Both pieces strike the listener as being extraordinarily angry, with a great deal of unrelenting hammering at the piano. Page after page of Rihm's *Klavierstück* is marked *fff*, reinforced often by *sffff* indications. Ferneyhough's much longer piece is surely as complex as any music ever written for the piano and is full of energy so intense and unremitting as to seem psychotic (example 25.8).

Perhaps this music properly reflects the socio-political fears of central Europe today. Possibly, however, it is self-indulgent complexity and sonic violence carried to an unnecessarily cruel level of intensity. In any case, it is difficult to justify this music as either an intellectual experience or as an emotional one.

If one can feel optimistic about the creative possibilities in the Far East, the opposite is presently true in Europe, at least insofar as piano music is concerned. The explosive fertility of the postwar years seems to have given way to a period of relative inactivity, now becoming more and more extended. What remains to be seen is if a revival of activity in this area takes place before the century ends. If not, one may well speculate that the life of the piano as a tool of European artistic and creative ingenuity may be over.

EXAMPLE 25.8. Ferneyhough, *Lemma-Icon-Epigram*, mm. 51–57. © 1976 by Peters Edition, Ltd., London. Used by permission of C. F. Peters Corporation.

CHAPTER TWENTY-SIX

Other Composers in America

Of the composers in the United States and Canada not already discussed at length, a large number have written at least one work for the piano in the 1970s and 1980s. Of this music, Elliott Carter's *Night Fantasies* (1980) will be considered by many to be the most significant (his earlier *Piano Sonata* is briefly discussed in chapter 20). This work, commissioned by four of the century's finest pianists involved in the performance of contemporary music—Paul Jacobs, Gilbert Kalish, Ursula Oppens, and Charles Rosen—is one of substantial length, complexity, and technical difficulty.

In his preface to the composition, Carter describes *Night Fantasies* as a "piece of continuously changing moods, suggesting the fleeting thoughts and feelings that pass through the mind during a period of wakefulness at night." He also writes that he wished to capture the "poetic moodiness" he hears in the music of Robert Schumann. Thus, *Night Fantasies* is constantly changing character, one episode interrupted by another in a fanciful, flighty way.

A problem for many listeners, even with repeated hearings, is to perceive coherent shape or growth in this piece, which lasts more than twenty-two minutes. Schumann, in most of his lengthy works, achieves poetic variety by creating a sequence of short, diverse pieces, each with its own romantic character. At the same time he creates a feeling of structure for the entire composition by writing each of these little pieces in a coherent, easily recognizable shape. Crumb does exactly the same thing to good effect in *Makrokosmos*, and Martino appears to have been far more successful with just such a procedure in *Fantasies and Impromptus* than he was in the equally long, single-movement *Pianississimo*. This is not to suggest that a composer of Carter's genius should not write an extended work in one movement; such an insinuation would be presumptuous. However, to carry the Schumann parallel just a bit further, one would like to hear Carter's "Florestan" and "Eusebius" characters more clearly drawn, or, to put it in more contemporary language, one would rather not have constantly to absorb so much diverse information without structural reference points. Certain kinds of compositional procedures may be effective for five minutes but do not sustain interest for twenty-two. Neither complexity nor incomprehensibility can ensure profundity, much less communication, though they may bring about a temporary awe among those who are impressed by obfuscation. Carter has a tendency, mentioned several times earlier with regard to the music of Xenakis and Babbitt, to "use up" the piano too quickly, and the constant alternations in his music tend to take on a certain grayness.

This does not happen with the splendid, amusing, challenging *Six Études* (1973–1976) by George Perle (b. 1915). Perle has been an important figure in twentieth-century music in a number of ways. He was, for example, one of the first composers in this country to be attracted to the twelve-tone technique and much of his career has been devoted to adapting Schoenbergian principles and procedures according to his own devising. His final conclusions in this are illustrated in his music and described in his *Twelve-Tone Tonality*,[1] published just after the completion of *Six Études*.

Perle has written a considerable amount of piano music in his highly developed, personal style. It is dodecaphonic, yet individual pieces tend to gravitate toward certain pitches as "tonics." There are neoclassic elements in his forms and textures, yet Perle does not fall into the clichés of the genre. His themes and (above all) rhythms are clear and comprehensible, and the music avoids sentiment to a fault.

This last attribute is not always a plus. The *Short Sonata* (1964) is a clever three-movement piece embodying Perle's style exactly as described. Possibly a bit more sentiment, perhaps in the middle movement, would have made the work more successful. Its wry humor wears thin simply because it lacks warmth.

Perle's austere emotional approach is never a problem, however, in *Six Études*. Here, form and content come together perfectly in these delightful (two-minute average) pieces.

The *Six Études* require superb control of touch and dynamics. Probably more important is the mental discipline required, especially if the music is to be played from memory. Perle does not allow the pianist to fall into rote finger patterns: similar passages repeat several times, but each time they begin on different chromatic degrees. To illustrate: a two-measure figure from the fourth *étude* (example 26.1), is heard again

EXAMPLE 26.1. Perle, *Six Études*, No. 4, mm. 1–2. Copyright 1977 Margun Music, Inc., assigned to GunMar Music, Inc. 1985. International Copyright Secured. Reprinted by permission.

moments later a half step lower (example 26.2). Then, after a passage including other material, it returns again, this time another half step lower. Much later in the same piece it appears a whole step higher than the original, then again a half step higher. This is just one example. Obviously the performer must remain vigilant to keep these transpositions straight.

EXAMPLE 26.2. Perle, *Six Études*, No. 4, mm. 8–9.

One of Perle's more extended piano pieces is the single-movement *Ballade* (1981), which lasts nine minutes. Here the composer appears to make an unabashedly lyric, romantic statement in a manner he previously seemed to avoid. Perhaps a lifetime study of Schoenberg and Berg had convinced him that such indulgences need do no injury to his compositional concepts! If there is a weakness in the piece, it is that the music is written almost entirely in the mid-range of the instrument. Somewhat more variety, especially later in the work, would have been welcome.

Six New Études (1984) return, for the most part, to the sparkling nature of the first set, with similar technical requirements.

Mario Davidovsky (b. 1934) was born in Buenos Aires and had most of his musical training there. During the summer of 1958 he attended the Berkshire Music Festival and met Milton Babbitt, who encouraged him to come to the United States.

In 1960 Davidovsky began work at the Columbia-Princeton Electronic Music Center. His skill as an electronic composer is demonstrated in his carefully wrought, imaginative *Synchronisms* series, which combines instruments and tape. *Synchronisms No. 6 for Piano and Electronic Sounds* (1970) deservedly won the first Pulitzer Prize ever given to a piano piece (example 26.3).

Of the hundreds of piano-and-tape pieces now in existence, *Synchronisms No. 6* may well be the most effective. Short and unprepossessing, it consists of a series of phrases, each of which electronically explores sounds related to those that can be made on the piano, turning and combining them in ways the piano cannot. For example, as the opening note of the piano part fades, the tape enters with a crescendo on the same pitch in a synthesized piano sonority, a simple enough idea, but one that indicates that the tape will complement the piano throughout, which it does in a very affecting way.

Much of the seven-minute piece requires split-second coordination, but there are moments at the ends of sections in which exact synchrony

EXAMPLE 26.3. Davidovsky, *Synchronisms No. 6 for Piano and Electronic Sounds*, mm. 22–24. © 1972 by Edward B. Marks Music Company. International Copyright Secured. Made in U.S.A. All Rights Reserved. Used by permission of Hal Leonard Publishing Corporation.

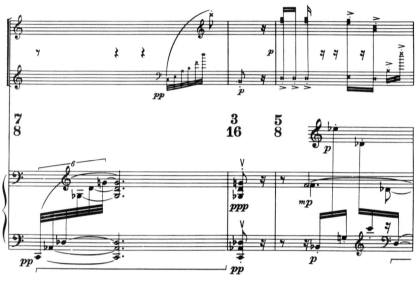

15590 - 21

is unnecessary, giving a sense of relaxation that actually helps to define the structure. Near the end there is an extended piano solo, a cadenza, so to speak, after which a short coda ends the piece.

The score is carefully notated, looking a bit like a standard piano concerto reduction for two pianos. The tape part is above, on smaller staves, with all rhythms and enough pitches indicated so the pianist has no problem coordinating properly.

William Bolcom (b. 1938) has written a number of works for the piano. A close associate of William Albright—both teach at the University of Michigan—Bolcom, too, has published several collections of ragtime pieces. His most substantial contributions to the piano repertoire, however, are two sets of studies. In 1966 he completed *Twelve Études for Piano; Twelve New Études for Piano* were finished in 1986 and, two years later, Bolcom received the Pulitzer Prize in music, the second work for piano to have done so.

In both sets of études a large variety of contemporary pianistic techniques is addressed. Rhythmic notation receives a particularly wide range of treatment, from very "tight," strictly metric writing in some études to free, "loose" presentation in others in which the rhythm is little more than suggested.

Overall, there is a pleasing casualness to the sound and flow of most of the études in both sets. The composer's superlative gifts as an improviser seem to be reflected everywhere. However, just as Bolcom has fooled many an audience into thinking that what he was doing at the keyboard was easy, these fascinating studies, whatever their apparent insouciance, are often devilishly difficult to play. As a result of mastering the études in either set, the pianist will find most of the music discussed in this book more approachable.

One of the most unusual piano pieces ever written is the four-movement *Rhapsodies* (1973) by composer-pianist Curtis Curtis-Smith (b. 1941). Seeking a way to do the impossible, a crescendo on a single note, Curtis-Smith experimented for a long time with the idea of bowing the strings. After much research and experimentation, he found that four-pound monofilament nylon fishing line, in groups of six to twenty strands (depending on the size of the strings to be activated) and held together at the ends with color-coded, tape-covered paper clips, gave the most satisfactory results.

The first movement of *Rhapsodies*, a quick-moving, improvisatory piece, is performed entirely on the keys, building slowly in asymmetrical groups of repeated notes and tremolos from the center of the keyboard up to the highest range.

The second movement introduces the first bowed note (the bows must be inserted before the performance as specified by the detailed drawings and instructions at the beginning of the score). It is a quiet pedal-point to the slow-moving chords that open the piece. The pianist slowly and steadily pulls the bow with one hand while playing the chords with the other. There are only three bowed notes in the movement, all acting as pedal-points. In addition, several bass notes are rolled with a timpani mallet, and there is considerable use of pizzicato, sometimes with the fingertip and sometimes with a guitar pick.

The third movement is the most complex of the four, employing many bows, almost all involving two or more pitches and requiring two hands to operate. Curtis-Smith has devised techniques by which notes can be plucked or otherwise played while one is bowing with both hands, a tricky procedure requiring a great deal of practice, especially because the bowing must be executed smoothly, fading gently in and out, emerging imperceptibly from previous sonorities.

The final movement is almost entirely bowed. Here the performer uses a very long, thick bow (alas, standing to do so), which is wound around two low bass strings very close to the tuning pins. By moving the bow back and forth laterally on the string, different partials can be obtained, some of which are very high and others close to the fundamental pitches of the two strings. There are several other effects, including whistling and a bottle glissando, which contribute to making the final movement an exotic sound experience.

One of the principal problems in performing *Rhapsodies* is a practical one. Lasting something less than twenty minutes, it takes at least that much time to put the bows in place. Because the bows tend to mute or deaden certain strings, they cannot be inserted until immediately before the performance unless (as mentioned earlier in connection with the prepared piano pieces of John Cage) one has two instruments available for a program or, as an alternative, *Rhapsodies* is the only piano piece in a mixed concert. Such problems, of course, can be solved.

A second problem, more difficult to resolve, may be less worrisome for some people than for the author. In a live performance, the piece seems so visually fascinating that many listeners turn into *spectators* and actually hear very little of the music. It may be that, for some, *Rhapsodies* is one of those rare pieces that works better on recording than in live performance.

The music itself is extremely intuitive, and the structuring of individual pieces is sometimes a bit unwieldy. But Curtis-Smith must be credited with a unique exploration of piano resonance—an exploration he carries on with more startling effect in two duos, *Five Sonorous Inventions* (1973) for violin and piano, and *Unisonics* (1976) for saxophone and piano, both of which are highly recommended.

One of the most beautiful and imaginative piano pieces of the 1970s is *Eclogue* (1974) by Richard Wilson (b. 1941). Wilson, a member of the music faculty of Vassar College, is himself an excellent pianist, and *Eclogue* reflects his intimate understanding of the instrument's sonorous possibilities.

Wilson brings together a highly chromatic Schoenbergian lyricism with a kind of Scriabinesque-Ravellian harmonic and pianistic style. There are long, beautifully written passages in which quiet, sensuous chords float under a repeated-note figuration (example 26.4), leading eventually to an extended arpeggiation passage that reminds one of the climax of Ravel's "Ondine" (example 26.5). Following an impressive climax, there is a particularly memorable quiet section in which guitar-like muted notes accompany simple melodic figures. All in all, *Eclogue* is the stunning realization of a well-conceived musical plan.

Of all the music discussed in this chapter, Wilson's is the most purely "pianistic." This is also true of two more recent works, *Fixations* and *Intercalations*, both of which were written in 1985. The latter, its four movements contrasting vividly, is wonderful, colorful writing. Many performers will, in fact, find it even more attractive than the masterful *Eclogue*.

Another fascinating piece of medium duration is *Appello* (1976) by Barbara Kolb (b. 1939). Kolb earlier had written a charming, atmospheric work for piano and tape called *Solitaire* (1971), a melange of quotations and semi-quotations from Scarlatti, Chopin, and others. *Appello* is a more ambitious kind of piece, exemplifying among other things the composer's eclectic use of different notational styles in a single, unified composition.

EXAMPLE 26.4. Wilson, *Eclogue*, mm. 85–87. © Copyright 1980 by Boosey & Hawkes, Inc. Reprinted by permission.

EXAMPLE 26.5. Wilson, *Eclogue*, mm. 105–106.

There are four different notational systems in the four movements of *Appello*. Some are rhythmically exact, such as the first, with its carefully specified repeated sonorities and, more particularly, the third, which is based on a sophisticated Boulezian time-point organization. The second and fourth movements are in a much freer rhythmic notation. Interestingly enough, in performance one hears a reversal of what the notation would seem to specify, probably because performers tend unconsciously to play music written with free rhythmic notation periodically, whereas carefully notated, aperiodic rhythms, played correctly, will often sound improvised and free.

Kolb has written a dramatic piece that mixes serial and minimalist techniques in an original and logical way. The four movements build effectively to a decisive close.

One of the most enchanting piano pieces of recent years is by Ann Silsbee (b. 1930) of Ithaca, New York. *Doors* (1976) is a sound-piece in which resonances created by clever use of the middle pedal make the piano's continuing sonorities as captivating during moments when the pianist is not playing as when he is (example 26.6). Borrowing a technique from Crumb, Silsbee begins *Doors* by depressing all the bass notes silently, catching them with the sostenuto pedal. She then begins the music with a series of clusters played in the upper registers of the keyboard, the resonances of which are picked up by the open bass strings. The effect is stunning. The heavy, curved lines are clusters rolled with either forearm; numbers under large fermatas between measures indicate the lengths of resonances.

EXAMPLE 26.6. Silsbee, *Doors*, lines 1 and 2. All Rights Reserved by the Composer, 1976. Reprinted by Permission of American Composers Alliance, New York.

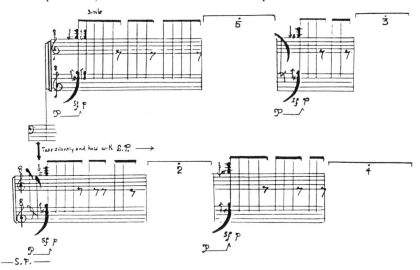

Soon after this passage, in a series of small rolled clusters played by the flat of the hand, she marks the music "quasi parlando" ("as if speaking"). Indeed, with their irregular rhythmic patterns, the rising and falling clusters seem to imitate spoken syllables grouped into words and phrases. Many types of "parlando" figurations, some quite different from those at the opening, are developed before the piece concludes. There is a genuine sense of adventure about this unique work. Silsbee, a fine pianist herself, has made some fascinating discoveries that she communicates skillfully in *Doors*.

Phrygian Gates (1978) is by John Adams (b. 1947), an easterner who, after studying with Kirchner at Harvard, migrated west, teaching for many years at the San Francisco Conservatory, directing the New Music Ensemble there, and eventually, in the mid-1980s, becoming composer-in-residence with the San Francisco Symphony Orchestra.

Adams is at the forefront of the minimalist movement, with orchestral and operatic works, noted for their color and rhythmic élan, to his credit. *Phrygian Gates* is one of his first minimalist compositions. Using "gating" procedures to move from one figuration to another (the word is derived from electronic music) he has constructed a *very* long piece—sixty-one pages, 1092 measures—in which, unlike most minimalist scores, every note is written out, there are no repeat signs, and dynamics and pedalings are carefully notated. Although the time-to-event ratio is high in this music, with its constantly flowing pan-diatonicism, Adams is not oblivious to the possibilities of an old-fashioned dramatic buildup, which occasionally saves the piece from being another repetitious bore. At the same time his reliance on the well-known minimalist hypnotic aura in order for one to be able to accept long stretches of unchallenging, pretty sonorities is not for everyone. It is undeniably true that there has been a great deal of overly intellectual music written in the present century; this is its opposite number, and its negative implications are just as disturbing.

The *Six Fantasy Pieces for Piano* (1982) by the Canadian composer-pianist Alfred Fisher (b. 1942) rank among the strongest piano works of the last two decades (example 26.7). Fisher, originally from the Bronx but now a professor of composition at the University of Alberta in Edmonton, is a man of deep social convictions and outspoken musical beliefs. These pieces brilliantly express the perceptions of a passionate, serious, introspective human being.

Some of the six pieces are portraits of Canadian Indians Fisher has known and with whom he has worked (one summer he was an "Indian" guide in the northern territories—"the only Jewish Caucasian Indian guide any of the tourists had ever seen"). Other pieces seem more abstract, but all of them, says the composer, are "confessional." The language is sometimes highly chromatic, as in the intensely animated, almost frenzied "Arik"; others, such as the mournful "There Is My People Sleeping," are folk-like in their simplicity. This is a remarkable set of heartfelt pieces.

Other works by American composers that deserve more than just the mention they receive here includes the brief but virile *Three Short Fantasies* (1971) by Yehudi Wyner (b. 1929), the effective *Phoenix* (1971) by Robert Moevs (b. 1920), which is surely one of the most impressive pieces of pure contrapuntal writing of recent times, the beautifully written *3 Hommages* (1973) by the composer-pianist Robert Helps (b. 1928), and the formally uneven but still dazzling *Fantasy* (1973) by Lawrence Moss (b. 1927). The irrepressible Tom Johnson (b. 1939), whose *Scene for*

EXAMPLE 26.7. Fischer, *Six Fantasy Pieces for Piano*, No. 1, "Arik," mm. 1–15.
Copyright 1983 by Seesaw Music Corp., New York. All Rights Reserved. Used by
permission.

Piano and Tape (1969) is one of the few genuinely funny theater pieces for
a pianist, has contributed several "straight" piano pieces to the repertoire, including *Septapede* (1973), the quintessential minimal piece in
which, over a quarter of an hour on a good day or five or six minutes on
a bad one, absolutely nothing happens (in tiny, tiny increments). David
Chaitkin's (b. 1938) somewhat over-refined but always expressive *Études*
(1974) should be mentioned here, as should the impressive *Étude Fantasy*
(1976) by John Corigliano (b. 1938) and the searing, vibrant *Hyperbolae*
(1977) by Shulamit Ran (b. 1949). Strong works from the 1980s include
such diverse compositions as *Masks* (1980) by the prolific Robert Muczynski (b. 1929), the granitic *Sonata* (1982) by Richard Wernick (b. 1934),

the lovely, romantic *Bagatalles* (1985) by Peter Lieberson (b. 1936), and the intense yet song-like *Five Pieces for Piano* (1986) by Leon Kirchner, whose fine *Sonata* was discussed in chapter 20.

On the basis of the evidence presented here, it would seem that the majority of good music for solo piano written in the 1970s and 1980s, and the most varied stylistic selection as well, comes from composers living in this country. The evidence may be at fault, of course; the author lives in the United States and it would be expected that he would have more contact with American composers and publishers than those from other parts of the world. Yet, on numerous trips abroad to lecture, teach, and perform, little has been found to contradict these conclusions.

Since 1970 in this country, the variety of styles employed in the composition of solo piano music has been both numerous and heartening. Serial music, best exemplified by the final piano pieces of Roger Sessions, has been composed by Babbitt, Wuorinen, Carter, Perle, Martino, and Kolb. Experimental sound-pieces by Curtis-Smith and Ann Silsbee complement the continued exploration of pianistic sonorities by Crumb, while the combination of piano and electronic sounds has been investigated thoroughly by Davidovsky, Albright, and countless others. Carry-overs from the indeterminate world of the 1960s still exist in the scores of Cage and Feldman at the same time that minimalism, probably a stepchild of Cage's own early prepared piano pieces, has been promulgated by such diverse composers as Tom Johnson and John Adams. Meanwhile, the "new romanticism" continues in piano pieces by Rochberg, Albright, Helps, and Lieberson, while strong, individualistic pieces, making eclectic use of all available styles, have come from Wilson, Fisher, and Rzewski.

Of course such categorizations are unfair and misleading. Arthur C. Danto has recently written that "the language of the critic is as dangerous as a paralyzing dart" in that "the critical designation of an artistic movement redirects the movement it intends to label."[2] But terms such as serialism, indeterminism, eclecticism, new romanticism, minimalism— none of them new—are used here only as an aid in illustrating the diversity that can be found in recent American piano music. If the pianist interested in new music had reason to be pessimistic at the end of the 1960s, those reasons evaporated a few years later. If, in fact, European composers no longer write so prolifically for the piano, their music from the 1950s and 1960s still needs to be assimilated better into the repertoire, as do the new sounds from the Orient and the ever-growing activity in South America, Australia, and nearly everywhere else.

Meanwhile, there is this wonderful body of literature from American composers that serious pianists need to make known to their audiences everywhere. If this book, a true labor of love, helps in even a small way to bring this about, it has been well worth the effort.

Selected Bibliography

Bartók, Béla. *A Memorial Review.* New York: Boosey & Hawkes, 1950. Includes: "The Influence of Peasant Music on Modern Music," 71–76.

Berger, Arthur. *Aaron Copland.* New York: Oxford University Press, 1953.

Bertensson, Sergei and Jay Leyda. *Sergei Rachmaninoff: A Lifetime in Music.* New, York: New York University Press, 1956.

Boulez, Pierre. *Conversations with Célestin Deliège.* London: Eulenberg Books, 1976.

Bunger, Richard. *The Well-Prepared Piano.* Colorado Springs: The Colorado College Press, 1973.

Burkholder, J. Peter. *Charles Ives: The Ideas behind the Music.* New Haven: Yale University Press, 1985.

Butterworth, Neil. *The Music of Aaron Copland.* London: Toccata Press, 1985.

Cage, John. *Silence.* Middletown: Wesleyan University Press, 1961.

Casella, Alfredo. *Music in My Time: The Memoirs of Alfredo Casella.* Translated and edited by Spencer Norton. Norman: Oklahoma University Press, 1955.

Collaer, Paul. *A History of Modern Music.* Translated by Sally Abeles. New York: Grosset & Dunlap, 1961.

Cone, Edward T., ed. *Roger Sessions on Music: Collected Essays.* Princeton: Princeton University Press, 1979.

Copland, Aaron, and Vivian Perlis. *Copland, 1900 through 1942.* New York: St. Martin's and Marek, 1984.

Cowell, Henry, and Sidney Cowell. *Charles Ives and His Music.* Rev. London: Oxford University Press, 1969.

Crow, Todd. *Bartók Studies.* Detroit Reprints in Music. Detroit: Information Coordinators, 1976.

Dallapiccola, Luigi. *Appunti, incontri, meditazioni.* Milan: Edizioni Suvini Zerboni, 1970.

Gartenberg, Egon. *Vienna: Its Musical Heritage.* University Park: The Pennsylvania State University Press, 1968.

Gena, Peter, and Jonathan Brent, comp. and ed. *A John Cage Reader.* New York: C. F. Peters Corp., 1982.

Gillespie, Don, ed. *George Crumb: Profile of a Composer.* New York: C. F. Peters Corp., 1986.

Griffiths, Paul. *A Concise History of Avant-Garde Music, from Debussy to Boulez.* New York: Oxford University Press, 1978.

Henck, Herbert. *Karlheinz Stockhausen's Klavierstück X: A Contribution toward Understanding Serial Technique.* Translated by Deborah Richards. Cologne: Neuland Musikverlag, 1980.

Hinson, Maurice. *Guide to the Pianist's Repertoire*, 2nd, rev. and enl. Bloomington: Indiana University Press, 1987.

Hitchcock, H. Wiley: *Ives: A Survey of the Music*. London: Oxford University Press, 1977.

Hull, A. Eaglefield. *Scriabin: A Great Russian Tone-Poet*. London: Kegan Paul, Trench, Trubner & Co., Ltd., 1927.

Ives, Charles: *Essays before a Sonata, The Majority, and Other Writings*. Edited by H. Boatwright. New York: Norton, 1970.

———. *Memos*. Edited by John Kirkpatrick. New York: Norton, 1972.

Johnson, Robert Sherlaw. *Messiaen*. Berkeley: University of California Press, 1975.

Krenek, Ernst. *Music Here and Now*. Translated by Barthold Fles. New York: Norton, 1939.

Leibowitz, René. *Schoenberg and His School*. Rev. ed. Translated by Dika Newlin. New York: Da Capo Press, 1970.

Lesznai, Lajos. *Bartók*. Translated by Percy M. Young. London: J. M. Dent & Sons, Ltd., 1973.

Mead, Rita. *Henry Cowell's New Music 1925–1936: The Society, the Music Editions, and the Recordings*. Ann Arbor: University Microfilms International, 1981.

Messiaen, Olivier. *Technique of My Musical Language*. Translated by John Satterfield. Paris: Alphonse Leduc, 1956.

Moldenhauer, Hans. *The Death of Anton Webern*. New York: Philosophical Library, 1961.

Myers, Rollo. *Modern French Music: From Fauré to Boulez*. New York: Praeger Publishers, 1971.

Nestyev, Israel V. *Prokofieff*. Translated by Florence Jonas. Stanford: Stanford University Press, 1961.

Nichols, Roger. *Messiaen*. London: Oxford University Press, 1975.

———. *Ravel*. London: J. M. Dent & Sons, Ltd., 1977.

Perle, George. *Serial Composition and Atonality*. 4th, rev. ed. Berkeley: University of California Press, 1977.

———. *Twelve-Tone Tonality*. Berkeley: University of California Press, 1977.

Perlis, Vivian. *Charles Ives Remembered: An Oral History*. New York: Norton, 1976.

Peyser, Joan. *Boulez*. New York: Schirmer Books, 1976.

———. *Twentieth-Century Music: The Sense Behind the Sound*. New York: Schirmer Books, 1980.

Reich, Willi. *Schoenberg: A Critical Biography*. Translated by Leo Black. Edinburgh: Longman Group Limited, 1971.

Riesemann, Oskar von. *Rachmaninoff's Recollections*. Translated by Dolly Rutherford. New York: Arno Press, Inc. 1979.

Roland-Manuel. *Maurice Ravel*. Translated by Cynthia Jolly. London: Dennis Dobson, Ltd., 1947.

Rosen, Charles. *Arnold Schoenberg*. New York: The Viking Press, 1975.

Rosen, Judith. *Grażyna Bacewicz: Her Life and Works*. Polish Music History Series, vol 2. Los Angeles: University of Southern California, 1984.

Salzman, Eric. *Twentieth-Century Music: An Introduction*. 3d ed. Englewood Cliffs: Prentice-Hall, Inc., 1988.

Shattuck, Roger. *The Banquet Years: The Origins of the Avant Garde in France, 1885 to World War I*. Rev. ed. New York: Vintage Books, 1968.

Shead, Richard. *Music in the 1920s*. London: Gerald Duckworth & Co., Ltd., 1976.

Skelton, Geoffrey. *Paul Hindemith: The Man behind the Music*. London: Victor Gollancz, Ltd., 1975.

Solomon, Maynard. "Charles Ives: Some Questions of Veracity." *Journal of the American Musicological Society* 40, no. 3 (Fall 1987): 443–470.

Stevens, Halsey. *The Life and Music of Béla Bartók*. Rev. ed. New York: Oxford University Press, 1964.

Stravinsky, Igor. *Poetics of Music: In the Form of Six Lessons* (1939–1940). Translated by Arthur Knodel and Ingolf Dahl. New York: Vintage Books, 1959.

Tannenbaum, Mya. *Conversations with Stockhausen*. Translated by David Butchart. Oxford: Clarendon Press, 1987.

Toop, Richard. "Stockhausen's Klavierstück VIII (1954)." *Miscellanea Musicologica* 10 (1979): 93–130.

Watkins, Glen. *Soundings: Music in the Twentieth Century*. New York: Schirmer Books, 1988.

Webern, Anton. *The Path to New Music*. Edited by Willi Reich. Bryn Mawr: Theodore Presser, 1963.

Westergaard, Peter. "Webern and 'Total Organization': An Analysis of the Second Movement of the Piano Variations, Op. 27." *Perspectives of New Music* 1, no. 2 (Spring, 1963): 107–120.

White, Eric Walter. *Stravinsky, the Composer, and His Works*. 2nd ed. Berkeley: University of California Press, 1979.

Wildgans, Friedrich: *Anton Webern*. Translated by Edith Temple Roberts and Humphrey Searle. London: Calder and Boyars, 1966.

Wörner, Karl H. *Stockhausen: Life and Work*. Translated by Bill Hopkins. London: Faber & Faber, 1973.

Xenakis, Iannis. *Formalized Music*. Bloomington: Indiana University Press, 1971.

Yates, Peter. *Twentieth-Century Music*. New York: Pantheon Books, 1967.

Chronological List of Works and Publishers

1886 Satie: Ogives (MCA)
1888 Satie: Trois gymnopédies (Salabert, G. Schirmer)
1890 Debussy: Suite bergamasque (Durand)
1892 Rachmaninoff: Prelude in C-sharp Minor,
     Op. 3, No. 2 (International)
1901 Debussy: Suite: Pour le piano (Durand)
     Ravel: Jeux d'eau (G. Schirmer)
1903 Stravinsky: Sonata in F-sharp Minor
     Debussy: Estampes (Durand)
     Scriabin: Fourth Sonata (International)
     Szymanowski: Four Études, Op. 4 (Universal)
     Bartók: Four Piano Pieces (Kalmus, Boosey & Hawkes)
1904 Debussy: L'isle joyeuse (Durand)
     Rachmaninoff: Ten Preludes, Op. 23
       (G. Schirmer, International)
     Bartók: Rhapsody, Op. 1 (Boosey & Hawkes.,
       G. Schirmer)
1905 Debussy: Images I (Durand)
     Ives: Three-Page Sonata (Mercury)
     Ravel: Sonatine (Durand)
     Ravel: Miroirs (Durand)
     Szymanowski: Sonata No. 1 (Piwarski)
1907 Bartók: Three Folk Songs from Csík County
     Debussy: Images II (Durand)
1908 Debussy: Children's Corner (Durand)
     Ives: The Anti-Abolitionist Riots (Mercury)
     Ives: Some Southpaw Pitching (Mercury)
     Ravel: Gaspard de la nuit (Durand)
     Scriabin: Fifth Sonata (International)
     Falla: Pièces espagnoles (Durand)
     Bartók: Fourteen Bagatelles, Op. 6 (Boosey & Hawkes)
     Bartók: Ten Easy Pieces (Boosey & Hawkes)
     Berg: Sonata, Op. 1 (Universal)
     Stravinsky: Four Études (Peters, International, Associated)
1909 Schoenberg: Three Piano Pieces, Op. 11
      (Universal, Belmont)
     Ives: First Sonata (Peer International)

Bartók: Two Elegies, Op. 8b (Boosey & Hawkes)
Bartók: For Children (Boosey & Hawkes)
1910 Debussy: Preludes I (Durand)
Rachmaninoff: Thirteen Preludes, Op. 32
    (G. Schirmer, International)
Busoni: Fantasia Contrapuntistica (Breitkopf & Härtel)
Bartók: Two Romanian Dances, Op. 8a (Boosey & Hawkes)
Bartók: Sketches, Op. 9 (Boosey & Hawkes)
Bartók: Four Dirges (Boosey & Hawkes)
Bartók: Three Burlesques, Op. 8c (Boosey & Hawkes)
1911 Schoenberg: Six Little Piano Pieces, Op. 19
    (Universal, Belmont)
Ravel: Valses nobles et sentimentales (Durand)
Scriabin: Seventh Sonata (International)
Bartók: Allegro Barbaro (Boosey & Hawkes)
1912 Ives: Étude No. 22 (Merion)
Satie: Véritables préludes flasques (Eschig)
Cowell: The tides of Manaunaun (Associated)
1913 Debussy: Preludes II (Durand)
Scriabin: Eighth Sonata (Boosey & Hawkes, International)
Scriabin: Ninth Sonata (Peters, International)
Rachmaninoff: Second Sonata, Op. 36
    (Boosey & Hawkes, International)
Prokofiev: Sarcasms, Op. 17 (Kalmus)
1914 Satie: Sports et divertissements (Salabert)
Satie: Valses distinguées du precieux dégoûté (Salabert)
1915 Debussy: Douze études (Durand)
Ives: Second Sonata ("Concord") (Arrow)
1916 Bartók: Suite, Op. 14 (Boosey & Hawkes, International)
Griffes: Roman Sketches (G. Schirmer)
Casella: Sonatina (Rocordi)
Nielsen: Chaconne (Hansen)
1917 Ravel: Le tombeau de Couperin (Durand)
Rachmaninoff: Études-tableaux, Op. 39 (International)
Prokofiev: Third Piano Sonata, Op. 28a (International, Boosey & Hawkes, others)
Prokofiev: Visions fugitives, Op. 22
    (Boosey & Hawkes, Kalmus, International)
Casella: A notte alta (Ricordi)
Busoni: Sonatina in Diem Navitatis Christi
    (Breitkopf & Härtel)
Bartók: Fifteen Hungarian Folksongs (Boosey & Hawkes)
1918 Falla: Fantasía baetica (Chester)
Bartók: Three Études, Op. 18 (Boosey & Hawkes)
Kodály: Seven Piano Pieces, Op. 11 (Universal)
Griffes: Sonata (G. Schirmer)
Poulenc: Mouvements perpétuels (Chester)
1919 Szymanowski: Sonata No. 3, Op. 36 (Universal)
Stravinsky: Piano Rag Music (Chester)

1920 Bartók: Improvisations on Hungarian Peasant Songs, Op. 20 (Boosey &
       Hawkes)
     Honegger: Sept pièces brèves (Eschig)
     Copland: The Cat and the Mouse (Durand)
1921 Stravinsky: Three Movements from Petrouchka (Boosey & Hawkes)
     Milhaud: Saudades do Brazil (Eschig)
1922 Hindemith: Suite "1922," Op. 26 (Schott)
     Bloch: Poems of the Sea (G. Schirmer)
     Copland: Passacaglia (Senart)
1923 Schoenberg: Five Piano Pieces, Op. 23
       (Wilhelm Hansen, Belmont)
     Schoenberg: Suite for Piano, Op. 25 (Universal, Belmont)
     Cowell: The Aeolian Harp (Associated)
     Ives: Varied Air and Variations (Merion)
1924 Stravinsky: Piano Sonata (Boosey & Hawkes)
     Chávez: Sonatina (Boosey & Hawkes)
1925 Stravinsky: Sérénade en la (Boosey & Hawkes)
     Prokofiev: Fifth Piano Sonata (Boosey & Hawkes)
     Cowell: The Banshee (Associated)
1926 Bartók: Sonata for Piano (Boosey & Hawkes, Universal)
     Bartók: Out of Doors (Boosey & Hawkes, Universal)
     Shostakovich: First Sonata (Boosey & Hawkes, Peters, Kalmus)
     Gershwin: Three Preludes (New World Music)
1928 Schoenberg: Klavierstück, Op. 33a
       (Universal, Belmont)
     Cowell: Tiger (Associated)
     Crawford: Four Preludes (New Music Editions)
     Nielsen: Three Piano Pieces (Hansen)
     Chavez: Third Sonata (New Music Editions)
1929 Szymanowski: Twenty Mazurkas, Op. 50 (Universal)
     Messiaen: Preludes (Durand)
1930 Kodály: Dances of Marosszek (Universal)
     Copland: Piano Variations (Arrow, Boosey & Hawkes)
     Sessions: First Sonata (Schott)
     Kabalevsky: Sonatina in C (Schirmer, Peters)
1931 Rachmaninoff: Variations on a Theme of Corelli,
       Op. 42 (Belwin-Mills)
     Schoenberg: Klavierstück, Op. 33b (Belmont)
     Antheil: Airplane Sonata (New Music Editions)
1933 Kabalevsky: Sonatina in G (Kalmus)
1935 Bloch: Sonata (Carisch)
     Enesco: Third Piano Sonata, Op. 24, No. 3 (Salabert)
1936 Webern: Piano Variations, Op. 27 (Universal)
     Hindemith: Three Sonatas (Schott)
     Poulenc: Les soirées de Nazelles (Durand)
     Casella: Sinfonia, Arioso, and Toccata, Op. 59
       (Carisch)
1937 Bartók: Mikrokosmos (Boosey & Hawkes)
     Ginastera: Danzas argentinas (Durand)

1938 Cage: Bacchanale (Peters)
1940 Stravinsky: Tango (Schott)
     Prokofiev: Sixth Piano Sonata (Peters, Boosey & Hawkes)
     Bloch: Visions et prophéties (G. Schirmer)
     Sessions: From My Diary (Marks)
1941 Skalkottas: Suite No. 4 (Universal)
     Copland: Piano Sonata (Boosey & Hawkes)
1942 Hindemith: Ludus Tonalis (Schott)
     Prokofiev: Seventh Piano Sonata (Peters, Boosey & Hawkes)
1943 Ruggles: Evocations (American Music Editions)
     Shostakovich: Second Sonata (Boosey & Hawkes, Peters, Kalmus)
     Dallapiccola: Sonatina Canonica (Suvini Zerboni)
     Cage: Amores (Peters)
     Cage: Our Spring Will Come (Peters)
     Cage: Tossed as it is Untroubled (Peters)
     Krenek: Third Sonata (Associated)
1944 Prokofiev: Eighth Piano Sonata (Peters, Boosey & Hawkes)
     Messiaen: Vingt regards sur l'enfant-Jesus (Durand)
     Cage: Root of an Unfocus (Peters)
     Cage: A Valentine Out of Season (Peters)
1945 Jolivet: First Sonata (Universal)
     Cage: Daughters of the Lonesome Isle (Peters)
     Finney: Fourth Sonata (Mercury)
1946 Boulez: First Sonata (Amphion)
     Sessions: Second Sonata (Marks)
     Carter: Piano Sonata (Mercury)
     Weber: Fantasia (Variations) (Marks)
     Kabalevsky: Third Sonata (Boosey & Hawkes, Peters, Kalmus)
1947 Cage: Music for Marcel Duchamp (Peters)
     Diamond: Sonata (Southern)
     Dello Joio: Third Sonata (Carl Fischer)
     Kabalevsky: Twenty-four Preludes (Peters, Kalmus)
1948 Boulez: Second Sonata (Heugel)
     Martin: Eight Preludes (Universal)
     Cage: Suite for Toy Piano (Peters)
     Cage: Sonatas and Interludes (Peters)
     Kirchner: Piano Sonata (Bomart)
     Krenek: Fourth Sonata (Bomart)
     Coulthard: Sonata (BMI Canada)
     Babbitt: Three Compositions for Piano (Bombart)
1949 Messiaen: Quatre études de rhythme (Durand)
     Bacewicz: First Sonata (unpublished)
     Barber: Sonata for Piano (G. Schirmer)
     Persichetti: Fourth Sonata (Elkan-Vogel)
1951 Cage: Music of Changes (Peters)
     Shostakovich: Twenty-four Preludes and Fugues (Boosey & Hawkes,
          Peters)
1952 Dallapiccola: Quaderno Musicale di Annalibera (Suvini Zerboni)
     Rochberg: Twelve Bagatelles (Presser)

Finney: Variations on a Theme by
  Alban Berg (Peters)
Ginastera: Suite de danzas criollas (Barry)
Ginastera: First Sonata (Barry)
Wolff: Suite I (Peters)
1953 Stockhausen: Klavierstück I–IV (Universal)
Berio: Cinque variazioni (rev. 1966) (Suvini Zerboni)
Bacewicz: Second Sonata (Polskie
  Wydawnictwo Muzyczne)
Cage: Music for Piano (Peters)
Dahl: Sonata Seria (Presser)
Brown: Twenty-five Pages for One to Twenty-five Pianists (Universal)
1954 Cage: 31'57.9864" for a Pianist (Peters)
1955 Stockhausen: Klavierstücke V–VIII (Universal)
Serocki: Piano Sonata (Polskie Wydawnictwo Muzyczne)
Lutyens: Piano e forte (Belwin-Mills)
1957 Stockhausen: Klavierstück XI (Universal)
Pousseur: Exercices pour piano (Suvini Zerboni)
Walker: Second Sonata (Galaxy)
1957 Bussotti: Musica per amici (Ricordi)
Jolivet: Second Sonata (Heugel)
Cage: Winter Music (Peters)
Copland: Piano Fantasy (Boosey & Hawkes)
Babbitt: Partitions (Lawson-Gould)
1958 Messiaen: Catalogue d'oiseaux (Leduc)
Nilsson: Quantitäten (Universal)
Yun: Fünf Stücke für Klavier (Bote & Bock)
Rochberg: Sonata-Fantasia (Presser)
Martino: Piano Fantasy (Ione)
Miyoshi: Piano Sonata (Ongaku-No-Tomo-Sha)
1959 Bussotti: Five Pieces for David Tudor (Universal)
Feldman: Last Pieces (Peters)
1961 Stockhausen: Klavierstücke IX–X (Universal)
Boulez: Third Sonata (Universal)
Xenakis: Herma (Boosey & Hawkes)
Pousseur: Caractères I (Universal)
Bussotti: Pour clavier (Moeck)
Cardew: February Pieces for Piano, and Octet '61 for Jasper Johns (Peters)
Takemitsu: Piano Distance (Salabert)
1962 Lutyens: Five Bagetelles (Schott)
Martirano: Cocktail Music (MCA Music)
Crumb: Five Pieces for Piano (Peters)
1963 Serocki: A Piacere (Polski Wydawnictow Muzyczne)
Wuorinen: Piano Variations (McGinnis & Marx)
1964 Durkó: Psicogramma (Kultura)
Eaton: Microtonal Fantasy (Associated)
Perle: Short Sonata (Presser)
1965 Pousseur: Miroir de votre Faust (Caractères II)
  (Universal)

Sessions: Third Sonata (Marks)
Johnston: Sonata for Microtonal Piano (Smith Publications)
Cardew: Three Winter Potatoes (Universal)
1966 Berio: Sequenza IV (Universal)
Pousseur: Apostrophe et six réflexions
    (Universal)
Rochberg: Nach Bach (Presser)
Bolcom: Twelve Études for Piano (Merion)
Babbitt: Post-Partitions (Associated)
Albright: Pianoàgogo (Jobert)
1967 Cardew: Memories of You (Universal)
Austin: Accidents (Composer/Performer Editions)
1968 Nørgård: Grooving (Wilhelm Hansen)
Nilsson: Rendezvous (Wilhelm Hansen)
Albright: Grand Sonata in Rag (Jobert)
1969 Johnson: Scene for Piano and Tape (218 Press)
Wuorinen: First Sonata (Peters)
1970 Martino: Pianississimo (Dantalian)
Albright: The Dream Rags (Marks)
Davidovsky: Synchronisms No. 6 for Piano and Electronic Sounds
    (Marks)
1971 Rochberg: Carnival Music (Presser)
Lockwood: Piano Burning (Source Magazine)
Kolb: Solitaire (Peters)
Wyner: Three Short Fantasies (Associated)
Moevs: Phoenix (Marks)
1972 Hamilton: Palinodes (Presser)
Crumb: Makrokosmos I (Peters)
Kocsár: Improvvisazioni (Editio Musica Budapest)
1973 Xenakis: Evryali (Salabert)
Crumb: Makrokosmos II (Peters)
Takemitsu: For Away (Salabert)
Miyoshi: Chaînes (Zen-On)
Tippett: Third Sonata (Schott)
Curtis-Smith: Rhapsodies (Salabert)
Helps: Trois Hommages (Peters)
Moss: Fantasy (Elkan-Vogel)
Johnson: Septapede (Associated)
1974 Babbitt: Reflections (Peters)
Wilson: Eclogue (Boosey & Hawkes)
Chaitkin: Études (Galaxy)
1975 Sessions: Five Pieces for Piano (Merion)
Cage: Études australes (Peters)
Rzewski: The People United Will Never Be Defeated! (Zen-On)
Rihm: Klavierstück n. 5 (tombeau) (Universal)
1976 Rochberg: Partita Variations (Presser)
Albright: Five Chromatic Dances (Peters)
Perle: Six Études (Margun)
Kolb: Appello (Boosey & Hawkes)

Silsbee: Doors (American Composers Alliance)
Corigliano: Étude Fantasy (Schirmer)
Wuorinen: Second Sonata (Peters)
1977 Ran: Hyperbolae (Israel Music Institute)
Martino: Impromptu for Roger (Dantalian)
Rzewski: Four Piano Pieces (Zen-On)
1978 Rzewski: Squares (Zen-On)
Adams: Phrygian Gates (Associated)
1979 Takemitsu: Les yeux clos (Salabert)
Rzewski: North American Ballads (Zen-On)
1980 Crumb: A Little Suite for Christmas, A.D. 1979 (Peters)
Carter: Night Fantasies (Associated)
Muczynski: Masks (Presser)
Xenakis: Mists (Salabert)
1981 Stockhausen: Klavierstück XIII (Universal)
Ginastera: Second Sonata (Boosey & Hawkes)
Crumb: Gnomic Variations (Peters)
Martino: Fantasies and Impromptus
    (Dantalian)
Ferneyhough: Lemma-Icon-Epigram (Peters)
Perle: Ballade (Peters)
Feldman: Triadic Memories (Universal)
1982 Ginastera: Third Sonata (Boosey & Hawkes)
Martino: Suite in Old Form (Dantalian)
Fisher: Six Fantasy Pieces for Piano (Seesaw)
Wernick: Sonata (Presser)
1983 Stockhausen: Klavierstück XII (Universal)
Babbitt: Canonical Form (Peters)
Crumb: Processional (Peters)
1984 Stockhausen: Klavierstück XIV (Universal)
Tippett: Fourth Sonata (Schott)
Perle: Six New Études (Gunman)
1985 Babbitt: Lagniappe (Peters)
Albright: Sphaera (Peters)
Lieberson: Bagatelles (Associated)
Ligeti: Études pour piano—premier livre (Schott)
Wilson: Fixations (Peer-Southern)
Wilson: Intercalations (Peer-Southern)
Messiaen: Petites esquisses d'oiseaux (Leduc)
1986 Bolcom: Twelve New Études For Piano (Marks)
Kirchner: Five Pieces for Piano (Associated)

Notes

Part 1 From 1900 to the End of World War I

Chapter 1: Debussy

1. Rollo Myers, *Modern French Music* (New York, 1971), 62.
2. Victor Seroff, *Debussy, Musician of France* (New York, 1956), 99.
3. Claude Debussy, "*Monsieur Croche the Dilettante Hater,*" in *Three Classics in the Aesthetic of Music* (New York, 1962).
4. Peter Yates, *Twentieth-Century Music* (New York, 1967), 85.
5. From a letter from Debussy to his publisher, Jacques Durand, quoted in Myers, *Modern French Music*, 98.

Chapter 2: Arnold Schoenberg

1. Willi Reich, *Schoenberg: A Critical Biography* (London, 1971), 7.
2. Ibid., 16–19. The statement is reprinted in its entirety.
3. Ibid., 48.
4. Ibid., 31.
5. Charles Rosen, *Arnold Schoenberg* (New York, 1975), 16. The quotation is from a letter from Schoenberg to Alma Mahler.
6. Reich, *Schoenberg*, 50.
7. Rosen, *Arnold Schoenberg*, 13.
8. Paul Griffiths, *A Concise History of Avant-Garde Music* (New York and Toronto, 1978), 26.

Chapter 3: Charles Ives

1. Charles Ives, *Memos* (New York, 1972), 79–80.
2. Maynard Soloman, "Charles Ives: Some Questions of Veracity," *Journal of the American Musicological Society* (Fall, 1987). See also J. Peter Burkholder, "Charles Ives and His Fathers: A Response to Maynard Solomon," *Newsletter of the Institute for Studies in American Music* 18, no. 1 (November 1988).
3. Vivian Perlis, *Charles Ives Remembered: An Oral History* (New York, 1976), 205.
4. Charles Ives, *Essays before a Sonata* (New York, 1970).

Chapter 4: Maurice Ravel

1. Roger Nichols, *Ravel* (London, 1977), 16.
2. Roland-Manuel, *Ravel* (London, 1947), 54.
3. Nichols, *Ravel*, 72.

Chapter 6: Other Composers

1. Ferruccio Busoni, *Selected Letters*, trans. and ed. Anthony Beaumont (London, 1987), 381–423.

2. Ibid., 386.

3. Eric Salzman, *Twentieth-Century Music: An Introduction*, 3rd ed. (Englewood Cliffs, N.J., 1988), 18.

4. Ibid., 20.

Part 2 Between the Two World Wars

Chapter 7: Béla Bartók

1. From a letter from Bartók to Kódaly quoted in Lajos Lesznai, *Bartók* (London, 1972), 51.

2. Béla Bartók, *Béla Bartók: A Memorial Review* (New York, 1950), 76.

3. Quoted in Todd Crow, ed., *Bartók Studies* (Detroit, 1976).

4. When the *Sonata* was much newer, many decades ago, several pianists, including Hungarian musicians who had worked directly with Bartók, told me that they considered the middle movement a mistake and that it should not be played!

Chapter 9: Arnold Schoenberg and Anton Webern

1. Readers unfamiliar with the nitty gritty of this much-discussed dodecaphonic method can find explanations and discussions in numerous books and articles. For short, thoughtful commentary, the following suggestions are offered: Eric Salzman, *Twentieth-Century Music: An Introduction*, 3rd ed. (Englewood Cliffs, N.J., 1988), Charles Rosen, *Arnold Schoenberg* (New York, 1975), and, for the more adventurous, George Perle, *Serial Composition and Atonality* (Los Angeles and London, 1962, rev. 1978).

2. Rosen, *Arnold Schoenberg*, 73.

3. Friedrich Wildgans, *Anton Webern* (London, 1966), 167.

4. Hans Moldenhauer, *The Death of Anton Webern* (New York, 1961).

5. I first became aware of this designation in May 1962, while attending the First International Webern Festival in Seattle. There I heard—among numerous noteworthy events—a fascinating "Concert of Post-Webern Music" given by the distinguished pianist Leonard Stein. Mr. Stein, at one time a pupil and associate of Schoenberg, is now director of the Schoenberg Institute in Los Angeles. I shall always consider his Seattle concert one of the most significant musical happenings in my life.

6. Peter Westergaard, "Webern and 'Total Organization': An Analysis of the Second Movement of the Piano Variations, Op. 27," *Perspectives of New Music* (Spring 1963), 107. This article thoroughly exposes various analyses of Webern's work which had made him seem to be the prototypical total serialist.

7. See the preface by composer Humphrey Searle in Wildgans, *Anton Webern*, 10.

8. Anton Webern, *Piano Variations*, Op. 27, ed. Peter Stadlen (Vienna: Universal Editions no. 16845).

9. Ibid., v.

10. Ibid.

Chapter 10: Paul Hindemith

1. Geoffrey Skelton, *Paul Hindemith: The Man behind the Music* (London, 1975), 43.
2. Ibid., 73.
3. Paul Hindemith, *The Craft of Musical Composition* (New York, 1942).

Chapter 11: Sergei Prokofiev

1. It is amusing today to read quotations from the early reviews of the piece, many of which are included in Israel V. Nestyev, *Prokofieff* (Stanford, 1960).
2. John Ogden, "The Romantic Tradition," in *Keyboard Music*, ed. Denis Matthews (New York, 1972), 256.

Chapter 13: Aaron Copland

1. For further discussion of the *Piano Variations* see Aaron Copland and Vivian Perlis, *Copland, 1900 through 1942* (New York, 1984), passim, but especially 173–4 and 178–84.
2. Arthur Berger, *Aaron Copland* (New York, 1953), 44–45.

Chapter 14: Other Composers in America

1. Rita Mead, *Henry Cowell's New Music 1925–1936* (Ann Arbor, 1981). A fascinating and detailed exploration of Cowell's life as well as an examination of every program and publication of the Society.
2. *The Piano Music of Henry Cowell*. Folkways FG 3349.
3. In chapter 22, in which the inside-the-piano music of George Crumb is discussed, there is a brief commentary on the techniques for—and perils of—performing this music. It is recommended that this be read before beginning work on *The Aeolian Harp, The Banshee*, or other pieces of this genre.
4. Henry Cowell, *Piano Music by Henry Cowell*. New York, n.d.
5. Henry Cowell and Sidney Cowell, *Charles Ives and His Music*, rev. (London, 1969).
6. See Glen Watkins, *Soundings* (New York and London, 1988), 302–305, for a brief but telling account of Gershwin's association with Ravel, Berg, Schoenberg, Stravinsky, and others, and for an assessment of his influences on his contemporaries.

Chapter 15: Olivier Messiaen

1. Robert Sherlaw Johnson, *Messiaen* (Berkeley and Los Angeles, 1975).
2. Igor Stravinsky, *Poetics of Music* (New York, 1959), 87.

Part 3 The Postwar Period

Chapter 16: Karlheinz Stockhausen and Pierre Boulez

1. Mya Tannenbaum: *Conversations with Stockhausen* (Oxford, 1987), 3.
2. Ibid., 87.
3. Karl H. Wörner, *Stockhausen: Life and Work* (London, 1973), 39.
4. Tannenbaum, *Conversations*, 54.
5. Wörner, *Stockhausen*, 32.

6. Richard Toop, "Stockhausen's Klavierstück VIII (1954)," *Miscellanea Musicologica*, 10 (1979): 93–130. A facinating analysis of *Klavierstück VIII* and valuable historical background on Stockhausen's pieces V–X by the composer's one-time assistant.

7. Wörner, *Stockhausen*, 36.

8. Herbert Henck, *Karlheinz Stockhausen's Klavierstück X*, English trans. Deborah Richards (Cologne, 1980).

9. Ibid., 52–54.

10. Karlheinz Stockhausen, *Klavierstück XI*, Universal Editions 12654 LW, "Performing Directions."

11. Joan Peyser, *Boulez* (New York, 1976), 125.

12. René Leibowitz, *Schoenberg et son école* (Paris, 1947). The English translation by Dika Newlin: *Schoenberg and His School* (New York, 1949, 1970).

13. Peyser, *Boulez*, 39.

14. Pierre Boulez, *Second Sonata* (Paris, 1950). The quotation is from the "Remarques" at the beginning of the score.

15. Peyser, *Boulez*, 49. These comments by Boulez, if they are accurate, conflict substantially with those in Pierre Boulez, *Conversations with Célestin Deliège* (London, 1976), 40.

Chapter 17: Luigi Dallapiccola and Luciano Berio

1. Luigi Dallapiccola, *Appunti, incontri, meditazioni* (Milan, 1970). See page 105 for an account of his first reactions to performances of the music of Webern.

2. Ibid., 166–167. English translation by the author.

3. In Berio's original manuscript of seven oversized pages, he arranged that there would be such a "cadence" at the end of every page except the sixth. Regrettably, this symmetrical configuration was not maintained in the engraved score.

Chapter 18: Other Composers in Europe

1. Iannis Xenakis, *Formalized Music* (Bloomington, 1971), 10. A diagram and photograph of the Philips Pavilion appear on pages 10–11.

2. Cornelius Cardew, *Octet '61 for Jasper Johns* (Leipzig, 1961) "General Performing Directions."

3. Judith Rosen, *Grażyna Bacewicz: Her Life and Works* (Los Angeles, 1984), 51.

Chapter 19: John Cage

1. Karl H. Wörner, *Stockhausen: Life and Work* (London, 1973), 236–237.

2. Joan Peyser, *Boulez* (New York, 1976), 85.

3. "Berio recalls the *Music of Changes* event [at Darmstadt in 1954]: 'I was bored to death. But it was the best moment for Cage to come. With his simplicity he accomplished a great deal. He proved to be a strong catalyst' " (Peyser, *Boulez*, 140).

4. See William Brooks, "Choice and Change in Cage's Recent Music," in Peter Gena and Jonathan Brent, *A John Cage Reader*, (New York, 1982), 99, n. 7, for a brief, clear explanation of Cage's use of the *I Ching*.

5. For an excellent how-to-do-it manual on the subject, consult Richard Bunger, *The Well-Prepared Piano* (Colorado Springs, 1973).

6. Peter Gena, "After Antiquity; John Cage in Conversation with Peter Gena," ibid., 170.

Chapter 20: Aaron Copland, Roger Sessions, and the Mid-Century Piano Sonata

1. Edward T. Cone, ed., *Roger Sessions on Music: Collected Essays* (Princeton, 1979).

2. Ibid., 179.

3. Ibid., 179–180.

4. President John F. Kennedy was assassinated in Dallas on 22 November 1963.

5. Ernst Krenek, *Music Here and Now* (New York, 1939).

Chapter 21: The American Avant-Garde

1. In a conversation with the author in the mid-1960s, Wuorinen commented, "We were the only group not to be funded by a foundation, too. We got started before the foundations thought of supporting new music. When they finally did, we applied, but were turned down. 'You're doing all right without us,' they said. We could certainly have used the money!"

2. Larry Austin, *Accidents, Source: Music of the Avant Garde* 2, no. 2 (1968): 21.

3. Anna Lockwood, *Piano Burning, Source: Music of the Avant-Garde* 5, no. 1 (1971): 48.

Chapter 22: George Crumb

1. My only objection to his written directions, which are otherwise both copious and clear, has to do with the marking of notes inside the piano. I believe my suggestions, detailed in the text, are simpler, more effective, and less potentially harmful to the instrument.

Chapter 26: Other Composers in America

1. George Perle, *Twelve-Tone Tonality* (Berkeley, 1977).

2. Arthur C. Danto, "Georges Braque," in *The Nation* (August 27–September 3, 1988), 174. A fuller quotation follows:

> It is fascinating to speculate upon what the subsequent history of art . . . might have been had this epithet [cubism] not fallen upon it to freeze it into a certain mold. Would Impressionism have existed as an artistic style without having been called Impressionism, singling out as salient the ephemeral and the sensory, and generating an entire agenda in the choice of the word? How many of the paintings of Abstract Expressionism would we have without the name? It is often as though name and substance penetrate each other; that the critical designation of an artistic movement redirects the movement it intends merely to label, giving it a consciousness, so that the language of the critic is as dangerous as a paralyzing dart.

Discography

A selected list of recordings of piano music written after 1945.

ADAMS:
Phrygian Gates · 1750 Arch: S 1874 · Mack McCray

ALBRIGHT:
Dream Rags · MHS 4253 · Wm. Albright
Grand Sonata
in Rag
Pianoàgogo · CRI SD-449 · Thomas Warburton
Five Chromatic
Dances

BABBITT:
Piano Works · Harmonia Mundi · Robert Taub
(nine pieces) · HMC 5160

BARBER:
Piano Sonata · Desto 7120 · John Browning

BERIO:
Cinque Variazioni · Candide CE 31015 · David Burge
(revised version)
Sequenza IV · Candide CE 31027 · David Burge
Sequenza IV · CP2/3-5 · Aki Takahashi

BOULEZ:
First Piano Soanta · Candide CE 31027 · David Burge
First Piano Sonata · CP2/3-5 · Aki Takahashi
Second Piano Sonata · DG 2530803 PSI · Mauricio Pollini
Second Piano Sonata · MHS 3874 · David Burge
Sonatas 1, 2, 3 · Wergo WER 60120/1 · Herbert Henck

BUSSOTTI:
Pieces for · CP2/3-5 · Aki Takahashi
David Tudor

CAGE:
Sonatas & Interludes · CRI SRD-199E · Maro Ajemian
Music for Keyboard · Columbia M2S 819 · Jeanne Kirstein
1935–1948
(twelve pieces)
Sonatas 1, 5, 10, 12 · New World · Robert Miller
& 2nd Interlude · NW 203
Winter Music · CP2/3-5 · Aki Takahashi
Études Australes · Tomata TOM 1101 · Grete Sultan

273

Études Australes	Wergo WER 60 152/5	Grete Sultan
A Valentine Out of Season	Toshiba TA-72034	Aki Takahashi
Music for M. Duchamp		
Music of Changes	Wergo WER 60 099	Herbert Henck
CARTER:		
Piano Sonata	Nonesuch 79047	Paul Jacobs
Night Fantasies		
Piano Sonata	Etcetera ETC 1008	Charles Rosen
Night Fantasies		
CHAITKIN:		
Études	CRI 345	David Burge
COPLAND:		
Piano Fantasy	Odyssey 32 16 0040	Wm. Masselos
CRUMB:		
Five Pieces	Advance FGR-3	David Burge
Makrokosmos I	Nonesuch H-71293	David Burge
Makrokosmos II	Odyssey Y 34135	Robert Miller
Gnomic Variations	Orion ORS 84473	Jeffrey Jacob
A Little Suite for Christmas	Bridge BCD 9003	Lambert Orkis
CURTIS-SMITH:		
Rhapsodies	CRI 345	David Burge
DALLAPICCOLA:		
Quaderno Musicale	Candide CE 31015	David Burge
Quaderno Musicale	Orion ORS 78299	James Avery
Sonatina	Italia ITL 70011	Lya De Barberiis
Quaderno Musicale		
DAVIDOVSKY:		
Synchronisms No. 6	Turnabout TV-S 34487	Robert Miller
GINASTERA:		
Sonatas 1 & 2	Elan: 1202	Santiago Rodriguez
HAMILTON:		
Palinodes	CRI 407	Lois Svard
JOHNSTON:		
Sonata for Microtonal Piano	New World NW 203	Robert Miller
KIRCHNER:		
Sonata	CRI SD 461	Robert Taub
KOCSÁR:		
Improvvisazioni	Hungaraton SLPX 11692	Adám Fellegi
KRENEK:		
Sonata 3	CBS M3 42150	Glenn Gould
Sonata 4	MHS 3874	David Burge
LIEBERSON:		
Bagatelles	New World NW 344	Peter Serkin

MARTIN:
    Eight Preludes   Orion 79328   Robert Silverman
MARTINO:
    Fantasies and   New World NW 320   Randall Hodgkinson
      Impromptus
MARTIRANO:
    Cocktail Music   Advance FGR-3   David Burge
MESSIAEN:
    Vingt Regards   RCA CRL3-0759   Peter Serkin
    Vingt Regards   Argo ZRG 650/1   John Ogdon
    Catalogue   MHS 1423/6   Yvonne Loriod
    Quatre études   Nonesuch 71334   Paul Jacobs
      de rythme
MIYOSHI:
    Sonata   Spectrum SR-301   Masa Kitagawa Fuku
MOEVS:
    Phoenix   CRI S-404   Wanda Maximillien
MOSS:
    Fantasy   Op. One 34   Dionne Weigert
MUCZYNSKI:
    Masks   Laurel 124   R. Muczynski
      (and other works)
NØRGÅRD:
    Grooving   Wilhelm Hansen: Elisabeth Klein
      (and other works)   LPWH 3013
PERLE:
    Ballade   Nonesuch 79108   Richard Goode
    Six Études   New World NW 304   Bradford Gowen
PERSICHETTI:
    Sonata 12   Orion ORS 84473   Jeffrey Jacob
ROCHBERG:
    Twelve Bagatelles   Advance FGR-3   David Burge
    Carnival Music   Grenadilla GS 1019   Alan Mandel
RZEWSKI:
    Four North American   Nonesuch 79006   Paul Jacobs
      Ballads
    Four Pieces   Vanguard 25001   F. Rzewski
    The People United   Vanguard VSD 71248   Ursula Oppens
SESSIONS:
    First Sonata   CRI 198   Robert Helps
    Second Sonata   New World NW 320   Randall Hodgkinson
    Third Sonata   New World NW 307   Robert Helps
SILSBEE:
    Doors   Pro Viva ISPV 110   David Burge
STOCKHAUSEN:
    Klavierstücke   Wergo WER 60 135-50   Herbert Henck
      I–XI
    Klavierstück X   Wergo 60010   Frederic Rzewski

Klavierstück VIII	Candide CE 31015	David Burge
Klavierstück IX	CP2/3-5	Aki Takahashi
TAKEMITSU:		
For Away	Toshiba TA-72034	Aki Takahashi
TIPPETT:		
4 Sonatas	2-CRD 1130/1	Paul Crossley
WEBER:		
Fantasia	Desto 7136	George Bennette
WERNICK:		
Sonata	Bridge BCD 9003	Lambert Orkis
WILSON:		
Eclogue	CRI 437	Blanca Uribe
WUORINEN:		
Sonata 1	CRI S-306	Robert Miller
Variations	Advance FGR-3	David Burge
WYNER:		
Three Short	CRI S-306	Robert Miller
Fantasies		
XENAKIS:		
Evryali	Toshiba TA-72034	Aki Takahashi
Herma	CP2/3-5	Aki Takahashi

Index